Martin's Dream

Martin's Dream

My Journey and the Legacy of
Martin Luther King Jr.

A Memoir

CLAYBORNE CARSON

palgrave
macmillan

MARTIN'S DREAM
Copyright © Clayborne Carson, 2013.

First published in 2013 by PALGRAVE MACMILLAN® in the U.S.—a division of
St. Martin's Press LLC, 175 Fifth Avenue, New York, NY 10010.

Where this book is distributed in the UK, Europe, and the rest of the world,
this is by Palgrave Macmillan, a division of Macmillan Publishers Limited,
registered in England, company number 785998, of Houndmills,
Basingstoke, Hampshire RG21 6XS.

Palgrave Macmillan is the global academic imprint of the above companies
and has companies and representatives throughout the world.

Palgrave® and Macmillan® are registered trademarks in the United States,
the United Kingdom, Europe, and other countries.

ISBN: 978-0-230-62169-5

Images in the book's photo section courtesy of the author.

Library of Congress Cataloging-in-Publication Data

Carson, Clayborne, 1944–
    Martin's dream : my journey and the legacy of Martin Luther King Jr. /
Clayborne Carson.
        pages cm
    ISBN 978-0-230-62169-5
    1. Carson, Clayborne, 1944- 2. Carson, Clayborne, 1944-—Friends and
associates. 3. African American civil rights workers—Biography. 4. African
American political activists—Biography. 5. African American historians—
Biography. 6. Stanford University—Faculty—Biography. 7. King, Martin
Luther, Jr., 1929-1968—Influence. 8. King, Martin Luther, Jr., 1929-1968—
Political and social views. 9. King, Coretta Scott, 1927-2006. I. Title.

E185.97.C273A3 2013
323.092—dc23   2012030145
[B]

A catalogue record of the book is available from the British Library.

Design by Newgen Imaging Systems, (P) Ltd., Chennai, India

First edition: January 2013

10 9 8 7 6 5 4 3 2 1

Printed in the United States of America.

Contents

Contents

Introduction: My Journey

On Friday, August 26, 2011, I saw, for the first time, the Martin Luther King Jr. Memorial that I helped to design. I was excited to be present at the National Mall with my wife Susan and several of my colleagues from the Martin Luther King Jr. Research and Education Institute at Stanford. More than most people, they understood the memorial's symbolic significance as the permanent manifestation of King's strong faith, expressed in his "I Have a Dream" oration, that "we will be able to hew out of the mountain of despair a stone of hope." As we gazed upon King's solemn image sculpted into the side of the memorial's Stone of Hope, I noticed that Dorothy Cotton, who had accompanied us, was especially affected as she looked up at the image of the man with whom she had worked closely during the 1960s. A park ranger who recognized me from my visits to the King Visitors Center in Atlanta excitedly came up to offer a warm welcome and have his picture taken with us. Although I was disappointed that the official opening of the memorial, which had been scheduled for the following Sunday, was delayed due to a hurricane approaching the Washington area, I appreciated the chance to walk slowly through the memorial with friends close by and, as I took photographs in the uncrowded space, I thought about all the remarkable events in my life that had brought me to this moment.

I realized that long before I founded the King Institute or met Dorothy and even before I met Susan, my life had become intertwined with King and his legacy. I thought back to the day, August 28, 1963, almost forty-eight years earlier, when I stood in front of the Lincoln Memorial just a short distance away, watching King deliver his "Dream" speech at the March on Washington for Jobs and Freedom. I was then a naïve, nineteen-year-old student attending my first demonstration. I had participated in the event without any conception of how it would affect my life and watched King's oration without fully understanding the meaning of his words. Afterward, I became involved in a tumultuous freedom struggle that radically transformed my aspirations. My life and my dreams for the future changed in ways that as a black teenager I could not have anticipated. I certainly could not have imagined becoming a professor at Stanford University, or being invited in 1985 by Coretta Scott King to edit and publish her late husband's papers, or later assembling *The Autobiography of Martin Luther King Jr.*, thereby enabling me to see the March on Washington through his eyes as well as my own. Nor could I have imagined joining more than a million people to witness the inauguration of Barack Obama, the nation's first president of African ancestry.

This book is about my journey during the past half century from novice activist witnessing King's greatest speech to veteran historian editing his papers. My journey has taken me to many parts of the world, but it has also often brought me back to the National Mall, where my life unexpectedly shifted course. Although I saw King only from a distance during his lifetime, my life became entwined with his enduring yet contested legacy. I have come to an even deeper understanding of his Dream during the decades spent reading about his life and ideas, probing the memories of his closest acquaintances, and most of all, studying the vast quantity of papers he left behind. I have learned that he was an imperfect man unexpectedly thrust into a leadership role that he performed with extraordinary, prophetic wisdom.

At first this deeper understanding eluded me. In 1963 I had only begun to feel "the fierce urgency of now" but would soon experience the "whirlwinds of revolt" that King mentioned in his speech. I admired his eloquence but at the time was more drawn to the courageous nonviolent radicals of the Student Nonviolent Coordinating Committee (SNCC or "Snick" as it was called), the group formed in 1960 by youthful sit-in protesters who saw themselves as the vanguard of the Southern freedom struggle. As I learned more about SNCC, I imagined becoming one of their "field secretaries," who were working closely with grassroots leaders in places where segregationist resistance was fiercest and most deadly.

I never joined SNCC's staff but instead engaged in part-time activism while working my way through UCLA. I became affiliated with a local group that adapted SNCC's tactics and organizing techniques to confront urban economic problems, and in August 1965 I witnessed a mass uprising in Los Angeles that revealed the limits of civil rights progress. Afterward, SNCC and the freedom struggle that had inspired me began to disintegrate as its staff members engaged in sometimes rancorous debates about racial identity and destiny.

At first exhilarated by Black Power militancy, I began to see the wisdom of King's warning against satisfying the "thirst for freedom by drinking from the cup of bitterness and hatred" and allowing "creative protest to degenerate into physical violence." The freedom struggle overcame the Jim Crow system, but activists did not agree on the answer to King's enduring question, "Where do we go from here?"

During the years after the March on Washington, I discovered that both SNCC and King were seeking, in their different ways, to achieve goals that extended beyond civil rights reforms. They realized that the march and the civil rights legislation that followed were only stages of a difficult, long-term experiment to determine whether this diverse nation could become truly just and democratic. SNCC and King left behind valuable insights about ongoing struggles to realize the aspirations of oppressed people throughout the world.

My own activism and the research I conducted for my first book, *In Struggle: SNCC and the Black Awakening of the 1960s* (1981), gave me a lasting appreciation for SNCC organizers who imagined a future in which previously powerless people could shape the nation's destiny. The techniques that SNCC developed have enabled people who once picked cotton and their descendants to help pick presidents. SNCC's bottom-up approach has continued to inform and inspire those still struggling to transform their lives and build a better world.

Once I turned my scholarly attention from SNCC to King, I realized that he shared SNCC's view that the radical transformation of American society should start with "the least of these." He risked the popularity he had gained at the March on Washington in order to "take a stand for that which is right," yet, at the end of his life he had not reached the Promised Land. Speaking to striking sanitation workers in Memphis on the night before his assassination, he anticipated a "human rights revolution" that would "bring the colored peoples of the world out of their long years of poverty, their long years of hurt and neglect."

I will likely spend more years studying King's life than he spent living it—a testament to the enormity of his achievements and the quantity of the historical materials he left behind. I have studied not only his great speeches but also his revealing sermons, letters, occasional diaries, and published as well as unpublished writings. I have talked with his widow and other family members, close friends, expert biographers, loyal admirers, and persistent critics.

My image of King is no longer the orator I glimpsed in front of the Lincoln Memorial. Instead, he has become the flawed, fallible, familiar figure at the center of my scholarship: a preacher's son with deep family roots in the black Baptist church; a skeptical college student who became a profound advocate of social gospel Christianity; an earnest young pastor, husband, and father unexpectedly thrust into the role of civil rights leader; a convert to Gandhian principles of nonviolent resistance; a leader always aware of his limited influence over a sustained mass protest movement; and a proponent of traditional American ideals who saw civil rights reform in the context of a global struggle for human rights.

Rather than a scholarly study of King, this memoir recounts my quest to understand him and shape his legacy. I have not provided footnotes or a bibliography, because my references are mainly from books that I have edited—especially *The Papers of Martin Luther King, Jr.*—which are readily available to those interested in studying the documentary record of King's life. Instead of adding to the list of King biographies and studies of his oratory, I have chosen to write about how I came to understand King's historical significance as a great leader of a great movement and the impact of both on my life. This memoir recounts dreams that were realized during the past half century and dreams that turned into nightmares. I have sought to reconcile my view of a freedom struggle initiated and sustained by self-reliant grassroots leaders with my growing understanding of King's unique, visionary contribution to that struggle.

I have had the privilege and pleasure of disseminating King's inspiring ideas to many parts of the world through multilingual publications, lectures, documentaries, and online educational efforts. I have seen my play *Passages of Martin Luther King* performed by Chinese and Palestinian theater companies as well as in many places in the United States. Seeing "Martin" speak in languages other than English has given me a greater understanding of the universality of his Dream.

As I have shared my insights about King with people throughout the world, I have also learned from those who follow in his footsteps. As I have grown older, he has become wiser, and my journey toward personal and historical understanding continues.

Part One

The Movement

Chapter 1

Alone at the March

I saw Martin Luther King Jr. proclaim his Dream at the 1963 March on Washington. King captured the nation's attention, and his legacy ultimately became the focus of my career. In the days before the march, however, my understanding of his significance changed when I met Stokely Carmichael, a young black activist affiliated with the Student Nonviolent Coordinating Committee (SNCC). Stokely made me aware that King was only one aspect of a sustained Southern freedom struggle to overcome the Jim Crow system of racial segregation and discrimination. Although I continued to admire King, I learned that the brash protesters and "field secretaries" of SNCC were key components of a community of dedicated activists I would come to know as the Movement. They exemplified the rebelliousness and impatience I felt as a teenager.

I had grown up as one of a handful of African American residents in Los Alamos, a small New Mexico town far from the frontlines of the Southern protest movement. Nonetheless, I paid close attention to news about civil rights activities—especially when black students near my own age were involved. When I was in eighth grade, the Little Rock Nine students were braving white mobs to desegregate Central High School. While I was in high school, I read about the student-led lunch-counter sit-ins and the freedom rides. During the months before the 1963 march, President John F. Kennedy stirred me with his televised speech urging Americans to see civil rights as a "moral issue," although I wondered why it took him so long to recognize this. While courageous young black activists were battling entrenched racial oppression and capturing the nation's attention, I resigned myself to return to Albuquerque for my second year at the University of New Mexico (UNM).

Several days before the March on Washington, I traveled to Bloomington, Indiana, as part of UNM's delegation to the National Student Association's (NSA) annual convention. Stokely, a Howard University senior, was representing SNCC. I was vaguely aware of SNCC's involvement in the sit-ins, freedom rides, and Deep South voting rights campaigns, but Stokely seemed to be a knowledgeable Movement veteran. His lanky build, intense demeanor, and copious confidence made him a magnet of attention at convention sessions and impressed me to the point of envy.

As the only black student on the UNM delegation to the NSA conference, I felt a special responsibility to inform myself about the convention's most contentious issue: whether the organization should support the upcoming March on Washington. I listened as Stokely insisted that the NSA not only back the march but also give financial support to SNCC. His arguments were peppered with sardonic criticisms of cautious liberalism. Some delegates warned that passing the resolution favoring the march would prompt the withdrawal of Southern white colleges from the NSA, perhaps fatally damaging the organization.

When I took part in an informal caucus of delegates supporting Stokely's position, I observed him up close as he guided the discussions. At first, his unfamiliar accent made me wonder whether he was a foreign student. I learned that his parents were immigrants from Trinidad but that he had spent his teenage years in New York. I wasn't surprised when he mentioned that he was a philosophy major. As he described SNCC's projects, I found it remarkable that a small group of young people had taken on the ambitious mission of overcoming Southern racism. I also realized how much I was missing while attending a predominantly white university so distant from the Southern, student-led protests of the early 1960s.

During the meetings I didn't feel confident enough to contribute to the discussions and hoped that my presence was enough to indicate support. When I had my only chance to speak privately with Stokely, I confided that I hoped to attend the March on Washington, perhaps thinking this would assure him that I was not a complete bystander in the Southern struggle. "Who cares about that middle-class picnic?" he retorted. "If you really want to help the movement, get involved in one of SNCC's projects and get a taste of the real movement." I said I would think about it but knew that I would almost certainly return to school in pursuit of becoming the first college graduate in my family. Although I had no quick answer to his challenge, his words stuck in my mind.

My understanding of SNCC was also affected by a long conversation at the conference with Lucy Komisar, the young white woman who edited the *Mississippi Free Press*. Lucy patiently explained the crucial, yet largely ignored, battles over black voting rights taking place in Mississippi. She told me about Bob Moses, a former high school math teacher from New York who had initiated SNCC's voter registration efforts in the state, and about the 1961 killing of civil rights advocate Herbert Lee by a white Mississippi legislator who was quickly exonerated by an all-white coroner's jury. Lucy even took the time to teach me some freedom songs.

Stokely and Lucy, in their very different ways, made me aware that people close to my age were moving beyond just voicing their support for civil rights by dedicating their lives to the struggle. They convinced me that SNCC was at the forefront of a nonviolent crusade against white supremacy in its Deep South strongholds. Although I was not ready to drop out of college to fight on the Movement's frontlines in the Mississippi Delta, Selma, Albany, Danville, Cambridge, and other places, my impetuous curiosity had a new focus. By the time NSA delegates voted lamely to back the goals of the March on Washington but not the march itself, my perspective had shifted toward SNCC's. I began to realize that King, the nation's best-known civil rights leader, was part of a freedom struggle seeking far-reaching changes and led by grassroots activists whose names were rarely in the newspapers. It would be three years before I saw Stokely again, but that first encounter strengthened my determination to find some way to connect with the Movement.

When I confirmed that a ride to the march was available on a bus chartered by an Indianapolis National Association for the Advancement of Colored People (NAACP) group, I eagerly agreed to go and told my UNM colleagues that I would not be returning to New Mexico with them. I didn't bother to tell my parents about my plans. Dad might not have objected, but Mom almost certainly would have insisted that I not participate in any demonstration, and she was the dominant, sometimes domineering parent.

I left my suitcase in a locker at the Indianapolis bus station and boarded a bus full of strangers that left early on the evening of August 27. I had less than fifty dollars in my wallet and a return bus ticket from Indianapolis to Albuquerque. It was my first trip to Washington, my first venture so far from home, and my first demonstration of any kind, but I don't remember feeling anxious or uncertain. I was confident that my impromptu adventure would turn out well.

The bus arrived in Washington the next morning, and I was exhausted by my choice to give up hours of sleep to talk to Sylvia, a winsome Jewish teenager. We promised to stay in touch but didn't. As I got off the bus, an elderly black man, who must have quietly observed me during the ride, pushed a twenty dollar bill into my hand, guessing correctly that I was worried about having enough money to return home.

My memories of the remainder of that day are a mixture of vague and vivid impressions. I was amazed by the multitude of marchers—many more black people

than I'd ever seen growing up in New Mexico. Accustomed to dry mountain crisp-
ness, I found it hard to adjust to the hot, humid air. I was impressed that most of the
adults were well dressed in the sweltering heat, but the sweat on my white cotton
shirt compelled me to take off my sport coat.

I decided against carrying one of the official printed placards offered to me so
that I could dart around the slowly moving marchers. Self-consciously aware that
I don't sing well, I only intermittently joined in the endless choruses of "We Shall
Overcome." I noticed a black contingent from Mississippi who energized the crowd
by snaking through the marchers shouting some of the spirited freedom songs that
Lucy had taught me. Although I imagined that most black Mississippians lived in
conditions only slightly removed from slavery, these demonstrators exhibited a
sense of freedom that I found enticing. My shyness inhibited me from talking to
other young marchers, who seemed to be with families or groups.

Approaching the Lincoln Memorial, I edged through the crowd toward the
speakers' platform to get a closer view of the famous people who were being introduced. I recognized some of the scheduled singers from appearances on *The Ed
Sullivan Show*, which my family regularly watched on Sunday nights. I never imagined seeing Marion Anderson, Mahalia Jackson, Joan Baez, Pete Seeger, and Bob
Dylan in person. Actor and playwright Ossie Davis announced that W. E. B. Du
Bois, the NAACP founder and famous author of *Souls of Black Folk*, had just died in
Ghana, having exiled himself there after becoming a victim of anticommunist hysteria. In the early afternoon, after the Tribute to Women Freedom Fighters (includ-
ing student activist Diane Nash Bevel and the recently widowed "Mrs. Medgar
Evers"), the sticky heat led me to join the people who removed their shoes to cool
their feet in the Lincoln Memorial reflecting pool.

Because of my new awareness of SNCC's significance, I felt a special sense of
anticipation when march director A. Philip Randolph introduced John Lewis,
SNCC's newly elected chairman and, at twenty-three years old, the youngest
speaker on the program. I knew by then that he had been a Nashville sit-in leader
and one of the freedom riders who were imprisoned in Mississippi during the
spring of 1961.

His rural Southern cadence contrasted sharply with Stokely's urbanity, but
Lewis also exemplified SNCC's militancy and took the risk of alienating some of his
listeners. Rather than merely calling for passage of the Kennedy administration's
civil rights proposal, he drew attention to its lack of provisions to protect peaceful protests from police brutality or to enable black residents of the Deep South to
register to vote. "One man, one vote is the African cry," he announced. "It is ours,

too." Departing from the bland tone of preceding speakers, he insisted, "The revolution is at hand, and we must free ourselves of the chains of political and economic slavery."

Lewis expressed a sense of urgency that I would soon share: "We want our freedom, and we want it now." Rather than depending on the two major political parties ("both the Democrats and the Republicans have betrayed the basic principles of the Declaration of Independence"), he placed his faith in grassroots militancy. "We all recognize the fact that if any radical social, political and economic changes are to take place in our society, the people, the masses, must bring them about," he explained. I was pleased that Lewis's call for a nonviolent revolution elicited a few bursts of enthusiastic applause.

By the late afternoon hour when King was introduced to speak, I was preoccupied with thoughts of finding the bus that had brought me, but I didn't want to miss his remarks. I edged my way toward the rear of the crowd, so that I could quickly depart when he finished speaking. His initial words confirmed that my decision to attend the march was wise.

"I am happy to join with you today in what will go down in history as the greatest demonstration for freedom in the history of our nation," he began. I had no basis for determining the march's historical significance, but I wanted to believe King. Many of the previous speakers had lauded Kennedy's proposed civil rights legislation, but King's address instead suggested a broader transformation of the nation's race relations. At the time, I didn't fully understand his challenge to "the architects of our republic" or his cascade of biblical and historical references, but his metaphorical, tradition-laden diction strengthened my sense of the march's importance. John Lewis's call for radical change had disrupted my complacency, but King transformed "Freedom Now!" into passionate poetry:

> Now is the time to make real the promises of democracy. Now is the time
> to rise from the dark and desolate valley of segregation to the sunlit path
> of racial justice. Now is the time to lift our nation from the quicksands of
> racial injustice to the solid rock of brotherhood.

How could I have known then that I was listening to a great speech rather than simply the last in a long program on a sweltering day? I cannot remember exactly when I learned that King's address even had a name, but I later discovered that the "I Have a Dream" refrain was extemporaneous—a last-minute extension of his prepared remarks. I couldn't imagine having the confidence to speak to so large an audience on such an important occasion and then make up a new ending on the spot.

King's rousing conclusion would soon become embedded in my memory, but discovering its deeper meanings would take many decades. It is likely that my immaturity, my lack of historical and religious knowledge, and the distraction of finding a ride prevented me from fully appreciating King's "dream deeply rooted in the American dream."

Failing to find my original bus, I impulsively accepted an invitation to ride with a group from Brooklyn. Still half asleep when I arrived at Penn Station, I took the subway to Harlem, guessing that I could find an inexpensive place to stay for the night. After asking for directions to a cheap hotel, I instead paid a few dollars to sleep on a stranger's couch. I spent the next morning gawking at the skyscraper canyons of central Manhattan before exchanging my bus ticket from Indianapolis to Albuquerque for a ticket from New York to Indianapolis.

Only then did I call Mom collect to explain, as imprecisely as possible, my sudden detour. I told her about finding a ride to the march and then meeting a group from New York, but said little about how I planned to return home. I didn't really have a plan—only that I would figure things out after getting some much-needed rest on the bus. The tone of her voice told me that she was not pleased, but fortunately she didn't want to run up a large phone bill talking to me.

I would never tell my parents that I hitchhiked the remaining 1,300 miles from Indianapolis to Albuquerque. A succession of short rides brought me to Illinois, where a black couple offered a ride to St. Louis. When they awakened me well after midnight, I was too groggy to understand where I was and had to walk for several hours to find the interstate highway.

The next night, I survived a harrowing experience in Oklahoma when a middle-aged white man stopped for me and then immediately warned, "I'll shove you out of this car, if you cause any trouble." I wondered why he gave me a ride, but surmised that he wanted to talk to someone. His slurred voice and erratic, high-speed driving betrayed that he was drunk. "Don't worry," he assured me. "I helped design this highway. I know it like the back of my hand." Predictably, he hit a median curb, and the car careened across the roadway before he regained control. Even though it was past midnight, I insisted that I would rather walk. I found a place to rest until the next morning.

After a few more rides, I reached the Albuquerque bus station. When my parents met me there, I had already claimed my luggage and changed into fresh clothes. I did my best to disguise the fact that I was dead tired after more than two days on the road.

The march became the link between my childhood and all the remarkable and unexpected things that later happened to me as an adult. Yet, after spending decades trying to make sense of my experiences there, I still had some unanswered questions. If I had been unable to find a ride to the march, would my life have been very different? Why was I so unconcerned about how to return home? Why did I accept a ride from the march to New York, even though I had little money, and my bus ticket was from Indianapolis back to New Mexico? Why didn't I call my parents to ask them for bus fare to get home? And why was I so attracted to SNCC's worldview, so ready to change the course of my life?

My march memories began to make more sense as I came to see them through a historical lens. At the march, I didn't yet have a historian's habits—I didn't think to keep mementos or even take snapshots to preserve the details of the experience. My fleeting memories are frail pillars to carry the weight I have since placed on them. Most of what I now know about the march comes from research, not memory, but I've learned that history and autobiographies are edited versions of the past that always leave unanswered questions. When people ask me how it felt to be at the march, I find it hard to give an answer. It would be years before I grasped the full significance of that special day.

Chapter 2

Leaving Home

*A*fter returning from the March on Washington, it was difficult to readjust to ordinary life following my cross-country adventure. I had just witnessed what Martin Luther King Jr. called "the greatest demonstration" in the nation's history, but few people I knew seemed to have noticed it. I felt strangely different inside, although people who knew me probably wouldn't have noticed that either. Returning for my second year at the University of New Mexico, I was no longer an anonymous face on campus. I moved into a dorm room with a friend from high school, enrolled in classes, reconnected with former acquaintances, and quickly became involved in campus activities, including student government. Graduating from college was still my overriding ambition.

Despite the familiar surroundings, I was more aware than before that a historic freedom struggle was happening elsewhere. I thought often of the courageous SNCC freedom fighters living extraordinary lives while I was attending classes. My new subscriptions to SNCC's *Student Voice* newsletter and Lucy Komisar's *Mississippi Free Press* kept me informed about often violent segregationist resistance to desegregation and black voting rights, especially in the Deep South. Still far from the frontlines, I read about battlegrounds such as Selma, Alabama, Albany, Americus, and "Terrible" Terrell County in Georgia; and McComb, Greenville, Greenwood, Jackson, and Ruleville in Mississippi. I followed the national political debate about the Kennedy administration's proposed civil rights legislation and lamented that civil rights reform was long overdue.

A few weeks after returning from the march, I was shocked to learn that a bomb planted at Birmingham's 16th Street Baptist Church had killed four black children. Angry that the murderers were unlikely to be caught and punished, I was also dismayed that few other students shared my sense of outrage. I suspected they would have cared more if the children had been white. I wondered why white Americans were so complacent about the continued existence of the Jim Crow system of racial oppression. Lingering in my mind was James Baldwin's observation in his recently published jeremiad, *The Fire Next Time*: "How can one respect, let alone adopt, the values of a people who do not, on any level whatever, live the way they say they do, or the way they say they should? I cannot accept the proposition that the four-hundred-year travail of the American Negro should result merely in his attainment of the present level of the American civilization."

Many students were grief stricken following the assassination of President Kennedy on November 22, 1963. After hearing news of the killing in Dallas, I watched the campus mood suddenly change. Some students cried openly. Perhaps because of my prior private grief over the Birmingham bombing, I maintained a measure of emotional distance. I spent the day recording student responses to the assassination for the first of a series of weekly radio programs I had convinced student government leaders to sponsor. Editing the audio montage became a way of expressing my own feelings.

While still wondering whether Lyndon Johnson's sudden ascension to the presidency would affect prospects for passage of civil rights legislation, I jumped at the chance to represent the UNM student government at a New Orleans gathering called by the Council of Federated Organizations (COFO), which coordinated the activities of various Mississippi civil rights organizations in helping local blacks register to vote. Even more than in other Southern states, Mississippi segregationists used violence and economic intimidation as well as literacy tests to discourage black residents from registering to vote. COFO leaders had decided that a new strategy was needed to attract national attention and bring about federal intervention to protect voting rights.

Taking place just months after the NSA conference, the New Orleans meeting once again brought me in touch with the Movement. I listened intently as Bob Moses, the twenty-eight-year-old SNCC organizer who directed COFO's voting rights program, presented a bold plan to enlist hundreds of student volunteers for an ambitious project the next summer. The volunteers were expected to assist local COFO projects in various ways, such as teaching in "freedom schools" and helping black residents fill out voter registration forms. I wanted to take part in the 1944 Mississippi Summer Project, but volunteers were expected to provide their own financial support, and I needed the income from my summer job to return to school in the fall. I also surmised that COFO needed white rather than black volunteers to carry out their somewhat cynical strategy to attract public sympathy outside the South.

Moses spoke softly and slowly as he retraced his involvement in the Mississippi voting rights campaign. In 1961 he left his position as a high school math teacher in New York to launch SNCC's first organizing effort in McComb, Mississippi. Overcoming initial setbacks, he recruited a staff of "field secretaries"—mostly young black Mississippians affiliated with SNCC—and forged close ties with veteran NAACP activists, including COFO's president Aaron Henry and Amzie Moore, who put him in touch with grassroots leaders, mostly in the Mississippi Delta region. Moses was articulate and clearly well educated, yet I was struck that he wore overalls with shoulder straps and buckles in the front—the kind I imagined were worn by Mississippi sharecroppers. Even as he appealed for outside support, he emphasized the crucial roles played by black Mississippians in the voting rights struggle. He mentioned in particular forty-six-year-old Fannie Lou Hamer, who, after attempting to register to vote, was jailed, beaten, and told to leave the cotton plantation where she had worked most of her life. Rather than giving in to intimidation, she became SNCC's oldest staff member.

Although Moses sought to deflect attention from his own contribution to the Mississippi struggle, I was deeply impressed by his unassuming courage. He immediately became a new role model—someone more in tune with my reserved personality than Stokely. Disappointed that I didn't have a chance to talk with him—it would be a decade and a half before our first conversation—he remained for me an exemplar of SNCC's distinctive cadre of grassroots organizers.

While in New Orleans, I briefly experienced the Southern Jim Crow system when I joined members of the Congress of Racial Equality (CORE) who were protesting one evening outside a segregated movie theater. It was the first time I had ever carried a picket sign, and I felt relieved when the picketing ended without incident. I also accompanied a biracial group to a jazz performance at Preservation Hall, which circumvented laws forbidding racially integrated seating by not providing any seats at all.

A few weeks later, during the year-end holiday break, my political awareness expanded still more after I attended a World Ecumenical Conference held in Athens, Ohio. There I listened not only to representatives of the Southern freedom struggle but also to speakers representing freedom movements in Africa and Asia. Within just a few months, my understanding of the changes occurring in many parts of the world had grown. I felt vicariously connected to a global human rights campaign in which people my age were playing crucial roles. Though still a student, I was being drawn into the Movement. When *Time* magazine named King as its Man of the Year for 1963, I rushed to buy a copy to read about the nation's best-known civil rights leader, but I knew that other activists were more responsible than King for the sustained grassroots struggles that were challenging the Southern system of racial domination.

By the beginning of the spring semester, I had become determined to leave New Mexico but was still uncertain how to do it. Although I valued my friendships at UNM, I continued to feel isolated—as if I were missing an opportunity that I would never have again. I considered transferring to Howard University, where I could connect with the Movement, but, with only minimal financial support from my parents, I could barely afford my expenses as a resident student at UNM. While mulling my options, I applied for the Peace Corps, reasoning that I could at least do something worthwhile for two years while satisfying my desire to travel. Afterwards, I would still have saved enough money to return to college. In the spring of 1964, I was pleased to learn that I had been accepted to a Peace Corps training program at Arizona State University that would prepare volunteers to be public health workers in the Brazilian state of Moto Grosso.

After finishing my classes, I returned home to Los Alamos. As in previous summers, I worked at the Los Alamos Scientific Laboratory, which was by far the largest employer in the small, isolated town in the Jemez Mountains of northern New Mexico. My workdays were spent conducting physical tests on materials intended for a hydrogen bomb, although I had decided by then that I would not pursue a career in science. I did not pay much attention to the irony of playing a minor role in nuclear weapons development while at the same time preparing to become a Peace Corps volunteer.

Though my job absorbed much of my attention, my final summer at home provided ample time to reflect about my decision to spend the next two years in Brazil. The choice had been a compromise of sorts. I had decided against satisfying my curiosity about the Southern freedom struggle in favor of something safer and more conventional—easier to explain to my family and friends. Joining the Movement would have been the first time I had done anything to call attention to my racial identity. Yet I realized that my rapidly growing interest in racial issues was rooted in my increasing awareness that I was different in many ways from those around me. After attending the March on Washington, I knew that this difference offered appealing and exciting possibilities.

The significance of my choice became clearer at the beginning of the summer, when I learned that three young Mississippi civil rights workers—one of them a recently arrived volunteer for the Summer Project—had not returned from investigating a church burning near Philadelphia, Mississippi. The likelihood that they had been kidnapped or killed by segregationists made me more aware of the risks I might have faced as a volunteer. Subsequent news reports indicated that hundreds of other volunteers had resolved to continue the summer effort, despite the disappearance of the three. Although I assumed that I would have done the same, how could I know? Was I deserting the Southern struggle for a less risky sojourn in rural Brazil?

Even as I made plans to leave for Peace Corps training, I followed news reports about the search for the missing civil rights workers and the discovery early in August 1964 of their bodies near their torched car. By this time, federal officials had learned from informants that the three men were abducted by Ku Klux Klan members after being held in the Neshoba County jail and then released late at night. My parents were undoubtedly aware of the Mississippi murders, but I did not tell them that I had wanted to participate in the Mississippi Summer Project. I suspected that they found Peace Corps service in Brazil far more understandable than going to Mississippi for any reason.

I didn't know for sure why we were the first black family to move to Los Alamos, but I assumed that my parents were seeking a better life for themselves and their children. They wanted to find a place free of the racial barriers and hardships facing black Americans elsewhere. King's speech at the march had envisioned a mass struggle to achieve racial equality, but they had chosen migration rather than civil rights activism as a way to pursue their version of the American dream.

Dad—Clayborne Carson Sr.—was born in Tuscaloosa, Alabama, but grew up in Detroit, where his father had migrated during World War I to work at Ford Motor Company. His siblings would remember him as a voracious reader—he was especially well-informed about history and current events—but also as an indifferent student in high school. During the Great Depression, he took a few college courses at Wayne University while struggling to find a decent job. At the time of the 1940 census, he was twenty-four years old, still living with his parents and working part time as a bellhop on a ferry between the city and Belle Isle Park on the Detroit River.

As was the case for millions of other men mired in the Great Depression, his life changed course when he was drafted in early 1942. After he scored well on an aptitude test, the Army selected him for officer training at the Quartermaster School at Fort Lee, Virginia, which had just been opened to black candidates. He was undergoing more training at Gunter Field in Alabama when he met my mother, Louise Lee.

Mom was born in southern Mississippi but had grown up in the rural town of Century, Florida, in the northwest part of the state. The 1940 census reported that she was a cook in a private home. She came to Montgomery in the early 1940s to take advantage of the job opportunities associated with the military buildup in the area. I never knew exactly how they met, but their courtship must have been brief. When Dad was sent to another military base in New Jersey, she followed, and they were married on October 29, 1942.

I was born on June 15, 1944, in Buffalo, New York, where Mom was staying with her relatives while Dad was taking part in the Allied invasion of Europe. During my early years, Mom took me to Century for a while and then to Seattle, where Dad joined us when he returned from abroad in November 1945 as a first lieutenant. He accepted a civilian job as a security inspector for the Atomic Energy Commission at the Los Alamos laboratory, which had been secretly established in during the war to design and build the atomic weapons that destroyed Hiroshima and Nagasaki. In 1947 Dad went alone to his new job while Mom and I stayed in Seattle with my brother, Michael, and sister, Gail, until our family housing was built in Los Alamos.

A family photograph taken soon after the war on a busy downtown Seattle sidewalk became my ideal image of my parents as they were before I formed enduring memories of them. Dad looks handsome and confident in his dress officer's uniform. Mom is pretty and poised in her long dark overcoat, knee-high dress, and sporty pillbox hat. Although Dad stood only five feet seven inches, he appears taller in the photo. Walking between them, holding both of their hands is the well-dressed two-year-old me, wearing a jacket, matching short pants, and white shoes. Even after I learned more about the complexities of my parents' marriage and of the war experience for black soldiers, I would still feel certain that no couple of that time, black or white, could have been a better symbol of postwar optimism.

In 1949 we moved into a newly constructed two-story, three-bedroom, wood-frame house—half of a duplex on a corner lot on the northwest edge of Los Alamos, more than seven thousand feet above sea level in the Jemez Mountains. Although Dad's salary at the facility was substantially less than what most scientists there made, our rented home was spacious and featured a scenic view across one of the canyons between the mesas that extended east from the mountain range. The laboratory and the town's ten thousand residents were, until my teenage years, surrounded by a fence with guard stations where Dad and other security inspectors checked entry passes. Initially a military community built to defeat fascism and sustained to defeat communism, Los Alamos had become, by the time we arrived, a safe, comfortable, suburban community—the kind of place to which millions of white Americans but only a few black Americans migrated during the decade after World War II.

In the years before I began to see the fence as confinement rather than protection, I thrived in this strangely conventional setting. By the time I entered Mountain elementary school, Mom had already nurtured my interest in reading by providing a set of Childcraft readers that introduced me to nursery rhymes and classic children's stories. Although my parents themselves had few books, I remember even as a young child immersing myself in the books, magazines, and newspapers that were around our house. My insatiable curiosity drove me to explore my initial areas of interest—especially anything I could find about the various countries in the world. In one burst of investigative energy, I sent letters to numerous travel bureaus and embassies to assemble maps and brochures from more than fifty countries. This inquisitiveness tended to guide my education more than assignments from teachers. My fifth grade teacher perceptively noted in his year-end report that I had "great powers of concentration but not always on the assigned work." Lauding my "burning curiosity about the world he lives in both socially and from a scientific standpoint," he observed that I failed to "understand that this search for knowl edge and understanding can be accomplished more when directed." When I was about ten, Mom began buying volumes of the *Funk and Wagnall's Encyclopedia* that were selling for $1 each at the grocery store, and in a year we had the full set. The encyclopedia quickly became my convenient, oft-consulted source of miscellaneous information. Only as I began to wonder about the significance of my skin color, which set me apart from almost everyone I knew outside my family, did I become dissatisfied with its paltry coverage of black American life and culture. Many years later I would accept an assignment to rewrite the encyclopedia's African American history entry.

Mom also nurtured my early interest in music. Her favorite genres were jazz and classical, especially opera. After we acquired a Sylvania combination television, radio, and record player, she filled Sunday afternoons not only with a fried chicken dinner but also with a dose of cultural edification. Around the time I was eight, she convinced Dad to purchase a piano and paid for my piano lessons by sewing clothes for the piano teacher and her daughter.

As I gradually expanded my social world beyond home, I participated in the socializing activities that were typical for white children growing up in small-town America during this period. Known mainly by my nickname "Pete"—chosen for reasons I never understood to distinguish me from Dad—I progressed from Cub through Explorer Scouts and delivered newspapers from about the age of ten (I can still mentally retrace my paper route and recall some of my longtime customers). I played Little League baseball and then participated in the Babe Ruth league in my early teenage years. During my high school years, I was the center fielder on the town's only American Legion team, taking advantage of the opportunity to travel to games against teams from throughout the state. I also played basketball on the high school team but spent most of my time on the bench, not being quick enough to play guard or tall enough at six feet to be a good forward. Because my 130 pounds did not fill out my frame, my prospects for football were even less promising. Although Mom rarely found the time to watch me play, Dad was always at my games whenever he could get away from work. Sports brought us closer. Normally quiet, he became animated when we talked about his favorite team, the Detroit Tigers. He also had a strong interest in boxing and told me about the Detroit ties of former heavyweight champion Joe Louis.

Although I became adept at fitting into the surrounding social world, by the time I reached my teenage years my daydreams often took me elsewhere. Once I realized the limits of the encyclopedia at home or became bored with my classes in school, I read books from the Los Alamos Public Library or purchased paperbacks for my own library. Given the proximity of the Los Alamos Scientific Laboratory, it was hardly surprising that I had a strong interest in science, mathematics, and science fiction. I imagined becoming a scientist, like those who had been responsible for the key theoretical breakthroughs in atomic physics. Among my ambitious teenage intellectual quests was to learn enough math and science to understand Albert Einstein's original papers on relativity.

My interests were eclectic and wide-ranging. In addition to my curiosity about science, I was especially drawn to books about history, although it never occurred to me that I might become a historian. As for literature, I experienced the intellectual rites of passage—such as the temporary thrall of J. D. Salinger's *Catcher in the Rye*, Ayn Rand's *The Fountainhead,* George Orwell's *1984,* and Aldous Huxley's *Brave New World*—that broadened the imaginations of many precocious teenagers then and now. I was also drawn to writings by black authors, such as Richard Wright's *Black Boy* and *Native Son* and W. E. B. Du Bois's *Souls of Black Folk*, which, along with Lerone Bennett's occasional pieces in *Ebony* magazine, provided my first exposure to the serious study of African American life.

As a teenager, my budding interest in racial issues was linked to my increasing realization that my beliefs on many topics were somewhat unconventional, although hardly radical. Racial prejudice was merely one of many problems that seemed to be rooted in ignorance, intolerance, and antiquated ways of thinking. On religious matters, I was skeptical about what I learned in Sunday school at the local Baptist church where Mom took me—she had attended a black Baptist church as a child. After she switched to the interdenominational United Church, I enjoyed the social environment it offered, but remained skeptical about some aspects of Christian dogma, especially the notion that Jesus was literally the son of God. My religious doubts led me to read Bertrand Russell's *Why I Am Not a Christian*. I concluded that atheism was the most logical belief system, but was nonetheless drawn to the moral and ethical concerns associated with Christianity. I decided that the beliefs of Unitarians were closest to my own, and joined the Liberal Religious Youth group at the local Unitarian Church. In college I would continue to search for a hospitable religious community even as my beliefs remained somewhat heretical.

My political beliefs similarly gravitated toward liberalism because I associated conservatism with close-minded intolerance and indifference to matters of social justice. I read John Hersey's *Hiroshima*, with its horrifying descriptions of the destruction caused by the bomb made in Los Alamos, but only gradually began to question why the laboratory continued to design more powerful bombs to combat the Soviet menace. My beliefs about foreign policy were a mixture of utopianism, idealism, and anticolonialism. I hoped that the 1962 test-ban treaty was a first step toward the eventual elimination of nuclear weapons and the formation of a world government. I saw some merit in Marxism and socialism, but also felt that communism was totalitarianism. Nonetheless, I sympathized with Fidel Castro's successful effort to overthrow the pro-American Batista dictatorship. My unconventional ideas were not coherent enough to be called an ideology; nor were they part of a public identity as a free thinker or leftist. I saw myself as a liberal Democrat and favored John Kennedy in the 1960 presidential election. My beliefs did not keep me from unsuccessfully seeking an appointment to the Air Force Academy or West Point—I was selected as an alternate—or from working at the Los Alamos laboratory during the summers of 1962, 1963, and 1964.

By the end of my final summer at home, I realized that Los Alamos was not the idyllic place I remembered as a child and that my parents were themselves isolated from the kind of social life they had experienced growing up. Although they did not often volunteer information about their racial experiences and had many friends who were not black, I noticed that they had a special affinity for those they identified as "Spanish," a term applied to those who were descendants of the Spanish-speaking natives of northern New Mexico. They also made a special effort to establish contact with the few other black people who lived in or happened to visit Los Alamos. They appeared to know a large proportion of the black residents of northern New Mexico. I sensed that they wanted us to read the *Ebony* magazines that always featured profiles of successful black Americans. Yet they gave no indication that they missed or wanted us to experience life in a predominantly black community. Instead they encouraged me and my six siblings to mind our manners in public and to embrace the advantages of living in a generally affluent town in a region with unique scenic and cultural richness. On holidays, we often crowded into our Ford station wagon and drove to Santa Fe or Taos or one of the nearby Pueblos or to one of New Mexico's national or state parks.

The only indication that my parents felt any unhappiness with their life in New Mexico were their arguments that happened with increasing frequency and ferocity during my teenage years. They usually argued about money, but sometimes Mom's resentments focused on how Dad's parents had treated her when he was away at war.

She had a hard side to her personality and was always willing to express strong opinions on any subject that interested her. I never heard her speak out against white racism, but I also couldn't imagine her willingly submitting to it. Standing four inches shorter than Dad, the emotional force of Mom's angry outbursts gave her the edge. In contrast to her forceful will, Dad was generally amicable and conciliatory, although his temper could be a slow-burning fuse when Mom lashed out at him. Sometimes the violence of their words frightened me. On one occasion she threatened to leave Dad, but they stayed together, as most married couples did back then.

I had also often argued with Mom during my teenage years. Although pliant as a young child, it was perhaps inevitable that my precociousness and increasingly rebellious spirit would also result in confrontations with her unyielding sense of rectitude. Nonetheless, as I prepared to leave home, my sometimes tumultuous relationship with my parents had settled into a kind of acceptance on their part of my desire to explore the world outside the state where they would live for the rest of their lives.

When I left Los Alamos at the end of August 1964 to begin Peace Corps training, I had internalized President Kennedy's call to national service and looked forward to the challenging twelve-week program of public health training and intensive Portuguese lessons. About halfway through the program, however, I was troubled when a substantial number of the trainees whom I liked were "deselected" from the program, despite performing well in classes. Some trainees speculated that the conservative Mormons in charge of our program were weeding out those with liberal views, but I was reassured when the only other black trainee and I made it through the first cut. Nevertheless, our political discussions afterward became more muted, even though the training coincided with news of King's receipt of the Nobel Peace Prize, Lyndon Johnson's landslide victory over Barry Goldwater in the presidential election, and the start of the Free Speech Movement spearheaded by Mississippi Summer volunteers returning to the University of California, Berkeley.

On the final day of training, I was stunned to learn that I would not be going to Brazil. I was not comforted knowing that one-third of the original group had also been deselected. I had performed well in classes, but the program director explained that I was a "loner" who hadn't "bonded with the other trainees." I wanted to point to my selection as "Best Personality" in high school and argue that I would have been more sociable if my friends had not been deselected. Expecting to spend Thanksgiving saying good-bye to my family, I returned to Los Alamos uncertain about my future.

Fortunately, my decision making was made easier when my older half-sister came to visit from Los Angeles along with her husband and infant daughter. I had not seen Dorothy since she left home during her high school years to live with Mom's mother in Florida and never fully understood her reasons for leaving, although I remembered her heated arguments with Mom. I figured out as a teenager that Dad was not her father. I guessed that this explained her discontent and perhaps also Mom's oft-expressed resentment of the way Dad's family had treated her while he was serving in the military. I welcomed the chance to become reacquainted with Dorothy and hoped that she might supply missing pieces of our shared past. When she invited me to return with her to Los Angeles for a visit, I quickly accepted.

Within days of my arrival at her bungalow in the West Adams district near La Brea Boulevard, I knew that I would not soon leave the ocean beaches, palm trees, and ample amusements of Los Angeles. I found a job working the midnight shift at the Donut Chalet on the corner of Fifth and Hill in downtown Los Angeles (my formative experiences had not prepared me for the youthful sexual hustling and homelessness I saw each night). I used my savings to rent a small apartment in West Los Angeles near Santa Monica and not far from UCLA.

After enrolling at UCLA in February 1965, I found a job at Audience Studies, Inc., an advertising research firm then housed in temporary buildings on the Columbia Pictures lot on Sunset Boulevard. It was only slightly closer to campus than my previous job, but my hours were more flexible and mostly in the afternoons. Although my work there was routine—tallying audience responses to television commercials—the job paid enough to cover my living expenses. It had the additional perk of admission to screenings of Columbia films before their release and the occasional glimpse of Hollywood stars on the lot. (I recall noticing a young Jane Fonda among the actors I recognized.)

Hollywood's grime somewhat belied its glittery reputation, and my classes at UCLA were hardly more appealing than those I had taken at UNM. During my initial months in Los Angeles, I sometimes felt lost and lonely in the vast, fragmented metropolis. Yet there was no doubt in my mind that I had made the right choice in leaving New Mexico for Los Angeles. I knew that I belonged in this fascinating, multifaceted place that promised to reward my curiosity.

Chapter 3

Finding the Movement in Los Angeles

A year and a half after the March on Washington and just months after my arrival in Los Angeles, the Movement I admired from a distance suddenly came closer, and I didn't want to miss a chance to connect with it. On March 7, 1965, I watched televised coverage of the "Bloody Sunday" assault by Alabama troopers and police who used tear gas and clubs to turn back hundreds of voting rights marchers leaving Selma on their way to the state capitol in Montgomery. SNCC chair John Lewis, the youthful speaker I had heard at the March on Washington, was one of those pummeled in the unprovoked assault on the Edmond Pettus Bridge. I initially considered answering SNCC's plea for outside help by going to Selma, but couldn't afford to lose the part-time job that enabled me to pay my rent and student fees. Instead, I took part in demonstrations at the downtown Los Angeles Federal Building that were intended to prod the federal government to act decisively on behalf of the voting rights campaign.

As was the case at the Washington march, I came alone and initially stood apart, watching the variously dressed demonstrators—black and white, young and old, most of them carrying signs proclaiming their views and affiliations. After convincing myself to join the picket line on Spring Street, I gradually became comfortable singing freedom songs and participating in the call-and-response chanting: "What do we want? Freedom! When do we want it? Now!"

Listening to the occasional impromptu discussions about whether to engage in civil disobedience, I learned that local activists were split over tactics. The United Civil Rights Committee, an umbrella organization headed by Dr. H. H. Brookins, supported the demonstrations but opposed disrupting the Federal Building's operations.

But many of the protesters—including members of the CORE and local Friends of SNCC groups—preferred more militant tactics, such as blocking entrances to the building. As a newcomer to Los Angeles, I was not yet affiliated with any group and was reluctant to risk arrest, but I felt drawn to the militants who reflected my own impatience with the pace of voting rights reform.

During the afternoon of Tuesday, March 9, sidewalk tactical discussions in Los Angeles intensified when demonstrators learned that a new march to Montgomery led by Martin Luther King Jr. had turned back after state troopers confronted marchers attempting to leave Selma. Ed Wilson, who said he was from SNCC's regional office in Southern California, denounced the retreat. He scoffed that King "was preaching at his Atlanta church, when he should have been with the marchers who were assaulted on Sunday." He then asked, "Who's going to join me when I go up to the U.S. Attorney's office and demand that the Justice Department do something?" I impulsively stepped forward, along with about three dozen others.

When we arrived at the office, Wilson and a few others barged inside, while the rest of us remained outside chanting slogans and singing freedom songs that echoed through the hall of offices. When about a dozen federal marshals arrived, I wondered whether it was too late to reconsider joining the sit-in and was relieved when Wilson emerged from the office to announce, without much explanation, that we should leave. Upon reaching the lobby, about a dozen members of our group suddenly sat on the floor and linked arms, ignoring warnings from guards that the building was closing for the day and anyone remaining inside would be arrested.

I watched quietly as the marshals dragged the protesters toward the door and then I walked sheepishly from the building along with office workers leaving for the day. Once outside, I pondered my indecision about going to jail. I admired those willing to be arrested but, at the last moment, I had backed away from joining the protesters. (Wilson, I noticed, was not among them.) Did I lack their courage and commitment? How could I be sure that my arrest would actually help the voting rights cause? Would it cost me my job? Was I thinking too much, as I often did in situations that called for spontaneity? I had learned some things about myself, and not all of them were flattering.

Since attending the March on Washington, I often imagined leaving college to become a full-time SNCC worker challenging the Jim Crow laws in the Deep South, but I had instead chosen to continue my undergraduate studies. The images of the Selma marchers being beaten and teargassed made me wonder whether I was ready to enlist as a foot soldier of the Southern struggle. If I had followed King on the second march, would I have been secretly relieved when he turned back? Despite my ambivalence about being beaten or arrested, I felt a sense of comradeship with the demonstrators who entered the building and was pleased that a few of them later recognized me.

On Thursday, March 11, the urgency of the voting rights issue became more evident after we learned that Reverend James Reeb, a white voting rights supporter, had died after being brutally beaten by Selma segregationists. Although the Alabama voting rights campaign had been energized a month earlier by the police killing of black activist Jimmie Lee Jackson, Reeb's death attracted far greater national press coverage and spurred new demands for federal action.

Since I didn't have classes or work that weekend, I again entered the Federal Building, this time with Lynelle, a white activist I had met on the picket line. I was impressed that she had worked with SNCC in Mississippi during the 1964 Freedom Summer, and her cool demeanor hinted at experiences I could only imagine. She suggested that we sit in the Federal Building lobby to test whether the authorities would overreact by shutting the entrances, even if only briefly. Our two-person protest surprisingly succeeded in closing the building for about an hour, longer than the larger sit-in had earlier in the week. We left when marshals gave their final warning that we would be arrested. Once again flirting with arrest—and perhaps with Lynelle—I had taken another small step toward joining the Movement.

During the weekend, the Federal Building demonstrations culminated into a rally on Saturday that attracted about six thousand people. Because the building was closed, I had no further opportunities to risk arrest, and, on Monday, March 15, President Lyndon Johnson announced at a joint session of Congress that he would introduce new voting rights legislation. Although previously skeptical of Johnson's commitment to equal rights, I was elated when he identified his presidency with the cause: "Really it's all of us who must overcome the crippling legacy of bigotry and injustice. And we shall overcome."

After Alabama voting rights advocates overturned a federal court injunction against resuming the march from Selma, bickering continued among the various civil rights groups in Los Angeles, and the Los Angeles Federal Building demonstrations dwindled in size. By then I realized that, even as my commitment wavered, my sympathies lay with the young people who favored militant nonviolent protests. I regretted that I did not find a ride to join the thousands of marchers who finally reached the Alabama state capitol in Montgomery on March 25, where King once again singularly expressed the meaning of the historical moment:

I know you are asking today, "How long will it take?" I come to say to you this afternoon, however difficult the moment, however frustrating the hour, it will not be long, because truth crushed to earth will rise again.

How long? Not long, because no lie can live forever. How long? Not long,
because you still reap what you sow. How long? Not long, because the arc
of the moral universe is long, but it bends toward justice.

By the time of the Federal Building demonstrations, I had become friends with
Charlie, a Jewish co-worker at Audience Studies who shared my interest in civil rights
activism. In contrast to my ingrained reticence about expressing unconventional
political views, Charlie startled me with his uninhibited verbal blasts against "fascist
pigs" who favored the status quo. He also railed against liberal Democratic politicians willing to compromise their principles. He identified himself as a radical, a label
preferred by many of the activists I would meet. Coincidentally, Charlie lived near
my apartment, allowing our office conversations to extend into the evenings. During
the spring, he introduced me to other (mostly Jewish) activists, advised me about the
relative merits of various leftist factions, and encouraged me to discover the unique
recreational virtues of marijuana.

Although I remained attracted to SNCC, Charlie pointed out that the Friends
of SNCC group in Los Angeles was mainly devoted to fundraising for SNCC's
Southern projects. He belonged to the Non-Violent Action Committee (N-VAC), a
group that adapted SNCC's militant protest tactics and grassroots organizing techniques to an urban setting. N-VAC's founders—Woody Coleman, Robert Hall, and
Danny Gray—were black activists who had left CORE to focus their efforts more on
the economic problems of poor and working-class black people. N-VAC's strategy
was to use boycotts and sit-ins to prod companies to hire more black employees.
Because the group was comprised entirely of those willing to "put their bodies on
the line" by going to jail, tactical discussions inside the group were usually short
and to the point: "Who's going?"

After Charlie introduced me to Woody Coleman, I decided that N-VAC was the
closest equivalent to SNCC that I was likely to find in Los Angeles. I was impressed
that N-VAC welcomed white as well as black members, although it was only the three
founders who focused on community organizing while most members, including
all of the whites, were involved in direct action. Organizing required a degree of
commitment that was difficult for those with full-time jobs or who lived outside the
predominantly black South Central area of Los Angeles.

As a full-time student living in a predominantly white neighborhood, I realized
that becoming an N-VAC community organizer was as unrealistic as my dream of
becoming a SNCC field secretary, but I wanted to contribute to the group in some
way. I soon decided that political activism in Los Angeles was almost as exciting

as participating in the Southern freedom struggle. Watching Martin Luther King Jr. speak at a well-attended UCLA event just weeks after the culmination of the Selma-to-Montgomery march seemed to confirm that I was well placed to take part in a freedom struggle that was becoming national in scope. I couldn't be Stokely Carmichael or Bob Moses, much less King, but N-VAC needed bodies for their demonstrations, and I had one to lend.

Late in the spring of 1965, after finishing my first term at UCLA, I agreed to join half a dozen N-VAC members who sat in at a Thriftymart grocery store in Santa Ana, about an hour's drive southeast from Los Angeles. The chain was targeted by N-VAC because of its discriminatory hiring practices. We arrived at the crowded store late on a Friday afternoon and took fully loaded carts to the counters, unloaded their contents, and then, after announcing our purpose, occupied positions in front of the store entrances. By the time a small contingent of Santa Ana police arrived, we had achieved our purpose. The store's business had ceased during a normally busy period, and the irate store manager demanded our arrest for trespassing. The police officers seemed unsure how feasible it would be to drag us all away. When they gave the final warning that we would be jailed, Woody calmly replied that we would leave.

We returned to our cars, which were driven by nonparticipants, and police escorted us from the city. I felt a mixture of emotions: relief that I wasn't in jail, a measure of guilt that our sit-in was coercive rather than persuasive, and regret that I had once again merely flirted with incarceration. Yet, almost two years after walking alone amid the thousands of marchers in Washington, I now had Movement friends and a closer vantage point for observing its urban dimension.

Curiosity and uncertainty about my Movement role prompted me to ask Woody if I could interview him for the *Los Angeles Free Press*, the "underground" weekly that had been founded a year earlier. I was somewhat surprised when he agreed and even more so when Art Kunkin, the paper's editor, reacted enthusiastically to my proposed profile, given that I was a newcomer to Los Angeles with no journalistic experience. The paper was attracting a rapidly growing readership interested mainly in the burgeoning Los Angeles music scene and nascent hippie counterculture. Kunkin, however, was a veteran leftist, and he was willing to pay nonprofessional writers very modest fees for articles on political topics ignored by the mainstream press.

Promising to present his ideas with minimal commentary by me, I convinced Woody to speak frankly. His bold prediction opened the article: "I'm looking for a bloodbath this summer. We're going to get tired of being peaceful and nonviolent without getting anything. We're still getting crumbs; we're going to get a big slice of that cake." The thirty-one-year-old unemployed construction worker told me that he had been arrested seventeen or eighteen times ("I can't remember exactly how many"). He acerbically dismissed the NAACP ("would do the civil rights movement a great service if they would dissolve") and King (a "misguided or misinformed individual" whose attitude was "don't do anything to make anybody mad"). He described SNCC in positive terms but was more impressed by the Nation of Islam. He faulted Malcolm X's former group only for lacking an "active program"—"If you stopped ten cats on the street and asked them where the NAACP office is, none of them would know, but four of five would know where the mosque is."

Woody intended N-VAC to be a black-led "mean and nasty organization, where people have everything to gain and nothing to lose." He said that its office at 4066 South Central Avenue (near what is now Martin Luther King Jr. Boulevard) offered a convenient place "where people can walk in off the street with their grievances." My article concluded with another of Woody's provocative forecasts: "We won't get a solution until we put enough pressure, until the politicians realize that there's not going to be any peace until the Negroes get their freedom. The movement will probably come to bloodshed. We've tried enough non-violence and seen that it doesn't work."

When Woody's pessimistic yet prophetic remarks appeared in the June 18, 1965, issue of the *Free Press*, I could not have predicted that less than two months later the arrest of a black driver would ignite a mass insurgency that would spread quickly from Watts to other black neighborhoods of South Central Los Angeles. The suppressed resentment felt by many black residents surfaced after police stopped Marquette Frye on August 11 and scuffled with Frye's brother and mother when they intervened in the arrest. Rumors of police brutality prompted looting of stores and attacks against police. By the following evening, black residents in the police-designated "riot zone" realized that white authorities could no longer control the contagion of anger and racial resentment.

The day after the rebellion began I left work and assembled with other members at N-VAC's office, which was several miles north of where most of the previous night's violence had taken place. As we discussed how to respond, sounds of shattering glass drew our attention outside. We saw gang members using crowbars to break open several nearby retail stores. By the time police cars arrived at the scene, the more expensive items had been taken. I looked on with horror as one of the youngsters picking over the remnants inside a store fled in panic by running through a display window. The police officers merely observed the brazen law-breaking for a few minutes and then drove away. By nightfall, nearly all of the retail stores in the area had been looted and some had been set on fire. Although we heard many sirens, we saw no firemen attempting to douse the flames that engulfed buildings to the north of the N-VAC office.

Our office and a few places with "Soul Brother" signs survived the night undamaged. I did not feel personally threatened by those milling on the street outside, but news reports of whites being dragged from their cars and beaten while driving through black neighborhoods caused me to fear for the safety of the few white N-VAC members in the office. Yet I understood why Carolyn, an N-VAC stalwart who had been arrested at the Federal Building, and Jon, a former Marine married to a black woman, wanted to remain outside the office. I realized that all of us were uncertain how N-VAC should respond to the unfocused anger and discontent of black residents.

After receiving a phone report about a wounded man stranded in a nearby alley, we jumped at the chance to do something other than watch. I left with Robert Hall and Jerry Farber in an unsuccessful search for the man, but, while returning to the office, we ran into a line of policemen patrolling the area on foot. Uncertain whether to retreat or move forward, we decided to stand still. As the police approached, we tried to explain our errand, but one of the officers cursed at us and several began beating us with their billy clubs. Groggy from a blow to my head, I decided to run away, even while fearing that I might be shot in the back. My two companions made the same decision. After sneaking back to the office, we felt fortunate to have avoided the fate of many unarmed residents who became victims of "justifiable homicide" after encounters with police. (I later learned that a short distance away on Central, at about the same time as our beating, police killed an unarmed man they suspected of looting.)

Early the next morning, I returned to my car which was parked on a side street near the office, only to discover that the windows were broken. Someone in the neighborhood told me that firemen had vandalized the car because of its "FREEDOM NOW" bumper stickers, but I doubted that firemen would notice this while much of the city was burning down. Taking care to avoid police and the glass that littered the streets, I drove slowly to the 110 Freeway, which was filled with its discordantly normal traffic, and made my way to my West Los Angeles apartment. I did not return to the N-VAC office until Sunday. By then, despite hearing radio reports of sniper fire, the arrival of National Guard troops brought a measure of calm to the Central Avenue neighborhood. Some residents expressed pride that the Los Angeles Police Department had required military assistance to restore order.

That afternoon, after listening to the radio as a military officer denied that National Guard vehicles were armed with mounted machine guns, we had fun prodding a reluctant white *New York Times* reporter sequestered at our office to come out front to confirm that the spokesman was lying.

The following Tuesday, I considered going to a community meeting in Watts featuring Martin Luther King Jr., who had been in Puerto Rico when the uprising began. I decided against attending because the meeting was intended for residents. I was also reluctant to go through roadblocks surrounding the "riot area" and risk joining the more than thirty people killed by police or guardsmen. Although several white officials, including Governor Pat Brown, publicly suggested that King's presence would worsen the situation, staying away would have been a far greater blow to his stature as the nation's most influential advocate of nonviolence. The *Los Angeles Times* reported some heckling, but most of King's listeners, according to the paper, "treated the civil rights leader with affection and respect."

Chapter 4

Bridging Racial Boundaries

*T*he Los Angeles rebellion marked the beginning of the Non-Violent Action Committee's swift decline. Although members of the group saw themselves as being in touch with black urban realities, and Woody Coleman had even warned of the impending violence, N-VAC's nonviolent militancy and biracial composition suddenly seemed tame and outmoded. Our protests had secured a few agreements to expand job opportunities for black workers, but we had done little to solve the problems of black residents in South Central Los Angeles. Woody and a few other members in the group remained committed to grassroots organizing and (somewhat) civil disobedience, but most white members began shifting their attention from civil rights concerns to the war in Vietnam. I still wanted to be part of the Movement, but the activist community that I had imagined existing in N-VAC as well as in SNCC proved to be elusive.

I didn't realize it at the time, but the summer of 1965 marked the end of the era of major nonviolent, interracial civil rights protests. The March on Washington and the Selma-to-Montgomery march captured the nation's attention more than any other black-led political protest before or since. Those involved in the long struggle to overcome the Southern Jim Crow system achieved their culminating victory when President Lyndon Johnson signed the Voting Rights Act in August 1965. Martin Luther King Jr.'s decision to become involved in the Chicago Freedom Movement along with SNCC's attempts to launch projects in Northern cities signaled a shift in the focus of African American militant politics from the Deep South to the urban North. The protest campaigns aimed at the Southern bastions of white supremacy would soon be overshadowed by varied new forms of political activism addressing concerns that were national and even global in scope.

During the months after the rebellion, I became increasingly aware of the divisions that existed among black activists who considered themselves militant or radical. Some black nationalist groups rejected the civil rights goals of N-VAC in favor of efforts to increase racial pride and create black-controlled institutions. Unlike N-VAC, which had welcomed anyone of any race willing to risk arrest during protests, black nationalists made clear that they wanted to work only with other black people or perhaps with other nonwhite oppressed groups. Before the rebellion, N-VAC had provided a way for me to learn about the black neighborhoods near its headquarters. I soon realized that it was rapidly being eclipsed by other organizations which had stronger black community ties and were more able to express the anger and discontent that fueled the summer's explosion of racial violence.

Like many black activists of the time, I was attracted to the ideas of the recently assassinated black nationalist leader Malcolm X. Malcolm's background was drastically different from my own; yet I was inspired by his evolution from hustler and criminal to Nation of Islam minister to advocate of grassroots militancy to Pan-African visionary—a story vividly related in Alex Haley's *The Autobiography of Malcolm X*, published early in 1965. I recognized important lessons that could be drawn from Malcolm's speeches and his efforts after leaving the Nation of Islam to forge ties with grassroots militants. During the fall of 1964, he met with SNCC's John Lewis while both were traveling in Africa, and in February 1965 he went to Selma to show his support for the Alabama voting rights campaign.

Although intrigued by Malcolm's political ideas, I was troubled by the anti-white sentiments that he had expressed as a minister of the Nation of Islam. I had been drawn to N-VAC and SNCC not because I wanted to separate myself from all white people; instead I wanted to connect with people of all races who were breaking free from the constraints of conventional American life. Nonetheless, my awareness of racial oppression in the North and the South caused me to wonder whether groups such as the Nation of Islam were a necessary part of the solution to America's race problems. Did I resist racial separation due to the fact that I had grown up more accustomed to living among whites than among black people? After the Los Angeles rebellion, I considered for the first time the possibility that racial integration was an illusory goal for many black people.

I became more aware of the volatility of my own racial attitudes when I attended the Los Angeles production of the controversial black playwright Leroi Jones's (later Amiri Baraka) one-act play, *The Dutchman*. Among a racially mixed audience crowded in a small theater, I was immediately struck by the main character being named Clay, a coincidence that heightened the play's emotional impact for me. Riding alone on a subway car, Clay encounters an attractive, uninhibited white woman, Lula, who flirts with him, invites his sexual interest, and then taunts him for being an "Uncle Tom." In a climactic monologue, Clay unleashes his long-suppressed racial anger: "You don't know anything except what's there for you to see. An act. Lies. Device. Not the pure heart, the pumping black heart." When Clay retreats from his brief outburst of rage—"I'd rather be a fool. Insane. Safe with my words"—Lula stabs him to death and then recruits white passengers to toss his body off the train car. I was both repulsed and fascinated by Jones's brutal yet poetic dialogue. I watched several other performances and pondered whether the play's depiction of black-white relations was overly pessimistic, or whether I was naïvely optimistic, having grown up sheltered from American racial realities.

I often thought about *The Dutchman* as I journeyed across the racial boundaries of Los Angeles. Uncertain whether there was a place for me in the rapidly changing world of the city's black politics, I realized that my involvement in N-VAC had been a diversion from my normal daily activities, which mostly involved interactions with white rather than black people. Yet I was fascinated by all aspects of the urban world I was discovering in Los Angeles, including the city's presumably nonhomicidal "Lulas." I had not left my life in a small town in order to become isolated in one of the city's black enclaves when there were so many other enticements elsewhere.

During the summer of 1965, I eagerly took advantage of opportunities to work overtime at Audience Studies, which relocated from the Columbia Pictures lot to a new building on Sunset Boulevard in West Hollywood. I rented a room nearby on Wonderland Road in Laurel Canyon, a pleasant, wooded neighborhood in the Santa Monica Mountains (although compared to my childhood surroundings, "mountains" was hardly a worthy designation). My landlord was an actress, and many of my neighbors worked in Hollywood or in the music industry. After working overtime through the summer months, I was earning more than enough money to buy a motorcycle (which I blithely rode without a helmet) to commute rapidly from my place to my job and to my UCLA classes, which I arranged to fit around my work schedule.

I remained interested in black political life and continued to write articles for the *Los Angeles Free Press,* but also became increasingly involved in the burgeoning antiwar movement. Even before the summer of 1965, I had taken my first step toward antiwar activism when I accompanied several N-VAC members to the San Francisco Bay Area. The trip provided us a chance to meet with Oakland civil rights activists and to visit the University of California's Berkeley campus to attend a "teach-in" on the Vietnam War. Thousands of people sat near Sproul Hall, where the rallies that ignited the Free Speech Movement had taken place. I listened to a long program of speeches criticizing President Johnson's decision to send troops to support the unpopular, anticommunist military regime in South Vietnam. I was impressed by the intellectual depth of the presentations, but realized that I had much to learn about the history of the anticolonial struggle led by Ho Chi Minh and about the American effort to prop up the anticommunist regime in South Vietnam.

Bob Moses was one of the speakers at the teach-in. I had not seen him since 1963 in New Orleans when I heard him describe plans for the Mississippi Project. I was intrigued by his current attempt to link the war issue to the Southern struggle. He contrasted the public outcry over the death of white minister James Reeb in the Alabama voting rights campaign with the muted response to the earlier killing of black activist Jimmy Lee Jackson. Moses suggested that most white Americans cared little about the deaths of black participants in the freedom struggle: "You've got to learn from the South if you're going to do anything about this country in relation to Vietnam," he concluded.

I also saw the war through a racial lens, and sometimes found it difficult to resist the tendency to view practically everything that way. I was pleased that President Lyndon Johnson had pushed landmark voting rights legislation through Congress, but I suspected that his war policies were motivated in part by racial arrogance rooted in the long history of Western domination of Asia and Africa. I was skeptical about the claim that the United States was bringing democracy to Vietnam when it was willing to support dictators in many nations, so long as they were anticommunist.

As antiwar protests increased during 1966, I noticed that the participants and major leaders were overwhelmingly white. Civil rights organizations, including King's Southern Christian Leadership Conference (SCLC), were reluctant to become identified with antiwar activism, but early in the year SNCC became the first major civil rights group to take a stand against the war. Many young male activists faced the threat of military induction, and SNCC workers often noted the hypocrisy of drafting black men to fight for democracy in Vietnam when black southerners still faced obstacles to voting. "Hell no, we won't go!" became a SNCC rallying cry.

My own vulnerability to being drafted spurred my participation in antiwar demonstrations, but I nonetheless felt isolated from the predominantly white leadership of the expanding movement. Working with a black-led group such as N-VAC had given me a sense of racial connection that was not possible in the Los Angeles antiwar movement, which became increasingly dominated by the various leftist factions competing for ideological control.

Like many of my activist friends, I was affected by the cultural changes that accompanied the political ferment of the first half of the 1960s. Living in West

Hollywood near the Sunset Strip, I had a close-up view of a multifaceted cultural transformation. Although many of the subsequent accounts of the "counterculture" of the mid-1960s would focus on white participants, I was far from the only black person shaping and being shaped by the new cultural currents. The Movement provided, at least during the first half of the 1960s, a setting in which black and white young people experimented with interracial relationships while fighting against segregation. The popular culture of the mid-1960s facilitated new kinds of black-white social interactions in neighborhoods such as West Hollywood or Venice, where I would later live. In many respects, the "countercultural" values of the mid-1960s were extensions of the questioning of conventional middle-class values that had occurred in the Movement. The overalls worn by SNCC field secretaries soon became models for the denim dress styles that later became popular among young people. More importantly, the central roles played by women in the civil rights and antiwar movements eventually encouraged the rise of the modern women's liberation movement.

These connections would only occur to me later. At the time, I was drawn to the aspects of the "counterculture" that confirmed the cliché of the 1960s as a time featuring hippies infatuated with sex, drugs, and rock-n-roll. I was eager to explore all the fascinating parts of the city that reminded me I was no longer in Los Alamos. The "Make Love, Not War" slogan became an appealing possibility as well as a popular political button. My social life was hardly promiscuous, mainly because my habit of thinking too much in situations calling for action applied not only to political activism but to my love life. During the summer and fall of 1965, I went out a few times with Lynelle, from the Federal Building protest, with Lori, one of the few black women in N-VAC, and had a brief infatuation with Susie, a white actress, whom I also met during the protest.

Drugs were also a major part of the Los Angeles social scene. I never bought marijuana, but I readily inhaled when a joint was offered to me. For most of my acquaintances, radical politics rather than pot was their primary avocation, nonetheless, I volunteered for a government-sponsored experiment at UCLA to test the effects of marijuana on my intellectual and physical performance. I was surprised that researchers released me while I was still high.

I also experimented with LSD came after attending a lecture at UCLA by Timothy Leary that ended with him handing out samples. Weeks later, I satisfied my curiosity when I ingested a vial while hiking in the mountains during a visit to Los Alamos. Just when I had concluded that the LSD had lost its potency, I noticed that the trees seemed to be growing leaves. The hallucination both excited and frightened me, but I was most worried by the possibility that I would have to return home for dinner still stoned. Fortunately, I returned to a sufficiently normal state just in time to avoid alarming my parents.

As for rock-n-roll, I enjoyed the new styles of popular music, particularly the free concerts at "Love Ins" in parks or on Venice Beach. My musical tastes were eclectic, often reflecting the varied musical interests of my female friends. Using my *Free Press* affiliation to gain access to entertainment venues, I saw Nina Simone perform "Mississippi Goddam"—"Alabama's got me so upset…and everybody knows about Mississippi goddam." I also met the SNCC Freedom Singers and Fannie Lou Hamer at a fundraiser, saw James Brown perform at Will Rogers Park in Watts, attended a wild concert by Frank Zappa's Mothers of Invention, and saw The Beatles trying to be heard over adolescent din at Dodger Stadium. Although I was only twenty-one, I felt significantly older than the white teenagers who followed the hot performers of the time. Riding my motorcycle, I often saw teens from the San Fernando Valley, some of them runaways, hitching rides along Laurel Canyon Boulevard to get to the clubs along the Sunset Strip.

My relationship with Lynelle was going nowhere and came to a memorable end in December 1965. I had invited her to a party given by Pat and Lauren, two women with SNCC ties who shared a house with my friend Charlie in Venice. I should have realized that something was amiss when Lynelle asked if she could invite a male friend, but I was nonetheless surprised when she suddenly left the party with the guy. I never saw her again, but her departure opened my eyes to Susan, a shy but attractive Jewish woman with long brown hair. Pat and Lauren had told me about their close friend in ways that made her seem admirable rather than appealing, but I was immediately attracted to her. Lightheartedly flirting, I found it easy to joke with her about being dumped and enjoyed coaxing smiles from her.

I knew that she liked me. I later learned that her friends had arranged the party so that we could meet. As the party wound down, we found a bedroom to talk privately and quickly pushed past superficial chatter to probing questions. She confided that her mother had died—a suicide, she later told me. She had become estranged from her father but remained close to her younger sister Jeanne. She was—as was I—working her way through UCLA and active in the protests. At some point, I kissed her gently, but thought it best not to rush things. Our extended conversation was the first of many more that we would have in the decades to come.

Even as Susan and I opened ourselves up to one another, I heard reports that SNCC was becoming increasingly divided over the issue of what role white activists should play in the group. Some black organizers on SNCC's staff had begun to argue that their white counterparts should focus their attention on white communities, while allowing black communities to gain confidence in their own leaders. Some white activists responded by launching modestly effective organizing efforts in Southern white communities through a SNCC offshoot called the Southern Students Organizing Committee (SSOC). The debate within SNCC became rancorous as some black members began to insist that the group should become all black. One black separatist said, "my loyalty is to black people and not to SNCC necessarily. It's to SNCC only in proportion as I determine its loyalty to black people." By the spring of 1966, this racially charged argument over the role of whites became one of the factors that led to the removal of John Lewis as SNCC's chair.

I was surprised when I heard that Stokely Carmichael had replaced John, whose speech at the March on Washington had exemplified SNCC's early nonviolent radicalism. Although Stokely had a forceful personality and verbal dexterity, most SNCC workers did not place much importance on leadership roles. Nonetheless, I heard about his growing influence in the group. After graduating from Howard University, he had directed SNCC's organizing efforts in Mississippi's second congressional district during the Mississippi Summer Project of 1964. He left Mississippi the following year to help launch an ambitious new project in Lowndes County, Alabama, whose black residents, although outnumbering whites, were prevented from registering to vote. The SNCC workers helped local residents form the Lowndes County Freedom Organization (LCFO), an independent political party that became known by its symbol, a black panther. Although the LCFO did not exclude whites, its all-black membership and independence from existing political parties signaled a decisive break with SNCC's past.

In June 1966 the implications of Stokely's election became apparent when he and other civil rights leaders, including Martin Luther King Jr., agreed to resume James Meredith's "March Against Fear" through Mississippi after he was wounded by a sniper on the second day of the march. Meredith's admission to the University of Mississippi had sparked riots in 1962. As the march continued through the Mississippi Delta towns where SNCC had established projects, Stokely used the nightly rallies to publicly display the extent of black support for the popular response to the Black Power slogan that SNCC workers had been using in Lowndes County. During rallies, Stokely shouted "What do we want?" The audience would yell back "Black Power!"

By the time Stokely came to Los Angeles later that summer, he had become—by a large measure—SNCC's best-known staff member and a central figure in a national debate about racial consciousness. His influence among young black activists would soon surpass that of King, who was forced to defend his commitment to nonviolence and interracial coalitions. When I greeted Stokely at a well-attended Black Power rally at Will Rogers Park in the Watts section of Los Angeles, I was pleased that he at least pretended to remember me.

As he stirred the racial emotions of the crowd, Stokely seemed like a younger version of Malcolm X. "The most important thing that black people have to do is to begin to come together, and to be able to do that, we must stop being ashamed of being black," he explained. "We are black and beautiful." Stokely drew a burst of laughter when he attacked "Negro leaders" who were on the defensive by the charge that they were seeking miscegenation: "Now I never get embarrassed when they ask me that question. I tell them: 'Your mother, your daughter, your sister is not the queen of the world; she's not the Virgin Mary. She can be made. Let's move on.'"

Stokely's visit to Los Angeles and the growing public interest in black militancy prompted Art Kunkin to pay me $75 per week to write regular articles for the *Free Press*. By then a decline in my work performance at Audience Studies caused me to be laid off. I didn't challenge the decision as I had become exhausted by the strain of holding a full-time job while also continuing to carry a full load of classes at UCLA. After a scary crash while riding to work destroyed my motorcycle and my desire to ride it, it had become impossible to get to and from work and classes. I radically reduced my expenses by moving to a small Venice apartment that rented for $75 per month, which I soon shared with Susan as well as with Dale and Jon, a couple I met through Charlie.

No longer balancing work and classes, I managed to combine my undergraduate coursework, participating in political activism and writing politically engaged journalism while still finding moments to enjoy Venice's ubiquitous casual beach nudity and ready supply of drugs (LSD was especially popular). On one occasion my younger brother Mark visited me from Los Alamos and was shocked when he sat down on a bench at Venice beach and a naked girl sat down next to him. I remember the summer of 1966 as my most enjoyable time in Los Angeles, but for Susan, who was working at a department store, it was much less so. I recall occasions when I spent afternoons debating political issues with Venice friends in our apartment while we waited for her to come home from work to make our dinner. (This was obviously before she joined a women's consciousness-raising group and then began to raise my consciousness as well.)

Even as I tried to bridge the widening gulf between black militants and the predominantly white antiwar movement, my *Free Press* articles explored the implications of the Black Power movement. My first front-page article, under the banner "Black Power Proposed for Watts," lauded the efforts of Cliff Vaughs, SNCC's Southern California chairman, to incorporate Watts and the surrounding black areas as a new Freedom City. A longer feature, my first published venture into historical writing, traced the history of the Watts black community from its origins in the late nineteenth century through the 1920s, and ended with a description of the neighborhood's gradual deterioration after World War II.

In one *Free Press* article I described the efforts made by Woody Coleman and Danny Gray to launch a campaign to convince voters to boycott the upcoming California gubernatorial election unless the candidates accepted N-VAC's sixteen-point program. The boycott effort had only a minor impact in the black community, but my involvement in the effort to draw attention to the campaign through provocative "B—, B—, B—" posters unexpectedly led to my first trip to jail. Although N-VAC leaders insisted that the posters were a call to Boycott, Baby, Boycott rather than an incitement to Burn, Baby, Burn, police were not amused in the aftermath of the previous summer's violence. They cited me after I put a poster on the side of an abandoned building. I was picked up and jailed for "defacing private property"—a misdemeanor that dashed my expectations for a grander cause for my first arrest.

Soon afterward, I was arrested again, this time for handing out antiwar leaflets to soldiers going through Union Station in Los Angeles. Charged with loitering and released on bail, I spoke out against the war a few days later at a rally on the UCLA campus. A decade later, after passage of Freedom of Information legislation, I would obtain my FBI file and learn that this arrest as well as my increasing interactions with leftist groups prompted an FBI investigation of my political activities and this led the Bureau to place me on its "Security Index" of "potentially dangerous" persons. The Special Agent in charge of the Los Angeles office reported to FBI director J. Edgar Hoover that Bureau informants had identified me—"aka Clyde Carson"— "from a photograph" as a participant at an antiwar demonstration against Vice President Hubert Humphrey at the Century Plaza Hotel.

Late in the summer of 1966, my long interview with Ron Karenga, a UCLA graduate student in African linguistics, who became one of the most influential black nationalist leaders in Los Angeles, appeared in the *Free Press*. He changed his name from Ron Everett and later adopted the title Maulana (revered teacher). I knew of him through the speeches he delivered at UCLA in his distinctively high-pitched voice. Following the previous summer's rebellion, he founded the all-black organization, Us—as in "wherever we are, Us is"—in order to "create a new sense of values" for black people. "I'm a cultural revolutionary in that we define culture as revolutionary—the overturning of ideas set down by men who never concerned themselves with our problems." Its members used Kiswahili terms to describe the group's guiding ideas and wore African-style green bubas. Karenga's top-down leadership contrasted with SNCC's emphasis on nurturing grassroots leaders, but he insisted that his group wanted to work closely with SNCC in the future. "What we would like to do is set up cultural and educational programs wherever they need them," he explained.

I admired Karenga's intelligence and confidence but was also troubled by his assumption that a single leader could or should reshape the values of black Americans. I couldn't imagine becoming one of his followers any more than I could consider joining the Nation of Islam or any group that required a high degree of conformity. I had begun to see myself as a journalist reporting the new currents of black nationalism, while still staying in close contact with the white New Left and the hippie counterculture. I felt vulnerable to the charge of being inauthentic, especially by black militants, because I lived among white people, and by the spring of 1966 I lived with one of them. The black-and-white-together ideal of the Movement's earlier period was giving way to derisive comments about black activists "talking black but sleeping white." I later realized that few black militants were as secure as they seemed in their newly adopted black identities but my border crossings also produced a constant sense of racial ambivalence.

As black militancy moved toward racial separatism, I persisted in supporting the efforts to build a black-white political coalition. I did not expect to play a prominent role in the effort, but my *Free Press* articles caught the attention of white antiwar activists who invited me to take part in planning a statewide New Politics conference. In August 1966, I flew to San Francisco in the private plane of Sy Casady, the former head of the California Democratic Council (a group of Democratic Party members urging state politicians to move to the left), to attend a meeting called by Californians for Liberal Representation to plan the future of liberal politics in California. Prominent white New Leftists were there—including Democratic congressional candidates Bob Scheer, Ed Keating, and Stanley Scheinbaum. Also attending were San Francisco State's Marshall Windmiller and Dave Jenkins of the International Longshore and Warehouse Union. I noticed that there was little nonwhite representation at the meeting. It was obvious that the participants didn't have a sense of how a broad coalition could be put together in time to affect the November gubernatorial election pitting Democrat Pat Brown against Republican novice candidate Ronald Reagan.

I was appointed as one of the two co-chairs of the California Conference on Power and Politics. Recognizing that black representation was a necessary component of the political movement they hoped to build, the white antiwar activists at the meeting turned to a twenty-two-year-old student who had never voted and had been in California less than two years. Although I was uncomfortable representing black militancy, I was at least in a good position to write an authoritative article for the *Free Press* about the conference that would launch the California New Politics movement.

The antiwar movement was well represented at the Los Angeles Conference on Power and Politics in October 1966, but the 2,500 people who attended the gathering included few African Americans (although the keynote speaker was SNCC's Julian Bond, who had been denied his seat in the Georgia legislature because of his antiwar stand). My participation in the conference predictably did little to increase black attendance. When attendees voted to support a motion rejecting both Brown and Reagan for governor, most of the liberal Democratic leaders who had financed the conference walked out. Nonetheless, the conference resulted in the formation of the California New Politics movement, which in turn led to the creation of the Peace and Freedom Party. The unintended result of these events was the election of Reagan as governor of California, which in turn led to the Reagan-led conservative revolt of the 1970s and 1980s.

A month after the Los Angeles conclave, Susan and I attended another conference at the Berkeley campus that similarly failed to bridge the racial gulf, despite the fact that it focused on the topic of Black Power and featured a keynote speech by Carmichael. Organized by the Students for a Democratic Society, the day of speeches at the Greek Theater attracted a large audience that approached ten thousand by the time Stokely began speaking. Mislabeled as a "Watts organizer," I was a warm-up speaker for Stokely's headlining slot, but my comparatively mellow show of black militancy did not persuade the mainly white audience that I was for real. They wanted to hear Stokely—the nation's most influential Black Power advocate. Ironically, Stokely's white listeners loudly cheered a message that was not meant to reassure them: that black-white alliances were "unrealistic" unless white radicals organized in white communities to build political support for civil rights reforms.

Later that night, Susan and I encountered Stokely at an interracial party in San Francisco's Haight-Ashbury neighborhood hosted by our friend Pat, who was now living in San Francisco. As I observed Stokely's evident close relationship with some of the white activists at the party, I sensed that he too was caught between the "black and white together" activism of the early 1960s and the new era of black separatism. My subsequent article on the event ignored the complexity of Stokely's private life while reiterating his public stance regarding the role of white activists: "The possibility of two separate radical movements, split on a racial basis, is a distressing but real possibility. A white radical response to Black Power is needed."

Few of those attending the conference noticed at the time, but one of the organizations represented was a black militant group that would become more successful than N-VAC in transferring SNCC's dynamism to the urban North. Shortly before the gathering, Huey Newton and Bobby Seale had formed the Black Panther Party for Self-Defense in Oakland, California, after reading a pamphlet about the LCFO party SNCC had helped to form in Lowndes County, Alabama. Among the black groups that emerged during the Black Power era, the Black Panthers were the most open to alliances with white leftists, particularly those willing to give the party contributions or publicity. One of several groups that adopted the Black Panther symbol and Malcolm X's rhetorical militancy, the party's ruthless discouragement of competing groups, their brash willingness to stand up to police, and their ability to secure white financial support enabled them to grow rapidly during 1967. The Black Panthers would soon become the largest black radical group and the most strident opponent of Karenga's cultural nationalism.

When the Black Panther Party expanded into Los Angeles during 1967, I became a supporter, but only from a distance. Despite my general agreement with their political program, they demanded a willingness to risk death through armed clashes with police and a degree of uncritical fealty that I was not willing to offer. I preferred their abrasive engagement with the American political system to the separatism of Karenga's Us, but I also recognized the difficulty of bringing together the Panthers—with their military-style leadership structure—with the antiauthoritarian idealism of the New Left. Black militancy was increasingly divided between self-described revolutionary nationalists, such as the Black Panthers, and cultural nationalists, such as Us members. I thought that both groups served a useful purpose that was undermined by the competition between dogmatic leaders seeking followers.

SNCC's shift from organizing efforts in the South to ideological bickering signaled the start of an era in which "the people" were no longer sources of innovative political ideals, but instead targets of "consciousness-raising." I heard that at one point a black militant in SNCC ridiculed veteran staff member Fannie Lou Hamer as "no longer relevant" and not at their "level of development." Black leaders competed to become the "messiah" that FBI director J. Edgar Hoover imagined "could unify and electrify the militant black nationalist movement." I admired the bravery and dedication of the Black Panthers and ignored signs that the party's leaders had little sympathy for SNCC's consensus style of decision making. Eldridge Cleaver would later explain to me that the difference between SNCC and the Black Panthers was that the former had long meetings, while the latter had very short meetings. Stokely and other SNCC veterans would later try to forge an alliance with the Black Panther Party, but ideological differences and FBI counterintelligence efforts quickly disrupted these ties.

My personal life mirrored this period of conflict among black radical groups. Having declined to apply for a student deferment, I had already received my induction notice, passed my physical for the military, and was almost certain that my belated application for conscientious objector status would be denied. My antiwar activities intensified as the war escalated. The antiwar movement had become the best available substitute for the community I had once found in N-VAC, but I continued to feel isolated as one of the few black activists to play a significant role in the California antiwar movement. I began to see that I could have very little impact on the divide between black racial separatism and white leftist sectarianism.

In June 1967, I took part in the UCLA commencement ceremony only because my parents had driven to Los Angeles to see the first member of our extended family graduate from college. On the morning of their arrival, Susan, who was also graduating but not participating in the ceremony, came over to the Venice apartment to greet them in an unconvincing effort to suggest that she was not a live-in girlfriend. Her being white was not much of a surprise to my parents, since I had dated white girls in high school, but I could tell that they were concerned about the apparent seriousness of the relationship. She sat with them as they watched the large and impersonal ceremony that conveyed the reality that my history degree had not improved my job prospects.

I got a job driving a taxi with the Yellow Cab Company after graduation. I might have eventually found something better, but I wanted a job that would provide a quick source of income before moving forward with a plan—one that I did not disclose to my parents. The draft board had rejected my plea as a conscientious objector to war, and even though I appealed the decision I realized that I had little chance of prevailing. After all, I had once sought an appointment to West Point and the Air Force Academy.

Facing the choice between military conscription or going to prison, I chose another alternative: emigration to Canada. I had heard that many American draft dodgers had taken this route, and, although Canada did not seem as attractive as California, I was gradually drawn to the idea of leaving. Realizing that I might not be able to return to the United States, I wondered how I would adjust to living in another country, but Canada did not seem that foreign, and race relations there were reputed to be better than in the United States. When I discussed the idea with Susan, I was somewhat surprised that she was willing to leave with me. On our application for landed immigrant status, we indicated that we would become teachers in the Northwest Territories. Surely, we thought, Canada wouldn't reject a couple volunteering to teach in such an inhospitable place.

We decided to travel abroad while waiting for a response to our application. Our expectation was that when our funds ran out, we would apply to become Canadians (or perhaps Swedes, if Canada rejected us).

Susan had a little money from an inheritance, and we also worked diligently during the summer to save as much as possible. We discussed another matter that I had purposely avoided as our relationship deepened. I loved her more than anyone else I had known but did not want to get married. My parents' marriage had deteriorated over the years into cohabitation punctuated by horrific arguments, and I was reluctant to make a lifetime commitment until I was certain that our love would endure. She reminded me that we had already been living together harmoniously for more than a year and that marriage wouldn't change our relationship. She pointed out—even more convincingly, I thought—that she was making a major commitment in following me to unknown destinations and that I should be willing to get married to make it easier to travel together. I finally agreed to legalize our ties, so long as I didn't have to take part in a wedding. On August 29, 1967, she left her job early so that a friend could drive us to Malibu, where a justice of the peace performed the ceremony. We spent the afternoon relaxing on Venice Beach while some of our friends gradually realized we were married. Our extended honeymoon, we told ourselves, would begin when we left the United States.

It may have occurred to me that I was escaping not only the draft but also the intensity of my two years in Los Angeles. I felt that there was not much of a role in the Black Power movement for a black kid from Los Alamos who was married to a white woman. And I was no longer eager to write about a freedom struggle that seemed to be split along ideological and racial lines.

I no longer dreamed of joining SNCC, either. John Lewis had quit the group after complaining that "speech-making" had undermined "on-going programs," and his successor Stokely Carmichael had himself been replaced by a little-known field secretary, H. Rap Brown, who soon established a reputation as a Black Power firebrand. I admired Stokely's accomplishments as a SNCC field secretary in Mississippi and Alabama but found it difficult to connect that little-known organizer to the media magnet who had conferred during the previous summer with Cuba's Fidel Castro, Vietnam's Ho Chi Minh, and Guinea's Ahmed Sékou Touré. Although Stokely's revolutionary rhetoric reflected the spirit of the times, the black militants attending the July 1967 national Black Power conference in Newark argued bitterly over the meaning of the Black Power slogan. The National Conference on New Politics held two months later in Chicago achieved the illusion of black-white unity only when white delegates gave in to the demand of the few black militants for equal voting power.

The sense of belonging I had found in N-VAC had been fleeting, and, in the aftermath of the 1965 mass rebellion, the group's goals were outdated when compared with the Black Panther Party's "pick up the gun" rhetoric or the widespread calls for a black revolution. I had learned much from my activism in N-VAC and the antiwar movement, including the difficulty of establishing a political movement that bridged the racial divide. I discovered that even among black militants there were significant differences. Whatever guilt I felt about leaving Los Angeles was matched by a feeling that I had failed to find my place there.

Chapter 5

Voluntary Exile

*W*hen we boarded the Santa Fe railroad's El Capitan train at Los Angeles' Union Station on the evening of October 17, 1967, Susan's sister Jeanne, her boyfriend Steve, and Al Parker, a UCLA friend, were there to say good-bye. Although our tickets were to New York, our destination was Europe for a stay of undetermined duration while we waited to hear whether we could emigrate to Canada. It was Susan's first trip outside of California and my most adventurous trip since the March on Washington four years earlier. As Jeanne cried uncontrollably over the departure of the older sibling who had cared for her for five years after their mother's suicide, I tried to suppress my lingering doubts. Had I fully considered the implications of leaving the United States, not only for me but for Susan and those who cared about us? Was I asserting a principle through my voluntary exile or deserting the black freedom struggle and the antiwar movement?

As the train pulled out of the station, I started a journal but couldn't express my jumbled thoughts about the venture we had embarked on. Why were we going to Europe? What was our goal? What were our career plans now that we had earned undergraduate degrees? We were married but had no place to call home. We had saved about $3,000; we were accustomed to living cheaply, and had no return tickets. We looked forward to the challenge of extending our voluntary exile through careful budgeting.

Our first stop was in Albuquerque, where we then traveled to Los Alamos to stay with my parents while sparing them the details of our plans. Mom and Dad greeted us at the station for the first time as a married couple, along with my sister Gail and brother Stephen. As we walked outside, I experienced a moment of dissonance when we noticed a group of distinctively dressed black Muslims among the other arriving passengers. It seemed that the militancy I had witnessed in California had unexpectedly followed me to New Mexico.

I learned later that Nation of Islam members as well as followers of Ron Karenga were in Albuquerque to attend a convention with the goal of forging ties with Native American activists and La Alianza, a militant group headed by Reies Lopez Tijerina that sought to reclaim land deeded to the Spanish settlers of northern New Mexico. Tijerina had recently gained notoriety when his group raided a county courthouse to free jailed compatriots and carried out a citizen's arrest of the local district attorney.

Once out of the station, I tried to avoid topics that would result in arguments and was relieved that Mom did not say anything critical about Susan's micro-mini dress. I answered questions about our travel plans by suggesting that we were leaving for a delayed extended honeymoon. After we settled into my child-hood home in Los Alamos, Susan gradually gained comfort in her new role as a daughter-in-law.

Conversations with my parents mostly danced around the details of my politi-cal activities. Mom viewed discussing politics as poor manners, and Dad's job as a security inspector with top secret clearance made him reluctant to discuss my antiwar views, especially when we could talk about sports instead. I spoke more freely with my sister Gail and her boyfriend Jeff, a white student she had met at the University of New Mexico. Although she was not politically active, Gail had become enthralled with California when she visited me the previous year.

As I spent the next week showing Susan around Los Alamos, hiking in the Jemez Mountains, and visiting nearby towns, I saw how little and how much the surroundings had changed from the place I had known as a teenager. The slow pace of small-town life reminded me why I had wanted to leave. Santa Fe and Taos still attracted affluent tourists seeking art galleries and museums. I became more aware of the cultural diversity I had not noticed while growing up in an Anglo outpost isolated from the Pueblo and Spanish cultures that predated the arrival of Pilgrims to North America. Yet, with the exception of Tijerina's somewhat quixotic cam-paign to reclaim ancestral land, northern New Mexico's complex intercultural rela-tions seemed peaceful when compared to the black-white rift in the nation's urban centers.

I was saddened by the thought of leaving, perhaps permanently, the world where I had come of age, but I was also eager to begin our adventure. On November 9 we flew out of Kennedy Airport on Icelandic Airways, the least expensive way to cross the Atlantic for those willing to go to Glasgow with a stop in Reykjavik.

The excitement of leaving the United States dissipated quickly when we reached the Glasgow passport control booth. The other passengers, including Susan, passed through without delay, but I was pulled aside for questioning.

The customs officer examined our tickets and then abruptly asked, "Are you coming here to avoid the draft? Are you here to demonstrate?" Confused, I asked, "Why do you want to know?"

"I'm the one asking the questions here," he retorted, before indicating that our one-way ticket had prompted his concern. "How much money do you have?"

"About a thousand dollars."

The officer carefully counted our traveler's checks. "Do you intend to work here?"

"I don't think so."

"What do you mean, 'I don't think so'?"

"No, I don't intend to work here."

"Who invited you here?"

"Nobody."

"What's the purpose of your visit? Where will you stay?"

I explained that we might stay with a friend, Mike Pollard, who lived in England, but admitted that I didn't know his address. I looked through my address book and found his mother's address. "I thought you had no address. You're not being frank with me."

I replied that I was doing my best but objected that none of the other passengers had been detained for questioning. I suspected that I was being singled out as the only black passenger on the flight, but tried to control my rising anger, realizing that we could be sent back to the United States. Susan also urged me to remain calm.

The interrogation went on for about two hours before officials relented to Susan's tearful pleas and allowed us to leave the airport. The feeling of powerlessness I had during that experience left me embittered, exhausted, and somewhat humiliated. Fortunately, we were able to locate a bed-and-breakfast. The proprietor, Mrs. MacCallum, cheerfully welcomed us. Without bothering to eat, we climbed into bed shortly after 6:00 P.M. and slept soundly until about 10:00 A.M. when Mrs. MacCallum thoughtfully had breakfast waiting for us.

We took a train to Edinburgh, where we established a pattern that would be replicated in London and many of the cities we would later visit: staying in

youth hostels or hotels without amenities such as bathrooms or hot water; buying groceries (bread, cheese, and water became our staples, although in Europe
we developed a taste for inexpensive wines) to carry in our rucksacks rather than
purchasing prepared meals (except for the occasional cheap meal out); and walking or taking public transportation to museums, historic sites, and special events.
Like other Americans going abroad for the first time, my eyes were drawn not
only to strange sights but also to the familiar things that confirmed that the world
was becoming surprisingly American. Chance encounters became answers to
unspoken questions: What were young people thinking? Did we attract special
attention as a black-white couple? How did the black people we sometimes saw in
urban areas differ from African Americans?

After a short stay in London, we spent a week in Hove on England's southern
coast with our Venice friends, Sandy and her English boyfriend Mike, who had
returned to his hometown after being drafted into the U.S. military as a resident
alien. Mike was good-natured, from a working-class background, and shorter
than Sandy, a red-haired California native. He introduced me to the various beers
and ales available at his local pub, and one evening took me to his evening class in
African history—my first exposure to the field—at the University of Sussex. When
a snowstorm arrived, all of us were reminded that we were no longer in Southern
California. The kitchen was so cold that we kept the milk in the cupboard. We
debated when to feed our precious shillings into the flat's sole heater to achieve an
acceptable level of comfort. We scheduled time to use the bathtub in the kitchen so
as not to interfere with meal preparation.

After the snowstorm, Susan and I left to explore southwest England, hitching
rides as I had done after the March on Washington. The purposely purposeless trip
gave us many opportunities to meet ordinary people. I recalled the vulnerability I
had felt after the 1963 March on Washington when I had hitched rides through the
Midwest and the Southwest. It would have been suicidal for Susan and me to have
hitchhiked together across the United States. We were doubtlessly an odd sight
in England and Wales, but we did not fear being lynched or violently assaulted or
even detained by police. One couple even invited us home for tea.

In contrast to my solitary march adventure, the haphazard days on the road
brought Susan and me closer together as we spent hours discussing our surroundings, where to go or stay, and whatever else came to mind. Our whimsical goal was
to reach Land's End on the southwest corner of England, but we changed course
impulsively whenever something caught our interest. After stops in Salisbury,
Stonehenge, Plymouth, and Penzance, we reversed direction and traveled to Exeter

and then Stratford-upon-Avon, where we treated ourselves to the Royal Shakespeare Company's performance of *The Taming of the Shrew*.

The next day in Oxford, we encountered a seventy-year-old man at Merton College who asked if we were visiting. When we said yes, he took us to his office, where he put our backpacks on a desk and gave us a short lecture about the history of the college. Afterward he guided us through a library where old books were chained to the cases. He showed us a Bible that he described as the second-oldest printed book and an encyclopedia from the fourteenth century.

After returning to London, we took a train back to Hove to see Sandy and Mike again while preparing to leave for France. We arrived in Paris on December 11 and found a room at the Hotel Olinda on Ile Saint-Louis and, the next day, an even cheaper one in the Latin Quarter. We belatedly discovered that the Hotel des 4 Nations—listed by Frommer's guidebook as a "sub-starvation option"—also served as a brothel. After discovering the pleasures of Parisian poverty, especially walking through the city's districts and eating at the Sorbonne student restaurant—I noted in my journal that our week in Paris cost $57.56 (less than the typical cost of an evening meal during our next visit to Paris three decades later).

On December 17 we boarded a crowded train for an overnight trip to Venice, where we endured several days of bitingly damp cold. After leaving our youth hostel each morning, the city's almost empty museums and its few inexpensive restaurants served as places to warm ourselves. On one occasion, we knocked on the door of a museum, where a kind caretaker allowed us to tour the otherwise empty building.

After a short stop in Florence, we arrived in Rome on the 23rd. We rented a room with the toilet on the balcony where we would stay for the next three weeks. During a time of year with few tourists, I enjoyed being able to leave behind my large backpack for the day as we explored the city. With an Italian phrasebook, we managed to communicate well enough to find inexpensive food and places of interest using public transportation. Despite our severely restricted budget, food was usually a pleasant part of our day. Keeping cheese, salami, fresh bread, water, and wine in the small backpack we carried around during the day, we searched for interesting, inexpensive restaurants for late evening meals.

Some days, especially when it rained, we rested in bed, reading in tandem John Barth's allegorical parody, *Giles Goat-Boy*. Barth's satirical observations about academic life and religion stimulated extended conversations about our uncertain future. Susan seemed willing to follow me anywhere, even though I didn't know where I was going.

•Because we were together almost all of every day, I found it difficult to find time for solitary reflection about the choices I had made since finishing college. For better or worse, I chose to become an exile, and Susan volunteered to join me. I had been reluctant to get married; yet we rushed into a commitment that extended beyond marriage.

On a few occasions, the tiredness and the stress of travel exposed and exaggerated our differences. Susan expressed her emotions; I kept mine inside. Her mother's death had left her with a deep-seated fear of abandonment; I had learned to appreciate moments of solitude. Even as she fearlessly revealed herself to me, I wondered whether she understood me and whether I truly understood her. One night she cried when we disagreed about where to eat. I didn't understand why she would cry over something so trivial.

We purchased train tickets to Barcelona but were able to debark at stops along the way. In part because we had enjoyed Matisse prints in our Venice apartment, we decided to stop in Nice to visit the museum housing the Henri Matisse collection donated to the city. The museum was especially attractive because it did not charge admission. After two days, we continued on to Antibes, where we waited two hours on the gorgeous beach before the Musée Picasso opened, and then to Cannes, where a friendly waitress gave us free food and beer.

We arrived in Barcelona early on the morning of January 15. Staying in a centrally located pension, we walked through the Gothic City ruins and Pueblo Español before Susan caught a lingering cold that grounded us for the remainder of our six days in the city.

Our three days in Valencia introduced us to *paella,* an inexpensive dish that came in many different varieties in the restaurants of southern Spain. Even as we enjoyed the increasingly warm days, I could see that our travels were taking a toll on Susan. She seemed exhausted and had trouble shaking her illness. We did little beyond going out in the evenings to eat and shop for the next day's groceries. By the time we arrived in Granada, I knew that Susan needed a period of rest to regain her energy. She spent much of the 24th sleeping. Although we enjoyed visiting the city's Cathedral and the Alhambra, Susan became sick again on the 29th, vomiting several times during the night and the next morning was too tired to get out of bed.

I knew by then that her illness was more than simply a cold. I suspected the flu and kept her well supplied with water, but she found it difficult to eat any solid foods. My concern was heightened when I saw that her already slender build appeared emaciated. I was upset with myself for failing to notice her weight loss, lack of stamina, and constant thirst.

While Susan rested at our Valencia apartment, I ventured out once a day to buy provisions and, for the first time since we went abroad, picked up a copy of the New York *Herald Tribune*. We had been largely out of touch with what had happened in the world since leaving California more than four months earlier, but the headlines about the major new Tet holiday offensive by communist-led Vietnamese forces caught my attention. This sharp escalation of the war belied the Johnson administration's optimistic predictions of military victory. The horrific rise in casualties on both sides signaled the beginning of a decisive phase in the war. For the first time, it seemed likely that the American military would not only fail to win the war but might actually lose it. I wondered about the impact of the offensive on the American antiwar movement and on the black freedom struggle.

I noticed that King had launched a Poor People's Campaign to bring thousands of protesters to occupy the National Mall until the federal government acted to end poverty. King's involvement in such a bold venture contradicted my view of him as a cautious civil rights leader. This new campaign seemed to reflect the confrontational approach of SNCC during its early years, as when John Lewis spoke at the March on Washington of a "revolution" to "free ourselves of the chains of political and economic slavery" and proclaimed that the "black masses" were "on the march for jobs and freedom."

I couldn't find any news about SNCC in the *Herald Tribune*. What had happened to Stokely Carmichael and H. Rap Brown? Was their Black Power notoriety fleeting or was I just out of touch?

During one of my daily ventures to the newsstand in Granada, I met Ira and Claire Garvin, a young couple from New York. When I told them about Susan's illness, they generously invited us to stay with them after we checked out of our hotel. In their more spacious place, Susan gradually began to recover some of her strength and felt well enough for us to leave. The Garvins offered to take us to Malaga in their land rover. After a leisurely drive through the Sierra Nevada Mountains, we arrived in Motril and then drove along the Mediterranean to Malaga, where Susan and I rented a small apartment on the eleventh floor of a pension. On our first night, a friendly neighbor invited us to join him to watch a televised boxing match involving American fighters—Jerry Quarry beat Thad Spencer. Our host didn't speak much English but forcefully expressed his views on one subject: "No like Vietnam."

On the morning of February 4, we were greeted by the bright sun, and from our balcony we could see the Mediterranean in the distance. Susan was able to join me in a walk through Malaga's downtown area. We bought a newspaper to read during a long lunch as we relaxed in the warmest weather we had experienced since leaving New Mexico.

The next day we took a bus to the village of Puerto de la Torre to meet Kevin Ryan to discuss the possibility of joining a rural commune called Centro San Jose Obrero. Kevin explained over a Spanish stew lunch that the community was open to anyone who felt "the necessity to serve God and their fellow human beings in a more direct manner, living and growing together." Many of the current members, we were told, were Catholics who had experienced a "crisis of faith" while training for the priesthood. Although neither Susan nor I were Catholics, we were open to the possibility that Centro San Jose Obrero might be a place where we could stay while we worked through our own crises of uncertainty about the future. Susan's health had become increasingly worrisome, and we decided it was best to visit Tangier, Morocco, for a week and then return to England to wait for Canada's decision about our emigration application.

After a short trip by hydrofoil on a rough sea from Algeciras to Tangier, we checked into the Hotel Fes in the Arab quarter, near the Kasbah, for our first night on the African continent. Our six days there were mainly spent enjoying Moroccan food (a three-course meal cost about 60 cents) and shopping for small presents that we could send back to the United States. Whenever we left our hotel, we would immediately encounter people trying to sell us something: "Want to see the Kasbah?" We explained that we had little money, but they were persistent nonetheless. "I'm not a guide. I'm a student, like you," one young man informed us. A multilingual child named Alexander took us to his father's shop, where we bought a few gifts. Alexander continued to serve as an informal guide during the next few days as we explored the fascinating city. On one occasion a man in a restaurant mistook me for Muhammad Ali; I was flattered, since Ali was much admired there.

After leaving Morocco, we took trains back to France and a ferry across the Channel and on February 24 reached Hove by late afternoon. That evening we joined Sandy and Mike to attend a performance of Samuel Beckett's *Waiting for Godot*. Although we couldn't make sense of its ultimate meaning, the unrequited expectation of Vladimir and Estragon that Godot would arrive seemed to speak to our plight. We also had similar thoughts about Franz Kafka's *The Trial*, which we were reading at the time, especially after we traveled on the 28th to the immigration section at the Canadian Embassy in London and were told that there had been no decision about our application.

By the time we returned to Hove the next day, both of us had bad colds that persisted for several days. Uncertain what to do next, we received a telegram from

Greg Wherry, an American minister living in Edinburgh. He had met us during our previous visit and had sympathized with my draft concerns. He invited us to visit him in Edinburgh, and we accepted his offer.

Wherry introduced us to the Bradfords, who offered to house us in an extra bedroom in their large flat, where we mostly rested and recovered during the next twelve days. On the Bradfords' television, we watched news of the New Hampshire primary election and were elated to learn that antiwar senator Eugene McCarthy had come close to defeating President Lyndon Johnson. While we had been abroad, it seemed that antiwar sentiment in the United States had grown dramatically for reasons we did not fully understand.

Back in London on March 17 we attended a "Solidarity with Vietnamese People" rally in Trafalgar Square with actress Vanessa Redgrave in the lead. It was the first demonstration we attended since the previous summer, and it felt odd to be among boisterous British leftists whose denunciations of American war policies seemed more trenchant than the American antiwar rhetoric. Two days later, we went for an interview at the Canadian Embassy and then waited in vain for their final decision on our application for landed emigrant status.

After extended talks about Susan's poor health and the apparent unwillingness of the Canadian officials to act promptly on our application, we decided to purchase Icelandic Airways tickets back to New York. We flew from London on Sunday, March 24. After a short layover in Glasgow, we arrived in New York on March 25. Excluding airfare, we had spent $1,078.65 during our 130 days abroad. Not wanting to spend more of our remaining funds in New York, we quickly boarded a bus back to Albuquerque.

We reached Los Alamos at the end of March, and I arranged to have Susan examined by a doctor at the local medical center. A few hours after returning from her appointment, Susan received a call from her doctor urging her to come to the hospital immediately. Her doctor informed her that she had diabetes and said that her blood sugar level was so elevated that she risked falling into a coma. She would have to check into the hospital to be tested and to stabilize her condition. I felt guilty that I had not paid sufficient attention to her declining health. She had become seriously ill while we were in Spain and might have died during the weeks before we returned to the United States and sought medical attention.

I recalled the risks I had taken while hitchhiking after the March on Washington, but in this case I felt guilty for unnecessarily exposing her to a possible medical emergency, especially during the days I wanted to spend in Tangier. My mother compensated for my neglect by insisting that Susan get the best possible care.

Because we had no health insurance and no bank account, my parents generously assumed financial responsibility for Susan's bill.

On April 4, three days after Susan entered the hospital, I was watching television with my parents when I heard the stunning news: Martin Luther King Jr. had been shot and killed at the Lorraine Motel in Memphis. As I listened to a succession of news reports about the shooting, I felt a profound sadness, as if I had lost someone close to me. The extensive racial violence that erupted in dozens of black urban communities reminded me of what I had witnessed in Los Angeles during the summer of 1965. It seemed as though that explosion of racial anger was being replicated in many of the nation's largest cities, including the predominantly black neighborhoods within a mile of the White House. Stokely Carmichael, I learned, had publicly warned that King's death removed the one advocate of nonviolence that "the militants and the revolutionaries" as well as "the masses of black people would still listen to."

I tried to formulate my own thoughts—perhaps for an essay for the *Free Press*—but found it impossible to capture my conflicting emotions. Although I had never written about him, King had been an unspoken aspect of everything I had experienced since going to the March on Washington in 1963. I had agreed with many of SNCC's criticisms of his top-down style of leadership. King seemed cautious when compared to SNCC's impetuous field secretaries, but he had been a standard of rectitude and courage that I and many other young black activists judged ourselves against. During a period when SNCC and the Movement as a whole were splitting into ideological factions, he had remained resolute in his commitment to nonviolent principles and ideals of social justice.

While I was in exile in Europe, he was launching the Poor People's Campaign and coming to the aid of beleaguered sanitation workers in Memphis. There was nothing I could write that could come close to matching the power of his final words, which were replayed on television again and again:

> And I've seen the promised land. I may not get there with you. But I want you to know tonight, that we, as a people, will get to the promised land! And so I'm happy, tonight. I'm not worried about anything. I'm not fearing any man! Mine eyes have seen the glory of the coming of the Lord!

It had been less than half a year since Susan and I had boarded the train from Los Angeles, but it seemed that, during the brief period we were away, black-white relations in the United States had changed for the worse. The community of activists I had once seen as the Movement had disintegrated into competing factions that insisted on ideological purity as the price of membership. My months abroad had provided ample time for reflection about the black freedom struggle, but I returned with little certainty about my relationship to the remnants of the struggle that still existed.

Chapter 6

A Not So Ivory Tower

*L*ate in April 1968, Susan and I stumbled back to Los Angeles with minimal expectations about our future. Her diabetes was under control with regular insulin injections, but both of us were weary from months of living peripatetically, often carrying our possessions. Our stay abroad had been shorter than we had expected, but we were also somewhat relieved that our separation from friends and relatives had not been permanent after all. We gave up on our plan to live in Canada as leaving again was hardly feasible, given Susan's fragile health, even though my draft status was still uncertain. With our remaining savings, we rented a cheap Venice apartment on Breeze Avenue near the beach and less than a block from our previous place.

A political transformation had occurred during the months since our departure. Like Rip Van Winkle in the Washington Irving short story, I sometimes felt as if I was awakening from an extended sleep during a period of revolutionary change. Since reading the *Herald Tribune* in Spain, news reports had repeatedly startled me: the Tet offensive, President Lyndon Johnson's announcement that he would not seek re-election, King's assassination and the widespread racial violence that followed.

Soon after returning to Los Angeles, I read news reports about a major student-led revolt in the Latin Quarter of Paris where we had stayed the previous December. Increasingly violent clashes with police soon escalated into a general strike of students and French workers. Other similar rebellions took place in Mexico City and Prague. The year of our return was a time of mass protests and tumult on a scale that would have been inconceivable the previous summer, but the mass movements also experienced major setbacks. In many parts of the world, protesters demanding radical change faced forceful and sometimes brutal opposition from authorities, and conservative politicians often successfully used calls for law and order to rally popular support.

The world seemed on the verge of extraordinary change, but our immediate goal was to return to an ordinary life with a job and a place to stay for a while. There were of course doubts about the future, including my draft status. I had not notified my draft board about our frequent changes of address, so I assumed that it would take several months at least before the board determined where to send another induction notice. By then I hoped that I could earn enough money to pay for a draft lawyer who could argue my case for alternative service as a conscientious objector. Rejecting the idea of serving in the military, I imagined the implications of going to prison.

Pushing this possibility out of my mind, I searched for a job with decent pay and medical coverage. I thought of once again driving a taxi but was pleasantly surprised when I quickly found something better—a statistical clerk position at the Survey Research Center on the UCLA campus. I qualified for the position because of my experience working at Audience Studies and my bachelor's degree, which became useful for the first time since my graduation. Although the work was only moderately interesting, I got along well with my French American supervisor, who encouraged me to learn how to program the computers that the Center was beginning to use to process survey forms. With his help, I soon learned how to write instructions in FORTRAN programming language for the IBM computers and, by the end of 1968, I had qualified for a higher-paying position as a computer programmer. At my urging, Susan successfully applied for an executive trainee position at Audience Studies.

Work and commuting on public buses absorbed most of our weekday time; it would be more than a year before we could afford a car. We soon left behind the excitement of our foreign adventure and felt fortunate to be settled in a familiar neighborhood.

Although I made no effort during the spring and summer of 1968 to become politically active, I could not ignore Robert Kennedy's attempt to win the California Democratic presidential primary. His campaign was fueled by the upsurge in antiwar sentiment, and Kennedy also voiced concern about the issue of poverty, echoing King's Poor Peoples Campaign. In the Democratic primary election on June 4, we strongly favored Kennedy over his main rival, Vice President Hubert Humphrey. Humphrey had been reluctant to break with Johnson's war policies. He had also opposed the effort of the Mississippi Freedom Democratic Party delegation to take the seats of that state's all-white "regular" delegation at the 1964 national Democratic convention. I knew that some movement veterans, including SNCC's former chair John Lewis, had joined Kennedy's campaign.

By the time Kennedy arrived in California, it was apparent that he had sparked the kind of enthusiasm among black voters that John Kennedy had garnered after announcing his support for major civil rights reform. With backing from Cesar Chavez, the leader of the farm workers movement, and other prominent Mexican American leaders, Kennedy seemed poised to prevail over Humphrey in the primary.

I was elated by the news that Kennedy did indeed win, but then I was brought back to earth when I learned of his assassination after making a victory speech at the Ambassador Hotel. Coming so soon after King's assassination, Kennedy's death provided another reminder that we had returned to a nation undergoing traumatic changes resulting from years of strife over racial inequities and the war. Nonviolent activism and conventional electoral politics no longer seemed to offer feasible avenues for achieving major social change.

SNCC, the group I had long admired, had come apart. John Lewis and other advocates of Gandhian nonviolence had left. SNCC's projects were in disarray, and I had heard nothing regarding the whereabouts of Bob Moses, its most influential organizer. SNCC's chair, H. Rap Brown, was facing federal charges of carrying a gun across a state line while under indictment. I was surprised to learn that Stokely Carmichael had allied himself with the Black Panther Party, which had grown rapidly in the months following an armed confrontation between Oakland police and the party's founder and defense minister, Huey Newton, on October 17, 1967—the day of our departure from Los Angeles. The incident left a policeman dead and Newton wounded and jailed on murder charges. Undeterred by his imprisonment, party followers launched a "Free Huey" campaign. Panther leaders Bobby Seale and Eldridge Cleaver recruited Stokely to be the party's prime minister and a featured speaker at "Free Huey" rallies held during February 1968 in Oakland and Los Angeles.

Members of the Black Panther Party reminded me of the rebellious and courageous SNCC field secretaries of the early 1960s. But, unlike my infatuation with SNCC, my admiration for the dedication of the young black men and women who joined the party did not mean that I wanted to join them. I had passed on the chance to join SNCC during its heyday, and now marriage and my approaching twenty-fourth birthday made me wary of potentially deadly militancy. Just days after King's assassination, an encounter between police and Panthers had resulted in the death of the party's seventeen-year-old treasurer Bobby Hutton and the wounding of Eldridge Cleaver.

I was also troubled by the Black Panther leaders' emphasis on the right of black people to carry weapons for self-defense. My dad had routinely carried a gun at his job and took pride in the awards he won as an expert marksman, but he had been trained in the military and practiced for years to hone his skills. The party's call for young black men without similar training to "pick up the gun" for self-defense seemed wrongheaded and even suicidal. When I discovered that the Panthers had formed an alliance with SNCC at the February rallies, I realized how far SNCC had moved away from the Gandhian ideals that had permeated the group during the early 1960s.

The SNCC–Black Panther alliance was short-lived. The remnants of the SNCC staff had abandoned nonviolent principles but resisted the notion of merging with the Panthers and severed ties with the party during the summer of 1968. Stokely chose to remain in the Panther Party, but he too found that his emphasis on racial unity put him at odds with the class analysis favored by most of the party's leaders. The breakup of the alliance was another sign that the black freedom struggle was continuing to disintegrate into warring factions, each claiming to represent the black masses.

Later that summer, my twenty-one-year-old brother, Michael, visited me following the completion of his basic training in the Navy. Although he was the sibling closest to my age, we had not talked much since he finished high school and enrolled at New Mexico State University. He had not come with my parents for my graduation from UCLA and had been away at the university when Susan and I had been in Los Alamos. I respected that he had chosen to enlist in the Navy rather than take the chance that he would be drafted into the Army. I was pleased that he was finally able to meet Susan and see California before beginning his service as an aviation electrician's mate on a ship he expected would be bound for Vietnam.

It was our first chance to speak to each other as adults, and I enjoyed talking to him in a way that was more frank and open than before. He told me that he had been bored in college and hadn't done well in his classes. I didn't want to make him feel uncomfortable by bringing up the subject of my antiwar views, but he volunteered that he had been reading with great interest Mark Twain's antiwar, anti-imperialist writings. He confided that many of his Navy friends were opposed to the war but saw military service as a way to get started in a career. When he left, I regretted that we didn't know each other better.

Michael's visit reminded me that I needed to decide what to do about my own draft situation. Using $200 of our meager savings, I retained J. B. Tietz, an anti-draft lawyer who didn't have much useful advice besides appealing the rejections of my application for conscientious objector status. As if I needed to be reminded, he noted that my earlier decision not to apply for a student deferment while a UCLA student had made me a target for induction sooner than would otherwise have been the case. He also mentioned that the same decision meant that I was still eligible for a fatherhood deferment. Susan and I had begun discussing when we would start a family, but the draft remained a constant cloud on the horizon.

I made no effort to contact my draft board, as I was legally required to do. Uncertain about how I would respond if inducted, I wanted to put off the decision as long as possible. The FBI, however, quickly discovered that I had returned from abroad, although I didn't know it at the time. An informant reported to the Bureau seeing someone he was "fairly certain was CARSON, walking in the beach area of Venice, California."

When UCLA students returned to campus for the 1968–69 academic year, I attended a few antiwar and pro-Panther rallies, but more out of curiosity than conviction. I heard a campus speech by Eldridge Cleaver, who had become the presidential candidate of the Peace and Freedom Party, which was an outgrowth of the New Politics movement with which I had been affiliated during 1966 and 1967. By then, I was no longer a political journalist or a member of any political organization. Although disturbed that Democratic presidential candidate Hubert Humphrey refused to take a strong stand against the war, I didn't share Cleaver's confidence that his candidacy provided a serious alternative. Nonetheless, I decided to cast my first ballot in a presidential election for a candidate I couldn't imagine ever becoming president, whereby I regrettably played a small role in making possible Richard Nixon's narrow victory.

As the nation turned to the right, UCLA's faculty and students turned to the left. When classes began in the fall of 1968, my campus job allowed me to observe that the campus political climate had changed dramatically in the year since I had been a student. Following several years of Black Power speeches and antiwar protests, King's assassination had been a catalyst for stimulating various kinds of student discontent. Like many other colleges and universities, UCLA administrators resolved to honor King and forestall further racial violence by increasing admissions of black students and encouraging departments to hire black faculty members. A few professors began offering courses concerning racial issues. Students mobilized around numerous demands, including the removal of the ROTC military program from campus, "open enrollment," the creation of Black—or African American or Pan-African—Studies programs, and the removal of "undercover agents" from campus.

I began auditing history professor Gary Nash's new class on race relations in the United States. Because of the flexible hours of my computer programmer job, I not only attended lectures but also took time to participate in the lively after-class discussions. Perhaps because I stood out as one of a small number of black college

graduates on campus, Nash recruited me as his informal teaching assistant, leading a section devoted to Black Political Thought. Among the fifteen students in the
section were the president and vice president of the Black Student Union as well as
members of the Black Panther Party, Karenga's Us, and the Nation of Islam. Intense,
sometimes angry exchanges gave me a brutal introduction to teaching; yet I found
that I enjoyed guiding discussions about the African American freedom struggle.
Despite my earlier feelings of being an outsider, I had learned much as a result
of activist journalism. Activism had once drawn me away from my undergraduate classes; now it gave me a reason to consider graduate studies and an academic
career.

With Nash's encouragement, I successfully applied to become a history graduate student starting in the fall of 1969. I realized that my admission was the result
of the affirmative action program instituted in the wake of King's assassination
and the student protests that followed. My undergraduate grades were not stellar, although better than could have been expected for a student living off campus,
working, irregularly attending classes, publishing journalistic articles, and maintaining a high level of political activism. My academic qualifications had apparently
improved during the time since my graduation.

In January 1969, I attended a meeting to discuss bringing a Black Studies program to UCLA. Students filled most of the seats in the classroom in Campbell
Hall, the building that housed minority programs. On one side of the room a few
Black Panthers wearing leather jackets stood glaring at African-garbed members of
Maulana Karenga's Us organization on the opposite side. Black Panther supporters
ridiculed Karenga's "cultural nationalism," describing him as a "pork-chop nationalist" allied with the "pigs"—police. Instead, the Black Panthers called for "revolutionary nationalism."

During the two years since I published my extended interview with Karenga
in the *Free Press*, he had become a prominent figure on the local black political
scene. Our occasional encounters had been amiable, and I doubted allegations by
Panther supporters that he worked with police, but I saw the Kawaida principles
that he taught to his followers as another example of a black group promoting
its own separate ideology. From my acquaintance with Clyde Halisi, a graduate
student who belonged to Karenga's group, I judged that Karenga's supporters were
very dedicated and more disciplined than their counterparts in the Black Panther
Party.

I was at my campus job when the simmering conflict between Black Panthers
and Us members came to a boil a few days later. The sounds of numerous police cars
arriving on campus alerted me to the fact that something serious had occurred. I

soon heard that an argument in the nearby Campbell Hall cafeteria had escalated into deadly violence. Two members of Us shot and killed two Panthers, Alprentice "Bunchy" Carter and John Huggins, and then fled. I would later learn that the FBI's secret counterintelligence program designed to "prevent the rise of a leader who might unify and electrify...violence prone elements" had used informants to exacerbate hostilities between the organizations. The killings and the subsequent police raids severely damaged both groups. They also reinforced my desire to distance myself from the Black Power movement that had descended into deadly rivalries.

Even as I watched the worsening of Panther-Us relations, my attention turned to my brother Michael, who had become seriously ill while stationed at a naval base in Washington. After he initially complained of debilitating headaches, doctors found that he had a congenital brain aneurysm that required surgery, which resulted in severe swelling of his brain. His doctors placed him in a coma until his condition could be stabilized. Mom flew to a hospital in Tacoma to be with him while he recovered. During a second surgery, Michael had a stroke that blinded him. I made plans to visit him but never had the chance. Mom and my sister Gail were there when he died early in March 1969.

Susan, who would soon learn she was pregnant, and I went to New Mexico for his funeral and his military burial at the Santa Fe National Cemetery. I noticed that Mom and my youngest brother Stephen cried the most; Dad and I kept our emotions inside. When I talked with two of his Navy friends who accompanied his body, I discovered that their views on the war were similar to those my brother had expressed during his visit the previous summer. They confided that Michael's headaches had begun after military police caught the three of them with marijuana. I wanted to believe that his fatal illness would have happened regardless of the added stress he faced. He was not a combat casualty, but I thought of him as a casualty of the times.

When I began my graduate courses in the fall, I was excited to be the first member of my family to undertake graduate studies but also felt a sense of panic. I was aware that admission to the program did not guarantee successful completion of a doctorate. I also realized that I would receive no financial support and would have to work part time as a computer programmer to pay expenses. Moreover, it soon became evident that some of the other first-year graduate students were far more prepared in the field of American history than I was. Many of them had teaching assistantships that allowed them to work closely with a professor and gain teaching skills. I recognized only a few of the books on the long list of readings intended to prepare me for the oral examination required of doctoral students. I had read a wide range of historical materials, but there were large gaps in my knowledge. I had taken only one undergraduate course in American history and even in my major field of Latin American history, my focus had been on Brazil. I didn't expect to be the top student in my graduate classes, but I was strongly motivated by a fear of failure.

On October 17, 1969, exactly two years after leaving the United States, I took a stack of books and scholarly articles into the maternity waiting room as Susan prepared to deliver our first child at Queen of Angels Hospital. From my Peace Corps training, I knew the essentials of delivering babies, but fathers were not allowed in the hospital delivery rooms. Moreover, because of Susan's diabetes, our baby had grown abnormally large, prompting her obstetrician to perform a caesarean section three weeks before the expected delivery date.

I tried vainly to push worries from my mind until a nurse came to inform me that I was a father. We eclectically named him David Malcolm Carson, giving him a racial-religious heritage he would have to come to terms with during the decades to come. He weighed nine and a half pounds, but his lungs were not fully developed, and doctors placed him in the premature ward, a giant among the tiny preemies. Even as I welcomed the idea of becoming a father, the prospect of supporting a family without Susan's income increased the urgency of completing my graduate studies. I was also now eligible for a permanent fatherhood deferment from the draft.

I was thankful that Mom came to Los Angeles to help Susan learn how to take care of an infant while she regained her strength during the weeks after surgery. Having a new grandchild helped Mom overcome the trauma of Michael's death, and I was grateful that she stayed long enough to help Susan gradually gain confidence as a mother.

Despite the distraction of fatherhood, my intellectual confidence grew during the first year of classes. My wide-ranging curiosity and readings proved to be better preparation for academic life than I could have imagined. My writings for the *Free Press* and other publications were hardly scholarly, but I had learned how to deliver short pieces on schedule without falling victim to writer's block. Failure in graduate school, I found, was often caused by an accumulation of incompletes rather than bad grades. As Susan assumed the primary role of caring for David, I voraciously consumed books and articles during most of the daytime hours when I was not in class, leaving the evening hours for my computer programming assignments.

My political activism paid unexpected dividends in my colloquia and seminars, where my SNCC-inspired insights about grassroots organizing fit well with recent scholarship in "bottom-up" social history. Most of my professors were sympathetic to the view that American history should be told from the perspective of those at the bottom of the social hierarchy rather than only from the viewpoint of elites. Furthermore, my exposure to New Left ideas encouraged me to move beyond stale Marxian class analysis toward an awareness of the cultural influences that affected liberation struggles. I was already familiar with UCLA professor Stephen Thernstrom's study of social mobility in Boston and Gary Nash's investigations of the lives of racial minorities during the colonial era. I attended Ronald Takaki's classes in African American history, and Paul Worthman, a recent addition to the faculty, introduced me to the pioneering scholarship of British and European labor historians, including E. P. Thompson's classic *The Making of the English Working Class*.

Although I tried to concentrate entirely on my classes, this proved difficult during a year when protests were an almost daily occurrence on the UCLA campus. In the fall of 1969, student protests erupted after the University of California regents fired Angela Davis, a recently hired black philosophy professor. A law student secretly working as an FBI informant had revealed that she was a Communist Party member. As Davis appealed her dismissal, black students and white sympathizers rallied behind her. Cheryl Dearman and Sonya Walker, two of the students in my Black Political Thought class, assumed leading roles in the campaign and convinced me to attend a public lecture given by Davis.

Convinced that she was unfairly fired because of her political affiliation, I came away impressed by her sophisticated Marxian psychological analysis of black liberation ideas. Yet I wondered why a woman with ties to the Los Angeles SNCC group and the Black Panther Party would join the moribund Communist Party. I introduced myself to her and attended several rallies where she spoke—usually in the company of Black Panther Party members—but resisted the temptation to become deeply involved in the campaign to save her job.

The following spring, President Richard Nixon's decision to send American troops into Cambodia sparked massive student protests at UCLA, as well as at other campuses. The protests were larger and more vehement than anything that had previously happened on the campus. I recall taking part in a demonstration directed against the building housing the ROTC program that culminated in a confrontation between angry students and overwhelmed campus police with weapons drawn from their holsters. No shots were fired, but it was the closest I had come to witnessing deadly gunfire since August 1965.

At the end of my first year of graduate school, I was offered a teaching assistantship that would pay some of my expenses during my second year. Although I had become used to earning a salary equivalent to that of a beginning assistant professor, I decided to give up my programming job to focus on my second-year research seminars. My seminar papers confirmed that I had a knack for choosing interesting and challenging topics. In a particularly ambitious paper comparing slavery in the United States to slavery in Brazil I made use of my rudimentary knowledge of Portuguese, gained from my Peace Corps training and a few UCLA courses. Consulting the research of Brazilian scholars, I explained why the slave system in the United States produced a rigid black-white divide that was quite different from Brazil's more fluid racial system, which offered greater opportunities for mixed-race people. A year after receiving an "A" grade for this paper, Stanford historian Carl Degler won the Pulitzer Prize for a comparative study of Brazilian and American race relations that reached conclusions similar to my own.

As I began to think seriously about a dissertation topic, I applied for a Fulbright grant to compare social mobility in Los Angeles and São Paulo, Brazil. After an interview with Fulbright representatives, I concluded that this project would require additional language training and several years of research abroad. Although disappointed that I would once again not be going to Brazil, I recognized the impracticality of completing such a project while supporting a family.

Soon afterward, Gary Nash invited me to meet with him in his office. The purpose of this meeting was unclear, and after seeing that most of the faculty in the U.S. history field were in attendance, I suspected that something important was afoot. "You've been doing quite well in your classes, and we're considering you for a faculty position in the department," Nash explained. "We'd like you to consider becoming an acting assistant professor in the fall."

He added that I would still have to pass my oral exam before the entire history faculty could vote on the appointment. The conversation continued for several more minutes before I realized that the position they had in mind was the one held by Professor Takaki, who, I was told, had been denied tenure by the senior faculty members. I was uneasy with the thought of replacing a popular teacher who had taken a supportive interest in me. I also knew that a year and a half of graduate courses did not make me as qualified as Takaki to teach African American history. I could not imagine a second-year white student who had not yet selected a dissertation topic being hired as a faculty member.

"I haven't given any thought about applying for a teaching position," I replied. "When do you want me to decide?"

"You can take a few days, but if this is going to happen, we'll have to schedule an oral exam soon."

I asked why Takaki was denied tenure. I knew that a few black students had complained that African American history should be taught by a black professor rather than Takaki, a Japanese American scholar. They explained that tenure discussions were confidential but assured me that the tenure decision had not been based on racial grounds.

I left the meeting in a state of disbelief and was unable to discuss the matter with other graduate students. Susan became my sounding board as I pondered the decision. How would I feel if my first teaching position came at the expense of a professor I liked? Was I being offered the position simply to placate black students? Would I later regret turning down a position that other graduate students elsewhere would eagerly seek once it became available?

I decided to accept the opportunity. The tenure decision was beyond my control, and someone was going to replace Takaki (he went on to a stellar career teaching at the University of California, Berkeley). I was not sure I was qualified to be a faculty member, but, if I passed my oral exams and did well in my remaining course work, that would be for others to judge.

Once I agreed to the proposal, my already intense graduate studies became even more accelerated. Oral examinations were normally scheduled during the third year in order to allow for the months of preparation necessary to display the competency across all major areas of American history, but in my case the exam took place with just a month of preparation. My committee consisted mainly of the faculty members who were already disposed to hire me as a colleague, so I was not surprised that I passed, but the unevenness of my answers also reminded me of how much I still needed to learn. I knew that I was probably the only second-year graduate student in the field of history to become a faculty member at a major research university.

Since returning to Los Angeles less than three years earlier without a job, I had benefitted from the rapid changes that had occurred on college campuses as a result of the nation's racial turmoil. Not much was being done to address the needs of the poor people that King had wanted to bring to Washington, but colleges and universities were admitting increasing numbers of black students and hiring at least a few black faculty members. Before his death, King had begun to speak of his Dream becoming a nightmare. But, even as the nation turned from racial reform to retrenchment, my once dim career prospects had unexpectedly brightened.

Chapter 7

SNCC's Legacy

*W*hen I began my graduate studies, I didn't consider the Student Nonviolent Coordinating Committee to be a topic for serious historical study. The group was far past its prime, but still existed. The institutional records and personal papers that historians normally use were not yet in archives. When my advisor, Stanley Coben, suggested that I write a dissertation on SNCC, I thought that the organization might be suitable for a journalistic book but not for a scholarly work that would earn a Ph.D. As I thought about Coben's suggestion, I realized that innovative research methods—oral history especially—could make up for the lack of archival sources. I knew that some historian would eventually write about SNCC's rise and fall. Why not accept the challenge myself? Historians were already writing about the 1960s. Lerone Bennett and David Levering Lewis had already written thoughtful biographies on King, and other scholars would undoubtedly follow. My dissertation would provide an alternative perspective to King-centered studies.

Studying SNCC also appealed to me as a return to the quest that started with the March on Washington. I had wanted to join SNCC but instead had participated in part-time civil rights activities and politically engaged journalism while pursuing my goal of graduating from college. During my self-imposed European exile, I had left behind my activism and SNCC dreams, but, after returning from abroad, I benefitted from the affirmative action programs established after King's death. I became a graduate student and now had the opportunity to study what I had been unable to experience. Having missed the chance to be part of SNCC, I could use my new skills to write its history. I could investigate what had become of John Lewis, Bob Moses, and other SNCC veterans I had long admired. How had Stokely Carmichael evolved from a grassroots organizer in a group that distrusted hierarchy to being a Pan-African ideologue?

Once I decided to go ahead with the dissertation on SNCC, I knew my teaching schedule would make it difficult for me to find time for research, including considering the travel involved. Even after negotiating a lighter than normal teaching load during my first year, I still had to teach during the fall and winter quarters. I also knew that I would have to devote considerable time to preparing lectures for my undergraduate survey course in African American history, having never taken a course in the field (simply sitting in on Takaki's lectures was hardly a sufficient substitute).

Once the academic year began, I found that lecturing to large classes was a skill that did not come easily. Looking back at my notes, I can see that I masked my lack of confidence by preparing—and often reading—overly ambitious lectures on slavery and the long history of African American resistance to racial oppression. My small-group courses were more successful since they allowed me to share with students my enthusiasm for research; yet even when I talked about the black freedom struggle—which I always distinguished from the more limited "civil rights movement"—I realized how difficult it was to translate experience and research into coherent lectures. My first years as a professor consisted mainly of unsupervised on-the-job training.

Once the winter quarter ended, I was eager to begin my research but not sure where to start. I wasn't even sure if the group still existed. During the late 1960s, a faction led by H. Rap Brown had changed the organization's name to the Student National Coordinating Committee. In 1970 the group briefly made news when two of Brown's associates, Ralph Featherstone and William "Che" Payne, were killed after an explosion ripped apart their car. They were apparently driving to a Maryland town where Brown was facing trial on charges stemming from the Cambridge racial violence of 1967. Brown went into hiding, but in October 1971 New York police wounded him in a shootout while responding to a reported robbery at a Manhattan cocktail lounge. I had never met Brown and did not know anyone still affiliated with SNCC, but I suspected that the group's beleaguered stalwarts would not have much interest in cooperating with me.

Even if I found SNCC's organizational files, I knew that SNCC field secretaries typically spent their days interacting with grassroots leaders and local residents rather than preparing daily reports. The qualities that made SNCC distinctive, particularly its decentralized structure, would make tracing its history difficult. Although a few archives, most notably the Wisconsin State Historical Society in Madison, had acquired SNCC-related collections, I decided that my best research strategy was to find former staff members willing to talk with me and perhaps share whatever documents they had kept. I hoped that these SNCC veterans could supply contact information about other former staff members.

In the spring of 1972, I left Los Angeles in a Volkswagen bus outfitted for camping. Needing to focus on my research and sensing that the South was not ready for my biracial family, Susan and David stayed with my parents in New Mexico while I drove to the east coast. Along the way, I stopped at libraries and archives in the upper South but found that their SNCC-related holdings consisted mainly of old newspaper clippings.

Once I reached Washington, D.C., I visited the National Mall for the first time since 1963. My first interview was with Marion Barry, the Mississippi-born veteran of the Nashville Student Movement who in 1960 became SNCC's first chairman. Listening to him describe his transition from nonviolent protester to Black Power advocate to successful urban politician helped me to understand the larger story of SNCC's transformation during the 1960s. Barry had been one of the Nashville students who prepared themselves for the sit-ins by participating in nonviolence workshops led by James Lawson, the Vanderbilt divinity student who had drafted SNCC's statement of purpose: "We affirm the philosophical or religious ideal of nonviolence as the foundation of our purpose, the presupposition of our faith, and the manner of our action." Like other SNCC activists, Barry had been deeply affected by Lyndon Johnson's failure to back the Mississippi Freedom Democratic Party's (MFDP) challenge to the seating of Mississippi's all-white "regular" Democratic delegation to the 1964 Democratic National Convention.

Barry was among the SNCC workers who shifted their focus from the rural South to urban areas where black residents had the right to vote but had little political power. In 1965, he helped rally residents of Washington, D.C., rally against a bus fare hike and later became a prominent figure in the Free D.C. Movement, a group that demanded representation in Congress and an elected city government for the nation's capital. After leaving SNCC in 1967, he co-founded Pride, Inc., an organization seeking to increase job opportunities for poor black residents, much as the Non-Violent Action Committee had tried to do in Los Angeles. When I interviewed him, he was serving on Washington's Board of Education, the first step of an ascent in Washington politics that would culminate in his election as the city's mayor in 1978. It seemed that Barry had made a successful transition from protest to electoral politics, although his subsequent checkered political career, which included a prison term for drug possession, demonstrated how difficult it would be to draw generalizations from the experiences of any one SNCC worker.

I completed other interviews and archival research in the Washington area and then drove to Greensboro to interview David Richmond, one of the four students at North Carolina A&T College who in 1960 ignited the lunch-counter sit-in movement. Although the students had been members of NAACP youth groups in high school, they formulated their plan for the protest in late-night discussions during their first semester in college. Richmond recalled his frustration hearing "how black folks were mistreated and nobody was doing anything about it." None of the four students joined SNCC's staff, and the Greensboro sit-ins confirmed that protest movements did not require direction from King or other national civil rights organizations.

In Atlanta, I met with Stanley Wise, one of a number of SNCC veterans who remained in the city where the group's headquarters had been located. Wise had been SNCC's last executive secretary before the group became debilitated by internal ideological warfare, and he told me that many of the group's records were still stored in his home. I excitedly went through the boxes, taking notes as fast as I could. He did not allow me to photocopy his collection, but these records provided me with an overview of SNCC's institutional history. He later sold these papers to the King Library and Archive at the King Center in Atlanta, where they became the largest collection of SNCC documents available to researchers.

The highlight of my stay in Atlanta was the interview I conducted with former SNCC chair John Lewis. The son of Alabama sharecroppers, he had followed news reports about the bus boycott movement that began in 1955 in nearby Montgomery. He met King in 1958 while attending American Baptist Theological Seminary in Nashville. Like Barry, he participated in Lawson's nonviolence workshops and in the Nashville student sit-ins of 1960. As one of the original freedom riders who set out to challenge segregation at Southern bus terminals, he suffered a horrific beating in Montgomery and served jail time in Mississippi's Parchman Prison. After being displaced as SNCC's chair in 1966 by Stokely Carmichael, Lewis left the group and became the director of the Voter Education Project (VEP) in Atlanta, which was formed to increase the number of black registered voters in the South. Arriving in his VEP office, I noticed a poster on his wall that proclaimed, "HANDS THAT PICKED COTTON NOW CAN PICK OUR ELECTED OFFICIALS." As I later recalled the words, they would come to summarize SNCC's remarkable achievement in the Deep South.

I asked Lewis about rumors that other organizers had censored the speech I had heard him deliver at the March on Washington. Having been greatly affected by his forceful critique of conventional American politics, I wondered what he had been prevented from saying. John told me that after an advance text was distributed to other civil rights leaders the day before the march, a Catholic archbishop insisted that John tone down his speech, especially his references to "revolution."

He recalled that King was one of those concerned about his call for nonviolent protesters to "pursue our own 'scorched earth' policy and burn Jim Crow to the ground—nonviolently."

In the original draft, Lewis questioned the Justice Department's commitment to civil rights: "I want to know, which side is the federal government on?" Although he epitomized the Nashville activists' fervent commitment to nonviolent principles, he nonetheless saw himself as part of a nonviolent revolution that would push aside political leaders who refused to act resolutely against injustice. "We will not wait for the President, the Justice Department, nor Congress," his draft warned, "but we will take matters into our own hands and create a source of power, outside of any national structure, that could and would assure us victory."

John recalled that he was "angry that someone would tell me what to say and what should be deleted." March director A. Philip Randolph, who had been a socialist firebrand himself during and after World War I, didn't object to the use of the word "revolution." The veteran labor leader noted that he had called for a similar march more than two decades earlier. Now on the verge of seeing his idea become a reality, he pleaded for a compromise: "John, for the sake of unity, we've come this far. For the sake of unity, change it." Lewis revised his speech inside the Lincoln Memorial, not far from where I stood in 1963.

After leaving SNCC, John Lewis continued to admire King and remained committed to Gandhian nonviolence even as Carmichael and other SNCC workers openly challenged King's principles. Although he had reason to be embittered by the "hard feelings" and "animosities" that accompanied his ouster, he remained convinced that SNCC had made a crucial contribution to the African American freedom struggle. "A whole thought pattern, a whole culture in some parts of the country, has been influenced by SNCC," he told me. It was the only organization, he said, that "had the audacity or the courage or foolhardiness—some people called us crazy—to go into certain areas of this country…and do something that the federal government wouldn't do and that certain other organizations wouldn't do." SNCC's legacy could be seen, he said, in the transformation of Southern black people from backgrounds like his own: "People that were sharecroppers and tenant farmers are now running for office."

John would go on to a successful political career, serving in the Jimmy Carter presidential administration, then as an Atlanta city councilman, and still later as a U.S. congressman representing a district in Atlanta. I would see him on a number of occasions in the years to come and would accompany him on a congressional tour of India to commemorate the fiftieth anniversary of Martin Luther King Jr.'s 1959 pilgrimage to "the land of Gandhi."

During my stay in Atlanta, I visited with my brother Chris, who was fulfilling his conscientious objector's service assisting in a day care center. I was pleased that he had been given an option other than enlisting in the military or leaving the United States, as I had done. He appeared to enjoy his work. When Susan and our then two-year-old son, David, joined me, they spent time with Chris while I completed my Atlanta interviews.

We returned to Washington during a massive Earth Day celebration on the National Mall before continuing on to New York. There I met with Ella Baker, the veteran organizer whose long career included serving as director of branches for the NAACP and setting up the Atlanta headquarters of the Southern Christian Leadership Conference (SCLC). Baker had by the late 1950s become disgruntled working under King and welcomed the student-led sit-ins. She used SCLC funds to pay for the April 1960 conference that resulted in SNCC's formation. Baker made certain that student activists were not encouraged to become the youth wing of one of the existing civil rights groups, which would necessarily curtail their independence and militancy. She became a trusted SNCC advisor. "She was much older in terms of age," John had told me, "but I think in terms of ideas and philosophy and commitment she was one of the youngest persons in the movement."

When I arrived at Baker's modest apartment in Harlem, she somewhat wearily greeted me wearing a robe and apologized for her appearance and messy place. "I'd forgotten that you were coming." I assured her that meeting her was an honor, given all that I had heard about her dedication and decades of activism. Many SNCC workers would cite her influence, along with that of Bob Moses, as crucial in the development of SNCC's distinctive community organizing approach. As we talked about SNCC's early days, she seemed to gain energy—I would later use the phrase "long-distance runner" to describe her resilience.

She recalled insisting that the student protesters at SNCC's founding conference should have "the right to direct their own affairs and even make their own mistakes." Remembering the frustrations of her years working with NAACP local branches and with King in the early years of SCLC, she feared that the existing civil rights groups would stifle student activism. "You see I've been around long enough and, I suppose, seen enough of what can take place, how people and their ideas can be captured by those who have programs of their own and who may not be as sensitive as they should be to what the other group that they are trying to capture is trying to do."

My next meeting with Baker would come in 1977 during a research trip through Mississippi and Alabama. She and filmmaker Joanne Grant were collaborating on the documentary *Fundi: The Story of Ella Baker* that would bring her ideas to a larger audience, including the students who would later watch the film in my classes. The last time I would see her was in December 1978, when I attended a celebration of her seventy-fifth birthday in New York. Few events in my lifetime have been as moving as witnessing speaker after speaker—representing American social justice movements of the previous five decades—express appreciation for Baker's selfless devotion to the idea that oppressed people can be mobilized to liberate themselves. Moses's tribute to her suggested the Kiswahili title for Grant's documentary:

> *Mfundi* is a person in a community who masters a given craft. And he mas-
> ters it coming up through the community...with the help of other people
> in the community who have mastered it. And he plies his craft and teaches
> it to other people in the community. And it goes on like that, without
> ever being institutionalized. And I've come to think of Miss Baker as our
> *mfundi* in the movement.

By the time I left New York, I had conducted more than a dozen interviews with key sources on SNCC's history. More important than the specific information I had gained, the interviews made me more aware of the strong personalities who had, for a brief historical moment, come together in an extraordinary community within a sustained freedom struggle. My 1963 encounters with Stokely Carmichael and Bob Moses had shaped my initial conception of SNCC, but each of my interviews with former SNCC activists would continue to enrich my understanding of this diverse and constantly changing group.

After driving on to Boston, I especially anticipated meeting Boston University historian Howard Zinn, the white leftist who had become closely associated with SNCC while teaching at the historically black Spelman College in Atlanta during the early 1960s. In 1963 SNCC activists asked Howard to become their historian, a testament to the trust they placed in him to explain their distinctive style of grass-roots organizing. Howard's involvement in SNCC in turn strengthened his own commitment to writing books such as *A People's History of the United States* that recounted American history from the perspectives of those struggling to overcome injustice and oppression.

When I arrived at his home, I was concerned that he might see me as a scholarly competitor, given that in 1965 he had written his own account, *SNCC: The New Abolitionists*, based on his close association with SNCC workers during his years at Spelman. The forty-nine-year-old scholar greeted me warmly, however, and gener-ously shared his memories of serving as SNCC's informal advisor. He then directed me to the boxes of SNCC materials he kept in his attic, which included numerous accounts of staff meetings, and position papers that staff members had prepared for the series of discussions about the group's future that took place in the crucial period after the 1964 Mississippi Summer Project. I was surprised that such meticulous records had been created by a group that I assumed lacked bureaucratic habits. "Take as long as you want to look through these materials," Howard told me. "There's a photocopy place not far away, and you're welcome to take the documents you need and make copies of them." I was elated that I had finally located a large body of revealing SNCC materials. Howard's openness and generosity impressed me and would later serve as a model for how I should treat the scholars who would request similar assistance from me.

Although in subsequent years I interviewed more SNCC veterans, this two-month trip provided the foundation for the dissertation I would write while teaching a full load of classes over the next three years. Even before I returned to Los Angeles, I had already begun to construct in my mind a basic narrative of SNCC's history, from its early years as a loosely structured coordinating committee of protesters mostly devoted to Gandhian-style civil disobedience, to its heyday as a cadre of full-time organizers seeking to mobilize black communities to overcome oppressive conditions; and finally to its later years as a rallying point for Black Power militancy. I wanted to understand why a group that seemed so effective and cohesive during the early 1960s would come apart just as landmark civil rights reforms were being enacted. Why had SNCC abandoned its early emphasis on grassroots organizing and nonviolent action and instead become mired in rancorous debates over issues such as the role of the declining number of whites in the black freedom struggle?

Early in 1973, I interviewed Stokely Carmichael, my first activist role model and the exemplar of the Black Power militancy of the late 1960s. After finishing his year as SNCC's chair, he had traveled abroad calling for revolutionary resistance to Western imperialism and capitalism. The product of a group that epitomized bottom-up organizing, he ultimately became a leader in search of a following. After a short stint as prime minister of the Black Panther Party, he moved to the West African nation of Guinea, where he studied Pan-Africanism under the tutelage of Guinean prime minister Ahmed Sékou Touré and exiled Ghanaian president Kwame Nkrumah. Adopting the name Kwane Toure Stokely, he became the most prominent figure in the All African Peoples Revolutionary Party. He spent most of his time in Africa, but in February 1973 he came to Los Angeles on a speaking tour.

I wanted to understand why he had abandoned the kind of grassroots organizing he had done so well in Mississippi during 1964 and in Alabama during 1965.

His shift from organizing to speechmaking seemed to symbolize a larger shift that had destructive consequences for SNCC. Breaking away from Ella Baker's notion of "group-centered leadership," Stokely had encouraged SNCC's shift toward becoming a "leader-centered" group of ideologues.

At the time I interviewed him, Stokely was still the engaging, outgoing person I had known in the 1960s, but his memories of his SNCC years were colored by the political positions he adopted during the late 1960s. Howard Zinn's 1963 interview with Stokely painted him as a product of New York's predominantly white Bronx High School of Science, where he had formed close ties with white leftists—including the son of a Communist Party leader—before enrolling at Howard University. Like Marion Barry, he had become disillusioned with liberal Democrats who had failed to support the MFDP challenge in 1964. The experience, he said, demonstrated that "black people in Mississippi and throughout this country could not rely on their so-called allies."

Along with other SNCC workers, Stokely left Mississippi during the Selma-to-Montgomery march to begin organizing in rural Lowndes County, a predominantly black area where local leaders had launched their own voting rights campaign. The formation of the Lowndes County Freedom Organization (LCFO) marked the beginning of SNCC's drift toward Black Power. Stokely told me that the Lowndes County effort was an outgrowth of the kind of organizing SNCC had previously done elsewhere. The new organization differed from the MFDP not only because of its lack of ties to liberal Democrats but also due to its all-black composition. He insisted that his Pan-African perspective was consistent with the "black nationalist" views that had led him to recruit an all-black staff to work in Mississippi's second Congressional district during the 1964 Summer Project.

Yet, I also knew that Stokely's reputation as a Black Power firebrand obscured his complex and somewhat ambivalent attitudes about the role of white activists in the movement. While urging white activists to organize white communities, Stokely had opposed the expulsion of white staff members, arguing that this debate had simply been a way for extreme racial separatists affiliated with SNCC's Atlanta project to assert control over the group. This debate, which exacerbated divisions among black staff members, culminated at a December 1966 staff meeting in an 18–17 vote in favor of expulsion.

When I asked Stokely about the relationship between SNCC and King, I could sense that he was still troubled by the perception that his differences with King were personal. "I was very close to King," he assured me. "He taught us how to confront the enemy without fear." He recalled that he opposed SNCC members who publicly attacked King during the 1965 voting rights campaign in Alabama and insisted that King's ability to "mobilize" black residents in the state paved the way for SNCC's Lowndes County project.

As I tried to bring together my research and interviews into a dissertation during the summer and fall of 1973, Susan and I decided to adopt a child. David's difficult birth and Susan's diabetes made another pregnancy risky. We applied to Los Angeles County to adopt a biracial child. Early in 1974, a social worker introduced us to our newborn, blond, blue-eyed girl. We learned that her birth mother was white, her birth father black. We named her Temera Lea—she immediately became Temie.

Temie's arrival coincided with an unexpected opportunity that suddenly shifted the course of my career. While attending a conference of historians in San Francisco during the Christmas break, I learned that Stanford's history department was seeking to fill a position in African American history. Stanford had already selected three finalists. After speaking with two members of its history department, I accepted their invitation to apply.

I wasn't unhappy at UCLA but sensed it was time to test whether another university was interested in me. Stanford would not have been my first choice. Although its history department was reputed to be one of the nation's best, "the farm," as it was called, seemed to me an elite, private institution compared to UCLA, a public university with a long history of admitting black students. I knew, however, that even a rejected offer from another university would be helpful if I decided to seek tenure at UCLA. I was pleased when I was added to the list of finalists and asked to deliver a lecture.

I decided against delivering a prepared text. Lecturing was not my strong point, and I learned that I was better at speaking informally about my scholarly interests. Once when I arrived at class with the wrong notes, I delivered my lecture as best I could from memory and was surprised when a student remarked, "That was the best lecture you've given this quarter." I realized afterward that I often relied too much on my notes rather than observing the reactions of my students. I still found it useful to prepare lectures, but I came to prefer consulting my notes only when necessary.

I chose not to speak about my dissertation, deciding instead to focus on the recent scholarship comparing slave systems in various parts of the western hemisphere. At the time, I was preparing my first publication as a scholar: a critical review of the controversial book *Time on the Cross: The Economics of American Negro Slavery* by Robert William Fogel and Stanley L. Engerman. During my talk I compared slavery in the United States to slavery in Latin America and more specifically in Brazil and the Caribbean. I felt relaxed giving the talk and responding to the questions that followed. I especially enjoyed exchanging ideas with St. Clair Drake, the director of Stanford's program in African and African American Studies and an anthropologist best known for his classic study *Black Metropolis*. His presence and that of African historian Kennel Jackson showed me that Stanford's faculty was becoming more racially diverse.

I was pleased that my first "job talk" went well, but I tried not to build up my expectations. Despite already having a faculty position, I soon worried that my UCLA colleagues would discover that I had tried and failed to get a job elsewhere. I was relieved when I received a formal offer to teach at Stanford. I might have been more excited by an offer from UC Berkeley, where I remembered seeing thousands of students attending a 1965 teach-in on the Vietnam War. Stanford's bucolic ambience and its proximity to Berkeley and San Francisco nonetheless made it an attractive destination. I had enjoyed my decade in Los Angeles but decided that it was the right time to leave. I looked forward to being in a new academic environment with a new set of faculty colleagues. Susan, who had grown up within a few miles of UCLA, was also eager to experience life in the Bay Area. We had grown tired of our apartment in UCLA's married housing complex on Sawtelle Boulevard right next to the San Diego freeway. When I told my UCLA colleagues that I was leaving, some tried to dissuade me but most wished me well.

We knew little about the Stanford area but were impressed by the beauty of its campus and surroundings. In June we traveled to Northern California to spend a week hunting for housing, only to find that my salary of $12,500, plus $2,500 for a summer stipend, did not qualify us to buy a house in Palo Alto. On the last day of our visit, a realtor told us that a two-bedroom house in nearby Menlo Park had just become available for "only" $32,000. We rushed over to buy it, using all our retirement savings from UCLA. It would be our home for the next five years.

Once we settled into our new house, I consulted an instruction book for the necessary skills to construct an office in the garage, where I quickly returned to writing my dissertation with the awareness that my new job was contingent on its timely completion. It was helpful that my Stanford classes were typically smaller than those at UCLA. Although I didn't notice a difference between the best students on each campus, there were fewer of the underprepared students who occupied a disproportionate amount of my time at UCLA. Stanford students were also more diverse in terms of racial and class backgrounds than I expected—a change accelerated by campus protests following King's assassination—and I was pleasantly surprised that many of them were politically active.

In the spring of 1975, I submitted my doctoral dissertation: "Toward Freedom and Community: The Evolution of Ideas in the Student Nonviolent Coordinating

Committee," which was accepted by my doctorial committee. I didn't attend the ceremony to receive my Ph.D. but felt good that I would no longer have "acting" before my assistant professor title. I didn't have to cringe when students addressed me as "Dr. Carson." I had reached a level of academic achievement that far surpassed my initial ambition had been to be my family's first college graduate.

Even after completing the dissertation, however, I was aware of its limitations. Although I saw myself as a social historian writing bottom-up history, my study of SNCC had focused mostly on its college-trained officers and staff rather than the grassroots leaders who made it possible for them to succeed. Most of my research had been conducted in libraries and cities—especially Atlanta and Washington, D.C.—rather than in the small towns and rural areas where SNCC's impact had been most dramatic. The dissertation was adequate, but I knew that much more research would be needed before I could expand my thoughts and observations on SNCC's historical significance into a book.

Chapter 8

In Struggle

*I*n November 1976, I traveled to Atlanta to attend a reunion of the activists who had once been associated with the Student Nonviolent Coordinating Committee. By the time of the gathering, few people who had not been part of the Movement remembered SNCC's important contributions to the Southern freedom struggle. So much had happened during the period since the group had exerted its greatest impact on black grassroots movements. As I noted in a *Nation* article published shortly before the reunion, "The 1963 March on Washington is separated from us by thirteen years and three Presidents and the rise and fall of a succession of movements, leaders and dreams." My article recounted that it had been ten years since Stokely Carmichael, just after becoming SNCC's chair, had garnered the attention of the nation's press by offering the Black Power slogan as a new response by black Americans to the enduring question: "What do you want?" During the decade following Carmichael's sudden rise to prominence, however, governmental repression and destructive ideological infighting had decimated SNCC and other militant black groups.

Carmichael remained in Africa rather than attending the reunion, where he might have faced sharp questions regarding his role in turning SNCC into a leader-centered organization. Those who did attend the gathering represented a wide variety of outlooks that were linked only by their involvement in a group that changed radically during its existence. Some were still committed to the Gandhian ideas expressed in SNCC's original statement of purpose, while others had become proponents of black nationalism, Pan-Africanism, or Marxism. A few former SNCC workers had been involved in the successful presidential campaign of former Georgia governor Jimmy Carter, who also drew support from former King aide Andrew Young—later appointed as Carter's United Nations ambassador. In the

1976 election, former SNCC chair John Lewis failed in his bid to succeed Young as a member of Georgia's delegation in the House of Representatives. Lewis later joined the Carter administration as director of the federal volunteer agency, ACTION, where he worked closely with another SNCC veteran, Mary King, ACTION's associate director. Julian Bond, SNCC's former communications director, won election to a new term in the Georgia Senate.

Attending the reunion helped me revise the generalizations I had reached while writing my dissertation. Although I realized that it would be impossible to interview every SNCC veteran, I was most concerned that I had not yet interviewed Bob Moses, the organizer who had initiated SNCC's voter registration effort in Mississippi and who subsequently influenced the development of SNCC's distinctive style of community organizing. The previous spring, he had returned from his voluntary exile in Tanzania (motivated, as in my case, by his desire to avoid military induction), but he and his wife Janet—also a former SNCC worker—had decided against attending the reunion.

I had also failed to interview James Forman, who had served as SNCC's executive director from 1961 to 1966 and thereafter remained affiliated with the group until the late 1960s. Forman attended the reunion but initially suspected that I was gathering information for the FBI. I would later learn that his paranoia was rooted in his experiences during the late 1960s, when he feared—correctly it turned out—that he was being threatened by FBI surveillance and retaliation from black militants in the Black Panther Party and other black factions. It would take another decade before he was willing to talk to me about his experiences and over time solicited my support for his antipoverty efforts. In 2002, just three years before his death, I would conduct an onstage public interview with him at a Smithsonian Institution event in his honor.

I was able to interview a few SNCC workers at the reunion and later used the reunion mailing list to contact veterans who were living in various places throughout the nation. I could see that SNCC did not simply consist of the courageous freedom fighters I had idealized after the March on Washington. Bob Moses had epitomized SNCC's distinctive ethos, but he was only one of many personality types who shaped the group's evolution. SNCC's greatest impact had been in the Southern Black Belt, where each of SNCC's projects had its own distinctive history. I had interviewed some of the most influential SNCC workers, but SNCC was also comprised of activists who never spoke at staff meetings or wrote position papers or produced the other documentary sources I had consulted.

During the summer of 1977, I visited many of the areas in the Deep South where SNCC had established projects. SNCC veteran Jean Wiley, who was making a film about the movement, joined me during parts of the trip. These interviews became windows into the ways in which SNCC's distinctive legacy still survived. Some SNCC workers had never left the places where they had struggled for voting rights. I interviewed some who had never accepted that the freedom struggle had ended. In Greenwood, Mississippi, Dewey Greene was still living in the same house where SNCC workers, including two of his own children, had been a target of bombings and nightriders during the 1960s. Jessie Morris, who arrived in Mississippi in 1963 intending to stay only a few weeks, was still politically active in the state. Charles Sherrod, who had directed SNCC's Southwest Georgia project, also remained in the area and became an elected public official in Albany, Georgia.

When I visited Bob Mants, who had worked with Stokely Carmichael in Lowndes County, Alabama, he was living on his small farm in the county. As we shared a lunch of catfish that he had caught, he told me about his continuing effort to build black political power in the county.

I found Maria Varela, once director of SNCC's literacy project, living in a small, isolated, northern New Mexico village not far from where I had grown up. She told me not only about her SNCC experiences, but also of her efforts to bring medical care to the Spanish-speaking residents in her community.

By this time, I had sent my manuscript to several publishers and was distressed to learn that University of Chicago Press had rejected it due to a negative report suggesting revisions that would require several years to complete. Normally such reports are anonymous, but in this case the author revealed that he was August Meier, a pioneering white historian who had specialized in African American history during a period when there were few black historians in the field. I disagreed with many of Meier's suggestions, believing that they were unnecessary or reflected a misunderstanding of SNCC's radicalism.

Soon after I read Meier's report, however, Harvard University Press responded to Pulitzer Prize–winning historian Louis Harlan's highly favorable report on my manuscript by agreeing to publish the book with only minor revisions. Meier would continue to object that I had not followed his suggestions and would later write a letter opposing my promotion to associate professor with tenure. Yet, ironically, if I had undertaken the additional research he had suggested, I would also have missed the chance to become tenured. Such are the dilemmas of academic life.

As I was completing my book manuscript, a tragic event occurred that reminded me of the intense emotions and interpersonal conflicts that eventually shattered the Movement. On March 14, 1980, I heard radio reports that former SNCC worker Dennis Sweeney had shot and killed former congressman Allard Lowenstein, who had once been Sweeney's political mentor. I had never met Sweeney, but I did know

Lowenstein, who had served as an assistant dean at Stanford during the 1960s. I saw him less than a year earlier when both of us participated in the fifteenth anniversary commemoration of the Mississippi Summer Project. On that occasion, I moderated the opening session and prepared to introduce him when two former Mississippi field secretaries stood up in the audience to denounce him for helping "destroy" SNCC. I was stunned by the vehemence of the verbal attack, which disrupted the session, but Lowenstein was eventually allowed to speak. Despite the fact that he had recruited many of the students who volunteered for the 1964 Mississippi Summer Project, I recalled from my research that some SNCC workers distrusted Lowenstein as an ally of the "liberal establishment" and believed that he undermined SNCC by telling his recruits that the group was becoming too radical.

At first I was uncertain how Sweeney fit into this long-standing antipathy, but my wife reminded me that Lowenstein had mentioned Sweeney during my 1977 interview with him at Stanford. I immediately located the recording of the interview and listened with rapt attention as Lowenstein described his deteriorating relationship with the person who would later kill him. He used Sweeney as an example of the way close friendships could be torn apart when the strains of activism in Mississippi "produced genuine paranoia and very often deeply bitter and permanently damaged people." A white student from Oregon, Sweeney was in his first year at Stanford when he met Lowenstein, who gained a following among white students because of his background as an officer in the National Student Association as well as his ties to Bob Moses and the Mississippi movement. When Sweeney volunteered to go to McComb during the 1964 summer, Lowenstein recalled that the violence and increasing racial militancy of the period pushed Sweeney gradually toward insanity.

He went to Mississippi during the period when SNCC was getting into black power:

> When I was becoming the sort of villain in their eyes. He became very much the spearhead of their campaign against me in a lot of ways....where he would attack me from a very personal feeling....He became very much involved with SNCC, ended up being thrown out of SNCC himself....They ended up accusing him of all the things that he had accused me of except it was done after he had put all of his emotion into SNCC, and it very, very badly damaged him.

After several of Lowenstein's other student followers at Stanford revealed that they had rejected sexual advances from him, I realized that his relationship with

Sweeney may have been even more complex than I had imagined. Lowenstein told me that he occasionally heard from Sweeney during the decade after the 1964 Summer Project. He told me Sweeney eventually "hacked out the fillings of his teeth," because, he said, the CIA was "using those fillings to damage his brain." I could not readily push from my mind an eerie feeling while listening to the recording of Lowenstein's unwitting attempt to explain the motivations of his murderer. Sweeney's apparent paranoia was an extreme manifestation of the loss of trust and mutual respect that led to the death of the Movement.

A year after Lowenstein's death, after going through the painful process of cutting my manuscript by about a third to satisfy my editor, Harvard University Press published *In Struggle: SNCC and the Black Awakening of the 1960s*. The cuts made the book more about SNCC's ideological and philosophical debates and less about the social history of the Southern freedom struggle. Despite its limitations, it remained for decades the only book-length scholarly study of SNCC. It was well received by most reviewers and received the 1982 Frederick Jackson Turner Award from the Organization of American Historians recognizing it as the best first book published that year by a historian.

I was generally satisfied with *In Struggle*, but I continued to regret that I had not interviewed Bob Moses, who many SNCC veterans mentioned as the key figure in SNCC's voter registration projects and the person who epitomized SNCC's ethos of encouraging grassroots leadership—"Our job is to work ourselves out of a job" was a popular slogan of many activists he influenced. As a teenager, I was inspired when I heard him discuss plans for the 1964 Mississippi Summer Project. I had listened intently when he spoke at an antiwar teach-in on the Berkeley campus in the spring of 1965.

I was not able to have my first talk with him until 1982, a year after the publication of my book. When I arrived at his Cambridge apartment, I noted that the clean-shaven voting rights worker in overalls I remembered from the 1960s had become a bearded, forty-seven-year-old Harvard graduate student, working on his dissertation in philosophy. He was nine years older than I was, but he was still lean and fit—the result, he later mentioned, of his vegetarian diet and yoga practice. I was pleased when he and Janet invited me to spend the night at their home with their four children. I treated the family to take-out Chinese food from a neighborhood place he recommended.

After explaining that I wanted to start by exploring his relationship with Ella Baker and the organizing principles he derived from her, Moses was strikingly forthcoming about every aspect of his life in the Movement. I found that we had a number of common threads in our lives, although in Bob's case the threads were longer and stronger. I had briefly been a math major in college; Bob had received a master's degree in math from Harvard and was a math teacher at New York's Horace Mann School, and his scholarly focus when we met involved comparing the epistemologies of mathematics versus other sciences. We both received draft notices in 1966; I traveled in Europe, Bob went to Canada, living there illegally during 1967 and 1968. Soon after I returned to the United States in March 1968, Bob left Canada for Tanzania. While I was becoming an academic at UCLA and Stanford, Bob was serving as a secondary-level math teacher in Tanzania and building a new life there with his family.

In his discussion of his experiences in SNCC, Bob rarely offered generalizations about organizing and instead stressed the practical lessons he had gained as a novice volunteer. I was struck that Bob saw organizing as an incremental process—like teaching students or nurturing children—in which the outcomes were often not evident until years later. He understood that the best organizers, such as Baker, managed to persist, despite many moments of disappointment and the inevitable frustrations that resulted from seeking radical social transformation. They were able to avoid the burnout that turns most activists into sprinters rather than long-distance runners.

Listening to Bob describe Baker's influence on him, I recalled the way in which she had impressed me when I interviewed her in the early 1970s. Sharing Baker's skepticism about charismatic leaders, such as King, he recalled that Baker often referred to the disillusionment that came when leaders are found "to have feet of clay." He remembered that Baker was "extremely matter-of-fact and level-headed about King as a person. She saw the struggle of our people, which was much bigger than any one person, was not to be encapsulated in some notion of a leader."

The most revealing part of our conversation, which stretched over two days, was Bob's description of his initial venture into the Deep South. Late in the summer of 1960, he had traveled by bus to Birmingham to meet with combative minister Fred Shuttlesworth, an SCLC founder who nonetheless questioned King's cautious leadership. Moses proceeded to Cleveland, Mississippi, where he met Amzie Moore, the forty-nine-year-old World War II veteran and NAACP activist, who enthusiastically agreed to attend SNCC's conference in order to recruit students for a voter registration effort in the Mississippi Delta. During several days of meetings late in the summer of 1960, the two men developed plans for an ambitious challenge to voter registration patterns in the Delta communities where black residents outnumbered whites. Bob recalled that the goal was to "gain political leverage" by registering black voters and ultimately electing black officials, especially in areas with black majorities.

Although I had written about Bob's return to the South in 1961, he surprised me when he admitted that he knew nothing about organizing before he arrived. He insisted that the essence of community organizing was in identifying trusted and respected local leaders and then learning from them. "Basically I did what Amzie told me to do," he related. "I just watched Amzie, how he moved. He very seldom told me what we were going to do in advance." I had often referred to local or grass-roots leaders, but Bob described how these leaders helped him to discover "all the ways community people interact with each other and the problems they might have with each other."

On many occasions during our extended conversation, I found myself wishing that I had been able to include Bob's reflections in my book. His thoughts would not have altered my overall view of SNCC's history but would have led me to be less inclined to suggest that Bob's success was due to a philosophical understanding of organizing methods. Instead I became aware of how much he had gained by working with experienced and self-reliant grassroots leaders such as Moore. Despite my belief in bottom-up history, I had fallen victim to the tendency to focus attention on the role played in mass movements by the well-educated, articulate outsider seeking to help the oppressed. Years later, I was pleased that historian John Dittmer published *Local People,* a detailed account of the Mississippi freedom struggle that devoted more attention than I had given to leaders such as Moore.

Looking back on the years I spent observing and studying SNCC, I recognize that I sometimes romanticized the Movement. Nonetheless, SNCC activists served as crucial role models, encouraging me and many others of my generation to identify with those at the bottom of any social order and to assume the risks of struggling against all forms of social oppression and injustice. At their best, SNCC workers exemplified the power that can be unleashed when people live according to their deeper convictions and higher values. As they became immersed in a sustained mass movement, they were transformed by their experiences, becoming more open to new ideas and more willing to question authority. Even now, SNCC's influence on my own identity and my worldview remains indelible.

Part Two

The King Papers Project

Chapter 9

Keeper of the Papers

One afternoon in late January 1985, my then-eleven-year-old daughter, Temie, answered a call from the King Center for Nonviolent Social Change in Atlanta. She neglected to relay the message that Mrs. Coretta Scott King would call me later that evening. The phone rang at 9:00 P.M. and I was surprised upon answering to hear a soft, distinctly Southern, somewhat recognizable voice. As I gestured for silence, Temie whispered apologetically, "Oh is that Mrs. King?" I strained to hear her during a call that would last about two hours (I later learned that she often had extended late-night telephone conversations). My prior acquaintance with her had been a single brief encounter years earlier when I was researching SNCC at Atlanta's Interdenominational Theological Center, where King's papers were housed during the construction of the King Center. Filling in a few inaudible gaps, I determined that she was exploring my interest in becoming the senior editor of the King Papers Project, which she had recently established to publish a multivolume edition of her late husband's papers.

As she slowly described the project, I recalled that a few months earlier the National Endowment for the Humanities (NEH) asked to review the King Project funding proposal that the King Center had submitted. I had responded positively but added that much would depend on whether an able scholar could be found to direct the project. Because I had never published even an article on King, it had not occurred to me that I might be a candidate for the position.

I was flattered to be considered but also confused. Why me? Mrs. King said that John Hope Franklin, the distinguished Duke University historian she had named to the King Project Advisory Board, had recommended me. I had met Franklin briefly when he came to the Bay Area to deliver one of a series of Thomas Jefferson Lectures sponsored by the NEH, and we crossed paths a few times at historical meetings. I was pleasantly surprised that he was familiar enough with my scholarly work to recommend me, and I knew I should seriously consider Mrs. King's proposal.

She described the research facilities at the King Library and Archive, and it became clear that she expected the editor to live in Atlanta. When I mentioned that I was a tenured professor at Stanford, Mrs. King assured me that she would help me find a comparable position at Atlanta's Emory University. I thought immediately of the drawbacks of giving up my hard-won job security for an uncertain role at the King Center. Moreover, I was looking forward to taking a sabbatical leave during the next academic year to work on a new book that would build upon my study of SNCC. Other considerations came to mind, especially the disruption of our children's education in Palo Alto's excellent public schools, of Susan's career in library science, and of our familial relationships. Susan's sister and my sister's families had followed us from Los Angeles to the Bay Area, and we enjoyed having an extended family nearby.

As the conversation meandered, I stated frankly that, although honored to be considered for the senior editor position, I was not willing to move to Atlanta. I offered to assist the project, perhaps as advisory editor, and suggested other scholars for her to consider. Why not David Garrow, the promising young scholar who was completing a major biography of King? Or perhaps other biographers such as David Lewis, the talented historian who had published *King: A Critical Biography* in the early 1970s. Even as I promised to send her a list of suitable candidates, I suspected that she must have already discussed other candidates with Franklin.

Within a day, I began to regret reacting so negatively to her query. Why wouldn't I be interested in studying King? As a historian of the African American freedom struggle, should I limit myself to SNCC's grassroots perspective or expand my focus by also exploring King's ideas? And why not consider leaving Stanford to take on a new challenge elsewhere? Had I lost my sense of adventure?

I realized that my single-minded focus on SNCC's grassroots perspective had caused me to neglect the most prominent leader to emerge from the Montgomery bus boycott movement. When Martin Luther King Jr. had delivered his "I Have a Dream" speech, I had been too distracted to give it my full attention. When he spoke at UCLA in 1965, I had felt smugly assured that he was not as radical as I had become. Yet, despite my long-standing admiration of SNCC, I had come to see its limitations, especially the tendency of SNCC workers to become absorbed in internal disputes that weakened the group's organizing efforts.

Even as SNCC faded from public view, King had remained the most visible symbol of the African American freedom struggle. Many of his erstwhile critics, myself included, had moved from political activism to more conventional lives, but King's commitment had endured. From the start of the bus boycott in December 1955 until his final day in Memphis, he had remained a key participant of the freedom struggle. Although I rejected the Great Man theory of history, I had to admit that there was something special about him. "I Have a Dream" had stuck in my memory as well as in the nation's consciousness. Moreover, it had been a moving experience to talk with the widow of a historical icon whose birthday was soon to become a national holiday. Honoring King, I also thought, would serve as a way to draw attention to other less-known activists.

I told acquaintances about the call from Mrs. King, and noticed that many of them were impressed in ways I had not seen when I mentioned SNCC. I persuaded myself that studying King would not mean turning away from SNCC; instead, it offered an opportunity to expand the scope of my scholarship. How could I pass up this opportunity to help carry on his legacy? As she often did when I faced crucial decisions, Susan put the matter bluntly: "Do you want to spend the rest of your career thinking you could have been editor of King's papers, and you didn't even seriously consider it?"

I sent Mrs. King a brief letter stating that I was open to discussing the senior editor position, if we could arrange for the project to be done both at Stanford and at the King Center. I then called Michael Jackson, a black aide to Stanford's president, Donald Kennedy. He quickly arranged meetings with Kennedy and Provost James Rosse, who promised funding for a King Papers Project office on the Stanford campus once we worked out a suitable relationship with the King Center. A few days later, I received a call from the King Center inviting me to meet with Mrs. King in person during her upcoming fundraising visit to San Francisco.

I was nervously excited that February afternoon as I entered the San Francisco Hilton wearing my only suit. (Although some Stanford professors routinely wore coats and ties, my attire, like that of most young professors, was typically more casual.) I wanted to see Mrs. King as merely another person, but could not help feeling a special sense of anticipation as I gave the desk clerk the false name her staff had used to register her. When I arrived at her suite, Mrs. King's assistant, Beni Ivey, greeted me and then took me inside.

I noticed that Mrs. King was impeccably dressed. Her luminous, light brown, clear skin belied the fact that she was fifty-eight years old at the time. She reminded me of my mother, and, from my preparatory perusing of her memoir, *My Life with Martin Luther King Jr.*, I had learned that she was born in rural Alabama near Marion, about 140 miles from the Florida town where my mother was born. As she began talking to me, it became apparent that Mrs. King, despite growing up in the segregated rural South, had taken advantage of educational opportunities that eluded my mother. She had attended Lincoln Normal School, where dedicated teachers nurtured her skills and made it possible for her to win a scholarship to Antioch College in Ohio. Aspiring to be a concert singer after graduation from Antioch, she entered Boston's New England Conservatory of Music.

She extended her hand, and I nervously shook it. She asked about my background, and I gave her a very brief overview of my childhood in Los Alamos, my attendance at the March on Washington, and my activism in Los Angeles. She expressed regret that we wouldn't have much time to talk privately but invited me to stay close to her while she attended the fundraising event at the hotel.

Once we arrived, I noticed San Francisco mayor Willie Brown was spearheading the effort to mobilize Bay Area support for the King Center, and I wondered what it would be like working with Mrs. King, who moved in such social circles. The crowd of people surrounding her did not leave many opportunities to move beyond the vagueness of our telephone conversation, I was encouraged when she introduced me as the Stanford professor who might become the "editor of Martin's papers." She later invited me to visit the King Center, I quickly accepted.

Although I had not yet received a job offer, I was pleased that Stanford administrators seemed willing to give the King Papers Project special support far beyond the norm for a humanities professor. I suspected that they were eager to signal the university's commitment to affirmative action at a time when I and many other black faculty members questioned that commitment. As at other universities, King's assassination had prompted Stanford to recruit black undergraduates and graduate students—there had been only a handful before then—but the pace of black faculty hiring had noticeably waned since I had arrived a decade earlier. Buoyed by promises of institutional support, I realized that Stanford officials would be greatly disappointed if the appointment fell through. In just a few weeks, my initial ambivalence had given way to a fear that I might not be chosen.

For the most part, my visit to the King Center in mid-March went well. I was impressed by the physical surroundings: the attractive three-story brick building that housed the Center's offices as well as its library and archive; the long reflecting pool surrounding King's crypt and the Freedom Walkway; and Freedom Hall, with its auditorium and nearby bookstore where I purchased souvenirs to bring home. The store clerks and National Park rangers stationed in Freedom Hall uniformly displayed the relaxed pleasantness that I associated with the South—Southern hospitality, I would find, was at times superficial but not mythical.

In the main building that housed the King Center's offices, I stopped by the historical exhibit on the ground floor that chronicled King's life. I was impressed, although it was quite modest in comparison to the one I would later help design for the National Park Service King Visitors Center constructed across the street. The exhibit space was publicly accessible, but I had to sign in with the receptionist to gain access to the rest of the building.

Louise Cook, the gregarious white woman who was the director of the King Library and Archive, escorted me to the archive on the third floor. We arrived at a large, well-lit room attractively furnished with tables for visiting researchers and a modest library along the wall. Once she took me inside her office, I could see, from the items piled on her desk, that Louise was a working archivist rather than simply an administrator. She seemed enthusiastic and full of energy as she discussed her initial funding proposal for the King Papers Project. I liked her informal, often jovial manner and began imagining her as a colleague. She took me to a large room that she opened with her key.

Inside was the King Center's archive: row after row of steel shelves holding hundreds, perhaps thousands of archival boxes containing not only King's papers but also the papers of SCLC and other organizations. For the first time, I saw SNCC's papers organized in acid-free document containers instead of the tattered boxes I had last seen in Stanley Wise's basement years earlier. I thought of how much easier—although far less exciting—my research would have been, if only this archive had existed then. In just a few years, the King Center, under Louise's guidance, had become a leading archive of the Southern protest movements of the 1950s and 1960s.

Louise also accompanied me to my first meeting with King's older sister, Christine King Farris, who served as the King Center's treasurer. I was only vaguely aware that King had a surviving sibling. Mrs. Farris invited us into her second-floor office for a meeting that was more a formality than about financial matters or her famous brother. Very protective about the family materials that she kept in her home, she ultimately proved generous in providing documents and photographs for the first volume of *The Papers of Martin Luther King, Jr.* She also possessed a quiet forcefulness that enabled her to keep firm control over the budgets of the King Center—and the King Project—while leaving Mrs. King to be its public face.

When the time came for my meeting with Mrs. King, Louise took me to a tastefully furnished waiting room. On the wall was a portrait of Mrs. King with her husband. Beni arrived to tell me that she was running late "as usual." She returned to retrieve me, and we walked by several of Mrs. King's aides, who offered their greetings. Inside her office, which overlooked the reflecting pool, I spotted her seated at her desk and walked toward her as she rose. "Welcome to the King Center, Dr. Carson." I felt happy to be there.

The center's chief operating officer, Dr. Chip Wheeler, was also at the meeting, although he did not contribute to our conversation. I would later learn that Wheeler—one of a succession of operating officers who would take on the challenge of improving the King Center's efficiency—was mostly concerned with bureaucratic matters rather than with the King Papers Project's mission.

Mrs. King relieved my lingering anxiety by confirming that I would soon receive a letter offering me the senior editor position with the understanding that I would do much of the work at Stanford. We did not discuss salary; she said it would be Wheeler's task to take care of those details.

The only surprise of the meeting came when Mrs. King nonchalantly informed me that she had asked Louis Harlan, the senior editor of the Booker T. Washington Papers, to become my co-editor. Until then, I had assumed I was her only candidate, but she explained that it was necessary to have an editor in Atlanta. "Perhaps Harlan's document editing experience would help the project get off the ground," she added. I struggled to get through the rest of the meeting without thinking of the implications of this news. Why hadn't I been told? How would the idea of a co-editor affect my feelings about the position?

After rushing to the airport (I would learn not to book flights directly after a meeting with Mrs. King was scheduled to end), I tried on the flight home to make sense of the new development. Harlan was a Pulitzer Prize–winning white historian more than two decades my senior. Although I knew him only by reputation—he had played a crucial role in furthering my academic career by backing the publishing of my book *In Struggle*—his qualifications clearly exceeded mine. Would I be viewed as Harlan's junior colleague? I considered the possibility that Harlan's presence might be helpful in relieving the pressure on me to spend more time at the King Center, but I wondered whether Stanford would maintain a high level of support for a project based mostly in Atlanta and co-directed by a prominent historian with closer ties to Mrs. King. Was he actually prepared to leave his position at the University of Maryland or was this a ploy by Mrs. King to pressure me into coming to Atlanta?

After talking with several of my Stanford colleagues, I concluded that the best course was to call Harlan. He lightheartedly acknowledged that Mrs. King had asked him about the position but added that he, like Franklin, had strongly recommended me. He said he had no interest in moving to Atlanta and was dubious about the feasibility of a collaboration involving two historians on opposite sides of the nation. He agreed to call Mrs. King to make clear that he was not a candidate and to offer instead to serve as an advisory editor.

In late March, Mrs. King formally offered me the position as editor. She also accepted Harlan's offer to serve in an advisory capacity and never mentioned the co-editor idea again. Harlan's wealth of experience as a documentary editor would become vital to me during the initial years of the King Papers Project. While reassured that the co-editorship arrangement was scuttled, I remained troubled that I had been caught by surprise.

Mrs. King's offer letter made clear that I would maintain my faculty position at Stanford and that she accepted that a cooperative arrangement with Stanford would be mutually beneficial. She wrote to Stanford's president inviting the university "to play a substantive role in the King Papers Project," and this letter led Stanford officials to promise to "devote a maximum amount" of Stanford's resources to the project. Mrs. King verbally accepted the idea that I would split my time between Stanford and the King Center. I realized, however, that she still wanted the King Papers Project to be seen as a King Center venture. Looking back, I can see that my eagerness to be offered the position clouded my perspective.

I returned to the King Center in mid-May to officially become editor of King's papers. As word of the impending appointment spread around the Stanford campus, several students indicated their willingness to remain for the summer to work in the King Papers office. Assuring Mrs. King in my acceptance letter that the project would "maintain a strong identification with the King Center," I was sure that she would be thrilled by the news that Stanford's Development Office promised to seek up to $250,000 per year for the project's first three years and that these funds could be used both at Stanford and at the King Center. "My goal is to bring together the moral vision of the King Center with the enormous financial and scholarly resources of Stanford," I enthused. The King Papers Project would, I confidently predicted, become "the most significant, historical project of our time."

On the surface, the meetings at the King Center on May 16, the day before my official appointment as editor, went smoothly. There were no noticeable hints of discord in the discussions about the King Papers Project's future plans. I winced, however, when I read a *New York Times* article announcing the project's launch. Pleased that the newspaper had given the project prominent coverage, I also noticed that the article featured a photograph of and quotes from Louise Cook, and there was even a reference to Stanford's financial support, but the single sentence about my appointment as director was buried deep in the piece.

I asked Louise why I hadn't been told about or interviewed for the piece; her explanation conveyed an implicit message that I should have been at the King Center rather than at Stanford. The first major article about the project hardly mentioned its director, but I tried not to allow this to douse my celebratory mood. After returning to Stanford, I saw that several local papers trumpeted my appointment on their front pages.

I was eager to begin work, but the arrival of a June 5 letter from Mrs. King dashed my hopes that the King Papers Project would have a smooth start. As I quickly read the typewritten letter, I took note of references to legal and administrative concerns relating to my "availability to be on-site in Atlanta." This issue had been discussed at every stage of my hiring, but now it was being linked to the King Estate's "lengthy and expensive litigation to establish its rights with regard not only to the King Papers, but also with the use of my husband's image and likeness."

After digesting the contents of the letter, I realized that I had touched on a sensitive issue by mentioning the need to make photocopies—at Stanford's expense—of King documents for my use at Stanford. "It became apparent to me that a significant proportion of the collection would have to be copied if the editor was off-site." Mrs. King indicated that concerns had been raised by the Estate's lawyer, who advised "that it would be unwise to make even selected portions of the collection available at another repository." On the final page of the three-page, single-spaced, typed letter, I had been presented with a stark ultimatum: "I have come to the difficult conclusion that the editor of the King Papers must be prepared to relocate to Atlanta and manage the project on-site."

I could not suppress my mixed feelings of dismay, embarrassment, and finally anger. How could Mrs. King change the basic conditions of my position after I had made a public commitment to direct the project? Why had she suddenly changed her mind and pulled the rug out from under me after months of negotiations during which I had made clear that work on the project would take place at Stanford as well as at the King Center?

Despite the headlines in the local papers at Stanford just a few weeks earlier, it now seemed unlikely that I would be editing King's papers after all. How would I explain this new turn of events to the Stanford officials who had given the project such enthusiastic support and the Stanford students who had volunteered to work with me during the summer? What would I do in the fall, now that I had just declined an NEH research grant in order to free myself to work on the King Project? What would I say to the dean who had agreed to cut my teaching responsibilities to two courses rather than four annually? Even if Mrs. King changed her mind, could I ever revive the enthusiasm that led Stanford's president and provost to pledge funding for a King Papers Project, especially when it was completely under the King Center's control? What would happen in the future if I ever sought institutional support for another project?

My first impulse was to respond emotionally to her letter, but Susan cautioned against doing anything precipitously. I explained the situation to Provost Rosse, who had been responsible for committing the funding needed to launch the project, and was reassured when he calmly advised me to consult Stanford's legal office to determine how to respond and counseled me to accept that it might take time to work out a mutually acceptable arrangement. I followed his advice and I also consulted with Bill Gould, the sole black member of the Law School faculty and a noted expert on labor law. A skilled arbitrator, Bill urged me to respond to Mrs. King's legalistic letter with one of my own, carefully reviewing the understandings we had reached during our spring meetings.

A week of intense discussions produced a reply that carefully retraced my interactions with Mrs. King from the initial phone call to my final letter concerning Stanford's promises of support. I reviewed the many occasions on which we had discussed and agreed to the notion of me directing the project while remaining based at Stanford. I quoted from Mrs. King's letter urging Stanford to support the project financially, with the understanding that much of the research would be done on the Stanford campus. Finally, I stressed that "on the basis of your assurance and those of other King Center officials, I have publicly associated my reputation and that of Stanford University with this project."

It was a cogent and forceful letter, but, even as I sent it, I was still unsure about my preferred outcome. Would I ever feel comfortable having my future career in Mrs. King's hands? Was I prepared to leave a tenured academic position for a subordinate role at the King Center? For several weeks, I waited in vain for a response, although I did notice news reports that Mrs. King and two of her children were arrested during antiapartheid protests at the South African Embassy in Washington, D.C.

Early in July I had a chance meeting at Stanford with Roger Bruns, the head of the federally funded National Historical Publications and Records Commission (NHPRC), which had provided the King Papers Project with its initial start-up grant. Bruns and a colleague were visiting the Bay Area and had intended merely to pay a courtesy call to check on the project's progress. When I told him about the impasse with Mrs. King, he was visibly upset and told me that my hiring and the Stanford ties had been crucial in convincing him to maintain support for the project. He promised to contact Mrs. King as soon as he returned to Washington and arrange a meeting to resolve the issue.

Bruns's call apparently gave added weight to my letter, because soon afterward I received a letter informing me that Mrs. King had agreed to a meeting in late August. I was pleased but hardly overjoyed at this news. Uncertain whether Stanford funds were still available, I was unable to move ahead with hiring student researchers for the summer. The new IBM personal computers that had been purchased for the use of the King Project remained in their shipping boxes. Many other aspects of my academic life—including the question of whether I would teach a full load of classes in the fall—remained in limbo.

By the time the meeting finally took place, Mrs. King had retracted her insistence that I move to Atlanta. I didn't feel a sense of triumph, when I met with her on August 26. Mrs. King greeted me cordially, but I could sense that the warmth that had existed when I was hired had been replaced by a cool correctness. She continued to insist that the King Center would have a "leading role" in the King Papers Project, even though we had already agreed to this during the spring. I asked her to write another letter to Stanford's president reiterating that the King Center welcomed Stanford's support. As if the summer's standoff had not happened, we were once again launching the project. I was only slightly encouraged by Beni Ivey's prediction that after six months on the job, Mrs. King would begin to view me as "part of the King Center family."

To the extent that we were able to discuss the King Papers Project's future at the meeting, it was evident there was much that needed to be done. I had assumed that accepting Mrs. King's offer to edit King's papers would mean that I would have her full support, but this was now far from certain. The project had no research staff at the King Center or at Stanford. I had only begun to formulate a research plan for the King Papers Project. My knowledge of documentary editing procedures was still minimal, although I had already spoken with Bruns to arrange visits to other papers projects. As had been the case at the start of my teaching career at UCLA, I would require on-the-job training.

Of even greater importance, documents needed for the initial volumes of *The Papers of Martin Luther King, Jr.* were not at the King Center. They were instead at Boston University, King's alma mater, where he had deposited his papers for the pre-1963 period. More troubling, I learned that Mrs. King was threatening to sue Boston University to force them to return her late husband's papers. Although having these papers at the King Center seemed beneficial to the project, Mrs. King had already signaled that she was reluctant to have the papers at the Center copied for my use at Stanford. I pondered the irony: What if Boston University gave me more access to King's papers than the King Center? What would happen if the Boston papers were tied up in an extended legal battle?

Bruns attended the August meeting but only intervened in the discussion when I requested payment of the salary I had expected to receive for the summer. When Mrs. King objected, Bruns noted that the NHPRC's grant to the King Center was intended to cover this expense. With some of the back pay, Susan and I were able to recover from the summer's stress by taking a two-week vacation in Kauai, the first of our many visits to that island. As much as I tried to relax, I could not clear my mind of the dispute and the difficulties that possibly lay ahead.

I sensed that enthusiasm for the venture had waned both at the King Center and at Stanford. Mrs. King would judge me according to how much time I spent at the King Center and would see Stanford's promises of financial support as a threat to the King Center's control of the project. In order to avoid offending her, Stanford officials would have to constrain efforts to publicize my role and that of the university. During a long walk with Susan on the beach near our condominium at Poipu, I came to the decision that I would remain with the King Project but only for a decent interval—perhaps a year or two—before resigning.

Yet, even as I resolved to leave on my own terms, I realized how difficult it would be to return to the more conventional scholarly life I had experienced before Mrs. King's phone call less than nine months earlier.

Chapter 10

Editing King

During the months after the unexpected impasse over Mrs. King's demand that I move to Atlanta, thoughts of resigning gradually gave way to a determination to move forward with the task she had assigned me. My ego was a bit bruised, but I was also eager to discover what could be learned from studying the thousands of documents that King left behind. I also appreciated the potential advantages of directing a project to publish an authorized edition of *The Papers of Martin Luther King, Jr.* I had written *In Struggle* without a full-time research assistant or major grant or access to a substantial archive of SNCC materials. Despite my efforts, SNCC's accomplishments remained little known. In contrast, the King Papers Project would be a collective venture sponsored by the institution created to preserve King's legacy. King's historical importance had been confirmed by the creation of a national holiday to honor him. Several King biographies had already been published, and two major Pulitzer Prize–winning books appeared soon after I became editor of his papers. Rather than wondering how long I would remain editor, I began to consider how long it would take before I could make a significant contribution to public understanding of King. What could the King Papers Project reveal that was not already known about the most famous African American?

I realized that there were many tasks to complete before I could actually begin studying King's papers. I had to develop positive relationships with Mrs. King and King Center officials, hire researchers at both the King Center and Stanford, and, most important, make copies of the documents needed for the initial volumes of the chronologically arranged *Papers.* Accomplishing the last task would be complicated because few of the early documents were at the King Center. Moreover, Mrs. King was disputing Boston University's ownership of the large collection of pre-1963 documents that her late husband had donated to the institution where he attended graduate school, claiming that the university was not giving the collection adequate care.

Aware that I needed Mrs. King's support, I traveled to Atlanta at least once per month during the first two years. Louise Cook usually arranged meetings with Mrs. King and other Center officials and, once I arrived, she offered helpful advice regarding how things were done at the King Center. Mrs. King made all policy decisions, and not always in a timely manner. Her calendar was crowded, and she had difficulty ending her conversations on schedule. "During the movement years," she once remarked to explain this tendency, "we did things on God's time."

Still somewhat insecure in my role as the project's off-site director, I diligently prepared for these visits, mentally rehearsing what I would say, deciding what to wear (I added to my meager wardrobe during this time), and making sure to get a haircut before traveling. I did my best to adjust to Southern mores—prayers before meetings and familial inquiries—before getting to the point. In my presentations to Mrs. King, I tried to explain what I thought was necessary for the King Papers Project to succeed and relied on Louise to translate those needs into items that required Mrs. King's approval. Although my relationship with Mrs. King gradually became more cordial, at first we treated each other with a mixture of formality and guardedness. I referred to her as "Mrs. King" and felt reassured when she addressed me as "Dr. Carson."

My frequent travels to Atlanta took a toll on my academic life at Stanford. I was expected to teach only two classes a year rather than the normal four, but unexpected problems at the King Center sometimes forced me to cancel classes, miss departmental meetings, reschedule meetings with students, and lose touch with friends. When I was on the Stanford campus, I was more often at the project's office in Meyer Library than in my history department office. I initially enjoyed aspects of my bicoastal life, but I also suffered from jet lag and symptoms of stress that worsened during trips to Atlanta.

My home life also suffered as I tried to balance competing demands on my time. While completing *In Struggle*, I had often cared for our children after school while Susan finished work on her master's degree and then began her career as a librarian. Because David had entered high school by the time I became editor of King's papers, he had less trouble adjusting to my travels than did our daughter Temie, who entered middle school in 1986. She missed the close relationship I once had with her as her soccer coach and often-at-home father. My absence exacerbated the difficulties that adolescent adopted children can experience—especially those from biracial backgrounds.

I was aware of the costs of my role as King's editor, and I also feared the consequences of failing to deal with matters that had to be addressed before I could actually study King's papers. The National Endowment for the Humanities had rejected the King Center's initial funding proposal, therefore I needed Mrs. King's prompt approval of a revised proposal that would enable the King Papers Project to hire a full-time assistant editor to work at the King Center in Atlanta. With help from chief operating officer Chip Wheeler, Louise and I revised the proposal in September 1985, and the NEH approved it the following spring, but this vital funding did not begin until July 1986. With funding in hand, the project hired Dr. Ralph Luker as an assistant editor. Although I was initially concerned that Mrs. King would impose nonacademic considerations on the search process, she deferred to my judgment and that of Louise that Ralph, a white scholar who had taught at Antioch College and was an expert on American religious history, was the best of the available candidates.

The delicate issue of the King Center's relationship with Stanford University also needed to be clarified. Mrs. King acceded to my request that federal grant funds intended to pay part of my salary be sent to Stanford, so that I could remain a full-time, tenured Stanford faculty member rather than a part-time employee of each institution. I did not, however, convince her to collaborate with Stanford to raise funds for the King Papers Project, despite a December 1985 visit to the King Center by representatives of Stanford's Development Office. The two institutions never forged the kind of cooperative relationship that might have enabled the project to raise an adequate endowment to replace year-to-year fundraising for the long-term venture, which I optimistically predicted would be completed in about fifteen years. I succeeded in getting Mrs. King to write a letter requesting that Boston University allow me access to the King documents archived there, despite her lawyer's concern that such a letter would weaken her claim of legal ownership of the documents.

While becoming comfortable in my relations with Mrs. King, my other scholarly activities showed how much I still saw the movements of the 1960s through the lens of SNCC. During the spring of 1985, I became one of four senior historical advisors for *Eyes on the Prize: America's Civil Rights Movement*, the documentary series on the black freedom struggle that Henry Hampton was producing at his Blackside film company in Boston. For the next year and a half I participated in meetings as a member of the "school" that Hampton created to bring together scholars and filmmakers. Those of us invited to work on the series agreed with me that it should focus not only on King's activities but also on the role of SNCC and grassroots activists, especially black students. I was pleased that the acclaimed six-part documentary, which would eventually be expanded to fourteen episodes, was seen by millions of viewers—far more people than would ever read *In Struggle*.

I also drew attention to SNCC's influence when I spoke at the University of Mississippi's civil rights movement symposium in October 1985. In my first scholarly talk as editor of King's papers, I criticized the tendency to highlight the role of national civil rights leaders and their organizations rather than "self-reliant indigenous leaders who were incorrectly portrayed as King's lieutenants or followers." Citing the examples of the Montgomery bus boycott movement, the lunch-counter sit-ins, and the freedom rides into Mississippi, I insisted that "local black movements produced their own distinctive ideas and indigenous leadership." King, I insisted, was "a source of inspiration rather than...tactical direction." I acknowledged that King had played a major role in the Albany, Birmingham, and Selma protest movements, but even in these places "he was compelled to work with local leaders who were reluctant, to say the least, to implement strategies developed by outsiders."

I would gradually modify such views as my knowledge of King increased, but I did not have an opportunity to examine King's papers at Boston University until January 1986, almost a year after Mrs. King's initial telephone call. Susan accompanied me when I arrived at Mugar Library for my first visit. Both of us appreciated the chance to combine her skills as a research librarian and archivist with mine as a historian. We began filling out forms requesting document boxes from the King collection. Uncertain how the library staff would treat us after Mrs. King's public statements suggesting that the King collection there was not being properly preserved, we were taken aback when Howard B. Gottlieb, the nattily dressed director of the archive, came over to our research table, cheerily introduced himself, and greeted us warmly. He then invited us for lunch, during which our voluble host proudly related stories of his success in acquiring the collections of well-known figures, especially Hollywood stars. He indicated that he was especially proud to have the King collection. "I'm saddened that Mrs. King would think that I would mistreat Dr. King's papers," he lamented.

Determined to avoid getting involved in the legal dispute, we said little of substance. By the end of lunch, he had made clear his strong opposition to returning his most notable collection to the King Center but also assured us that he would not stand in the way of our research. During this initial visit to the archive (which later became the Howard Gottlieb Archival Research Center), we selected several thousand documents to be copied and sent to Stanford, an arrangement meant to reassure Boston University that the copies were solely for the use of the King Papers

Project and not to supplement the King collection at the King Center. After many more visits, and telephone conversations, we identified tens of thousands of additional documents needed for our research. Although the Mugar Library staff sometimes failed to handle our copying requests as expeditiously as we would have liked, Gottlieb kept his commitment to facilitate our work.

The task of organizing the document copies that began arriving from Boston fell to the group of part-time research assistants I recruited at Stanford. I hired Penny Russell, a black graduate student in history who had been my teaching assistant in the African American history course I had taught the previous spring. Pete Holloran, a white undergraduate enrolled in the same course, also volunteered after hearing news of my appointment. Stanford law school graduate Rachel Bagby volunteered to handle personnel and financial matters and eventually became the project's associate director. Rachel's diverse talents—she was a gifted singer and writer as well as a capable manager—enabled her to increase the project's visibility on campus.

During the project's initial months, I worked closely with Penny and Pete as we learned the skills needed to produce authoritative documentary editions. Examining the practices of other papers projects, we saw that most of them published documents that were already assembled and organized in archives in order to make them more readily available to researchers. We quickly decided that our volumes should go beyond simply providing transcripts but should instead be extensively annotated, with headnotes to introduce documents and footnotes to provide background information. By providing biographical information about the people who corresponded with King and about the groups that worked with him, the volumes would shed light on the contributions of many activists in the Southern freedom struggle rather than focus narrowly on King.

We also began a systematic examination of the considerable literature of King-related books and articles. I was somewhat familiar with this literature, having already written reviews of Stephen Oates's biography of King, *Let the Trumpet Sound*, and David Garrow's *The FBI and Martin Luther King Jr.*, but our focus was less on scholarly interpretation than on the original source materials and archives King scholars had used. We then obtained copies of the King-related documents from the archives that held them.

One of our goals was to prepare a detailed chronology of every significant event in King's life, and thus we initiated a far-reaching document acquisition effort. After discovering that King had given a speech or a sermon at a particular time and place, we searched for the relevant recordings, transcripts, or news articles. We contacted friends and colleagues of King to ask if they had any correspondence with him and to request permission for the use of their documents.

As boxes of documents began arriving from Boston and other places, Susan's library science background and expertise in the use of computers in libraries became invaluable in helping us create a computerized database to manage the documents. While most archives kept track of documents through "finding aids" that identified the folders and boxes where documents on particular topics were stored, the system she designed allowed us to keep track of the archival source and the content of each document. Because such software was not commercially available then, developing this customized system was difficult and time consuming. The database was quite innovative for its time, and attracted the interest of research librarians elsewhere. Susan eventually became a full-time staff member contributing to the King Project's editorial work as well as its document processing.

My regular visits to the King Center provided many opportunities to expand my understanding of King's life and legacy. Meetings of the project's Advisory Board strengthened my friendships with scholars such as Garrow, Harlan, Bobby Hill, Ira Berlin, Darlene Clark Hine, and Vincent Harding. Over time I also forged enduring ties with a number of former King associates, including Harris Wofford, Andrew Young, and Lerone Bennett Jr. The King Center's summer programs on nonviolent principles and strategies attracted former SNCC stalwarts Bernard Lafayette and Congressman John Lewis, both of whom shared King's nonviolent ideals. In addition, I renewed friendships with several people I had met at the 1976 SNCC reunion, including Casey Hayden and Connie Curry. A King Center conference on the role of women in the movement enabled me to become acquainted with Rosa Parks and Dorothy Cotton, former director of SCLC's Citizenship Education Program. On another occasion I met Cesar Chavez and Dolores Huerta, co-founders of the National Farm Workers Association, the group I had briefly assisted in the 1960s.

Louise was neither a former activist nor a historian, but she facilitated my social outreach by introducing me to researchers and her own circle of friends. I often took her—as well as other King Center staff members—to lunch or dinner and discovered that outside the King Center's pious confines, she was willing to share her considerable store of gossip about the King Center and the King family. She sometimes displayed a ribald sense of humor, especially when David Garrow took part in our chats. They had become friends while Garrow was researching his biography of King. Listening to their conversations, I realized they knew more than I did about many aspects of King's life, especially the FBI's revelations about his extramarital affairs in documents released through a Freedom of Information Act request. Their casual references to King's promiscuity made me curious but also concerned that Garrow's disclosure of this information in his forthcoming book, and his friendship with Louise, would adversely affect Mrs. King's support for the King Papers Project.

Mrs. King's first opportunity to hear me speak publicly about her late husband occurred on October 15, 1986, at a conference on King sponsored by the Capitol Hill Historical Society in Washington, D.C. I brought my family with me so that Susan and our children would have an opportunity to attend the gathering and enjoy a few days visiting museums and historic sites on the Mall, including the Lincoln Memorial area where King gave his "I Have a Dream" speech. Our son David, who celebrated his seventeenth birthday while we were there, used the visit as an opportunity to stroll around the Howard University campus. He liked what he saw and would later decide to enroll at the predominantly black college.

The conference brought together several leading scholars and former activists who had influenced my life—notably Bob Moses, Howard Zinn, and John Hope Franklin. They were invited to comment on the speeches by King scholars, including myself and Dave Garrow, whose biography of King, *Bearing the Cross*, was about to be published. Because the conference proceedings were to be published as a book, I knew that my remarks would be widely disseminated. I struggled to balance appreciation of SNCC's importance against my increasing understanding of King's crucial role.

I delivered my paper, titled "Charismatic Leadership in a Mass Movement," mindful that this might be my only opportunity to address an audience that would include both Moses and Mrs. King. Could I find a way to reconcile her conviction that her late husband deserved a national holiday with Bob's skepticism about the need for charismatic leadership? I began by asserting that the holiday legislation "provided official recognition of King's greatness," but I insisted that "it remains the responsibility of those of us who study and carry on King's work to define his historical significance." Despite Mrs. King's presence, I restated in even more forceful terms the ideas I had presented at the University of Mississippi a year earlier:

> If King had never lived, the black struggle would have followed a course of development similar to the one it did. The Montgomery bus boycott would have occurred, because King did not initiate it. Black students probably would have rebelled—even without King as a role model—for they had sources of tactical and ideological inspiration besides King. Mass activism in southern cities and voting rights efforts in the Deep South were outgrowths of large-scale social and political forces, rather than simply

consequences of the actions of a single leader. Though perhaps not as quickly and certainly nor as peacefully or with as universal a significance, the black movement would have probably achieved its major legislative victories without King's leadership, for the Jim Crow system was a regional anachronism, and the forces that undermined it were inexorable.

I conceded that King "stood out in a forest of tall trees," among the leaders who emerged from the sustained mass movements of the 1960s, but added that his "involvement in a movement in which ideas disseminated from the bottom up as well as from the top down" transformed his leadership qualities and ideas. Not mentioning his "I Have a Dream" speech, I drew attention to his unpopular stands at the end of his life, such as his call for a Poor People's Campaign. Portraying King as "a product of the movement that called him to leadership," I nonetheless warned against the notion that "Great men (or great women) are necessary preconditions for the emergence of major movements."

Waiting for the Messiah is a human weakness that is unlikely to be rewarded more than once in a millennium. Studies of King's life offer support for an alternative optimistic belief that ordinary people can collectively improve their lives. Such studies demonstrate the capacity of social movements to transform participants for the better and to create leaders worthy of their followers.

Although the article based on my talk would often be reprinted and cited, my first effort to assess King's historical significance demonstrated how little I had learned during the previous year. Having spent the first decade and a half of my scholarly career understanding SNCC, I was still in the early stages of my effort to understand King's historical significance. Despite being curious about Mrs. King's reaction to my talk, I was reluctant to ask, and she never mentioned it.

Soon after the Washington conference, I invited Mrs. King to come to Stanford. I tried to make certain that Stanford accorded her the same treatment—limousine service and first-class lodging—as any other visiting dignitary. I didn't know how much could be accomplished during the brief scheduled meetings with Stanford officials, but I wanted to convince her—and perhaps myself—that the university strongly backed the King Papers Project. I knew that Mrs. King's demand that I move to Atlanta had dampened the initial enthusiasm of Stanford officials.

Mrs. King's meeting with Stanford president Don Kennedy went as well as I could have expected, but as we approached the project's office in Meyer Library, I became self-consciously aware that the lack of space would force the student researchers to sit on the floor outside as I gave Mrs. King a brief tour of the project's workroom. She seemed in good spirits as I showed her sample documents and the project's five computers arranged around the top of a meeting table. As she left the library, I was finally able to introduce her to Rachel Bagby, Penny Russell, and eleven of the students who were huddled outside. It would be several years before we moved to larger quarters on the outskirts of the Stanford campus where we remain today.

Mrs. King's visit ended with a talk to about a thousand enthusiastic students who crowded into a law school auditorium. After Kennedy opened the event with a warm welcome, I introduced her by suggesting that her accomplishments as the wife of Martin Luther King Jr. often obscured her achievements after 1968. I told the students that the Dream was "being kept alive" due to her "hard work, perseverance, and dedication." I was pleased that her remarks included an endorsement of me as the best choice to direct the King Papers Project, which she predicted "would be a long-term project," lasting perhaps fifteen to twenty years, adding, "Maybe more. Who knows?"

Soon after Mrs. King's visit, David Garrow's massive study of King was published. As I expected from my previous conversations with Dave, *Bearing the Cross: Martin Luther King, Jr. and the Southern Christian Leadership Conference* included references to King's extramarital sexual activities based on FBI surveillance files released through the Freedom of Information Act. The book described FBI director J. Edgar Hoover's efforts to use this information against King—most egregiously in late 1964 when Hoover's subordinates sent King a compilation of surveillance recordings along with an anonymous note suggesting suicide as King's only way to prevent having his "filthy, abnormal fraudulent self" publicly revealed. Dave had not heard the recordings themselves, which were not released but summarized in FBI reports, *Bearing the Cross* related that FBI bugs planted at a party held during King's stay at Washington's Willard Hotel earlier in 1964 and had picked up "dirty jokes and bawdy remarks" during a "drunken party" and sounds of "people engaging in sex." By this time, I was familiar with the FBI's files on King and therefore not surprised by Dave's revelations but I was far more concerned about his references to King's "compulsive sexual athleticism" and of Coretta as a nagging wife seeking a movement role despite being, according to an unnamed SCLC source, "completely and totally out of her depth in this milieu in which Martin moved and functioned." Another unnamed SCLC source judged the King marriage as doomed: "Coretta King was most certainly a widow long before Dr. King died."

I knew that the conclusions Dave drew from the FBI files would disturb Mrs. King, but only after examining his notes and the FBI files did I see that the evidence was not as definitive as his account suggested. The FBI files offered evidence that Martin Luther King Jr. likely was sexually involved with other women, but Dave seemed to accept Hoover's characterization of King as "a 'tom cat' with obsessive degenerate sexual urges." I wondered whether Dave had more explicit evidence that he had not disclosed or was simply offering an interpretation that went beyond his evidence. In the book he acknowledged but apparently dismissed Mrs. King's recollection that she listened to the recording but did not take it seriously—"I couldn't make much out of it: it was just a lot of mumbo jumbo."

After I accepted an assignment to write a review of *Bearing the Cross,* I asked Dave about his best source for his depiction of the King marriage. He sent me the transcript of his interview with William Rutherford, who served as King's chief aide from the summer of 1967 until King's assassination. The transcript made clear that Rutherford was shocked to discover that "the movement altogether was a very raunchy exercise" but also admitted he had no personal grounds to believe the stories about Martin until he encountered Mrs. King one evening and was surprised that she believed her husband was attending a meeting at Rutherford's place. After going through the evidence and finding it inconclusive, I wondered what I would do when faced with decisions about whether to publish FBI surveillance files in *The Papers of Martin Luther King, Jr.* I had long resisted the notion that King was a saintly leader. Was I beginning to feel protective of him and his widow? I later published the review of Dave's book, applauding its exhaustive research but questioning his uncritical handling of the FBI sources.

In my conversations with Mrs. King, she referred to *Bearing the Cross* only obliquely, suggesting to me that Garrow was untrustworthy and should be removed from the Advisory Board of the King Papers Project. I persuaded her that doing this might create a controversy that would draw even more attention to the book, which received a Pulitzer Prize in 1987. On another occasion, she brought up the matter during a brief conversation following meeting at the King Center that lasted into the evening. When I mentioned that I should call a taxi to return me to my hotel, she offered to drop me off during her drive home. The offer was quite unexpected, because I knew that an Atlanta police officer typically accompanied her when she traveled to and from the Center. I don't recall how the topic came up, but I remember that, while letting me off, she acknowledged that the sexual allegations bothered her. With an air of resignation, she said softly, "If all that had happened, don't you think I would have known?" Unsure whether she was asking me or herself, I couldn't think of a way to answer.

Even as I became somewhat distracted by the revelations in *Bearing the Cross,* my colleagues and I began studying the thousands of photocopied documents we had assembled from Boston's Mugar Library and other archives. I hoped that the King Papers Project would settle into a routine that would enable us to finish the first volume of *The Papers* in time for the fifth celebration of the King Holiday in 1990. I already realized that the schedule set in the Papers Project's original proposal to NEH—that is twelve volumes in fifteen years—was wildly unrealistic. The contributions of dedicated Stanford student researchers were essential to the completion of the volume. In addition to Penny Russell, Tom Jackson, another of my graduate students, had become an important part of the research staff, but because most Stanford graduate students had fellowships that covered their expenses, undergraduates did much of the project's work. Some were paid part-time wages, but others simply volunteered or worked in return for academic research credit. With guidance from Penny, they quickly acquired the skills needed not only to catalog the arriving copies of the King materials from Boston University but also to search in Southern newspapers to document King's activities during the 1940s and 1950s.

Occasionally some of the students became distracted by campus political activism. Some were involved in campus protests against apartheid in South Africa and in efforts to expand Stanford's multicultural course offerings. After a few student researchers were arrested in one protest, they arranged for their King Project work hours to be counted as community service in lieu of jail time. Political activism was by no means a requirement for involvement in the project. We attracted a wide range of students, including some majoring in science and engineering, who valued the opportunity to engage in research about King.

During 1987, with encouragement from several of my students, I became involved in the effort to alter Stanford's Western Culture requirement. I agreed that students should be exposed to a broader range of human experiences, including non-Western cultures. Although I found it difficult to devote sufficient time to teaching my required courses, I rashly agreed to teach an experimental course called "Western Culture: An Alternative View." The effort to replace the Western Culture courses with more inclusive ones soon escalated into a controversy that attracted national attention. After Jesse Jackson led a march on campus calling for reform, Ronald Reagan's education secretary, William Bennett, defended the existing program. The course absorbed unexpectedly large amounts of my time, but the lectures I prepared helped to broaden my understanding of Western culture as a product of not only white, male, intellectual elites but also oppressed people struggling to liberate themselves. This understanding would eventually inform my view of King as a global symbol of human rights.

As the project added new members to the King Center staff, it became increasingly difficult for me to manage the Atlanta office from three thousand miles away.

Ralph Luker was conscientious and productive, but he sometimes clashed with Louise and other staff members. I sometimes had to fly to Atlanta to resolve disputes. King Center rules—such as signing in and out—bothered researchers who were more familiar with academic environments. Morale in Atlanta improved in 1989 after Mrs. King agreed to let the project's staff move to Candler Library on the Emory University campus. The students recruited at Emory were as capable and dedicated as their Stanford counterparts.

Exacerbating the project's internal problems was the fact that it was the difficultly of getting prompt decisions from Mrs. King on key matters. By the time she visited Stanford, we had only begun the process of selecting a publisher for the volumes. After consulting extensively with Mrs. King and Joan Daves, the longtime literary agent for the King Estate, I solicited proposals from about a dozen academic and trade publishers. Stanford University Press made a strong effort to take on the project and having a publisher on the Stanford campus would have been convenient, but the press seemed understaffed and inexperienced in publishing a major multivolume edition. The Stanford Press director also indicated that they would need to undertake additional fundraising efforts, which I feared would compete with King Project fundraising. After careful consideration, Mrs. King and I agreed that the University of California Press would be best suited to the long-term publishing venture.

By the fall of 1987, it became clear that the legal dispute over the King Papers at Boston would not be settled amicably. In October I met with Archer Smith, the King Estate's head lawyer, who told me that the dispute would likely end up in court. I warned Smith that, if the library's staff stopped supplying the King Project with copies, there was no way we could complete work on the first volume of *The Papers*. He promised to do what he could to ensure that the library continued to cooperate with the project but also advised that I might have to testify in the legal case.

Fortunately, even as the King Estate and Boston University moved toward a decisive court battle, the King Project obtained most of the documents it needed for the first volume. I tried to stay uninvolved in the legal dispute, but on August 8, 1988, I reluctantly gave a deposition at Stanford. To prepare for my testimony, I consulted with attorney Deborah Zumwalt in Stanford's legal office, who also agreed to represent me when I testified. Aware that Archer Smith and Mrs. King wanted me to testify that Mugar Library was not offering the "scrupulous care" that Martin Luther King Jr. had stipulated should be given to his papers, I sought to limit my testimony to factual statements about what I observed while examining the papers.

Zumwalt was with me during the day-long deposition as I tried to respond as frankly as possible to questions from Archer Smith and Boston University attorney Larry Elswit. Concerned that my testimony might undermine the King Estate's case, I noted that the King documents at Mugar Library were often crammed together in folders and archival boxes but added that the library's practices were similar to those of other archives. The King Center's archival boxes and folders generally contained fewer documents, but this was because the documents at the King Center had been cataloged more recently and the containers were newer.

At the end of the exhausting day, Archer took Susan and me out to dinner and seemed pleased with my testimony. He appeared to appreciate the difficulty I faced in maintaining good relations with Mugar Library as well as with Mrs. King. I was later surprised when Elswit contacted me to express his own appreciation for my testimony. Both lawyers apparently understood that I was caught in the middle of a dispute that would not be resolved until 1993 when a Boston jury ruled in favor of Boston University. The King Estate unsuccessfully appealed to overturn the verdict. In the years to come, King's legacy would continue to become entangled in legal disputes.

Chapter 11

Unwanted Discovery

Like most previous King scholars, I did not pay much attention at first to his dissertation and most of his graduate school papers while working on the first volume of *The Papers of Martin Luther King Jr.* Given the quantity of revealing early correspondence with relatives and close acquaintances, I initially expected that the papers King wrote at Crozer Theological Seminary and Boston University served his academic needs but were not significant enough to warrant inclusion in *The Papers.* Nonetheless, as I read King's student writings, it became clear that they could not be ignored. They were, for the most part, unimaginative discussions of his assigned theological and philosophical readings; yet some of them clearly expressed King's evolving theological interests and religious attitudes. King did not often display scholarly brilliance, but he understood and made consistent judgments about theological ideas. He possessed an exceptional memory and paid special attention to pithy passages in his assignments that reflected his theological preferences. Some of these passages would later enrich his sermons and oratory.

King's dissertation, titled "A Comparison of the Conceptions of God in the Thinking of Paul Tillich and Henry Nelson Wieman," was, like most dissertations, written to satisfy a small academic audience. He added little to the existing scholarly literature about Tillich and Wieman, but he made clear to his mentors that he rejected abstract notions of divinity in favor of "personalism"—a theological preference for a God that, in his words, "both evokes and answers prayer." King criticized Tillich and Wieman for failing to develop conceptions of God that speak "to the deepest yearnings of the religious soul," but still applauded them for addressing important theological issues:

They do insist that religion begins with God and that man cannot have faith apart from him. They do proclaim that apart from God our human efforts turn to ashes and our sunrises into darkest night. They do suggest that man is not sufficient to himself for life, but is dependent upon God. All of this is good, and it may be a necessary corrective to a generation that has had all too much faith in man and all too little faith in God.

Although I initially believed that the few revealing passages in King's dissertation did not justify using more than two hundred pages of the first volume of *The Papers* to publish it in full, its derivative qualities ironically made it more important. In 1988, I asked Tom Jackson, a history graduate student and King Papers Project researcher, to check King's dissertation footnotes to determine whether they accurately reflected his sources. I expected that King's discussion of his subjects' views would consist largely of quotations from their writings and those of the scholars who studied them.

Tom found, however, that King's dissertation was even less original than I had imagined. Using colored markers to highlight passages in the dissertation that were identical to the wording of King's sources, he showed me vividly that when King had cited his sources with footnotes he had not always put quotation marks around all the words he had quoted. I knew that more research would be required to determine whether King had been careless in his note taking or had intentionally violated academic rules regarding plagiary, not only in the dissertation but also in dozens of other papers he had written at Crozer Seminary and Boston University. Before the Papers Project publicly claimed that King was guilty of plagiarism, we had to be certain of our facts.

While we continued our effort to document all aspects of King's formative years, I assigned key staff members to the tedious task of comparing every word of King's academic writings to the sources he consulted. I accepted that every "Great Man" had flaws but was disturbed that a central element of his public identity, the academic title that King and I shared, had been based on deception. If there was a pattern of plagiarism in his writings, we would have to address related questions: Why would he repeatedly risk exposure as a plagiarist? How had he avoided getting caught? Did his transgressions as a student detract from his later contributions as a leader? Would his plagiaries ever have been discovered, if he had not later become a famed civil rights leader who posthumously became the focus of the Papers Project's intensive research?

The investigation into King's plagiaries altered other aspects of our research, and added to the length of an already long-term project. If the dissertation became the focus of controversy, we would have to publish this tome as well as other plagiarized writings along with extensive footnotes. This in turn would require two volumes of *The Papers* instead of the one we had planned to devote to the years before he moved to Montgomery. Due to the chronological arrangement of the papers, the documents for King's graduate years in Boston would then have to appear in the second volume, which meant we would have to decide how to announce our plagiarism finding before the fully annotated dissertation appeared in print.

I put off telling Mrs. King until the extent of the plagiaries became clear, but I realized that she needed to know that our research had serious implications for her husband's reputation. She had launched the King Papers Project and selected me to direct it, and now I had to report that our first major discovery was that, during the early years of their relationship, her husband had violated academic rules.

In September 1989, I arranged a private meeting with her. Repeating the words I had rehearsed, I announced, "We've discovered that Dr. King did not adequately cite his sources," using his title but not the "p" word. She reacted calmly without probing to determine exactly what we had discovered. A thought entered my mind: Did she already suspect that Martin had cut corners as he struggled to complete his graduate work while serving as pastor of Dexter Avenue Baptist Church in Montgomery? (Only later did I learn from assistant editor Ralph Luker that he had informed Mrs. King without letting me know.) We discussed how to proceed, and she agreed that it was essential to publish an article before the news leaked out and made us vulnerable to the charge of a cover-up. She also accepted my suggestion to call an Advisory Board meeting to discuss the matter. Although my conversation with Mrs. King went more smoothly than expected, I thought back to the time in 1985 when she had masked her intentions in the days before suddenly ordering me to move to Atlanta.

When the Advisory Board met a few weeks later, I felt reassured that board members agreed with my proposal to write an article on the plagiarism issue. I was particularly pleased to have the support of the more senior scholars—especially John Hope Franklin and Louis Harlan—knowing that their opinions carried weight with Mrs. King. I realized that publishing a scholarly article was typically a drawn-out process, often taking more than a year from submission of a manuscript to publication. I contacted *The Journal of American History*'s associate editor Richard Blackett (the regular editor, David Thelen, was on leave for the year) and convinced him to agree to an expedited schedule so that my article would appear in the journal's December 1990 issue.

I wrote the article while teaching at American University in Washington D.C., where I had agreed to serve as Landmarks Scholar in History in place of historian

Nathan Huggins, who had accepted the visiting professorship but passed away before he could fulfill his commitment. With encouragement from Michael Kazin, who had been my graduate student at Stanford before joining American's faculty, I decided that a semester away from Stanford would be beneficial. Susan and I would be able to spend time with our son, who was a student at Howard University, where he started going by his middle name Malcolm and had joined in demonstrations that briefly shut down the campus. Our daughter Temie, then sixteen years old, was reluctant at first to leave her California boyfriend but ultimately enjoyed herself after becoming an important member of a championship high school soccer team in Bethesda.

Soon after our arrival, I was stunned to hear about the cocaine-possession arrest in January of Washington, DC, mayor Marion Barry, the former SNCC chairman I had interviewed during the 1970s. Given my knowledge of marijuana use in SNCC, Barry's offenses seemed slightly more explicable than King's academic transgressions.

As I pondered the significance of King's plagiaries, I searched in vain through his papers for hints that he was aware of his violations of academic rules. There were many questions that were difficult, if not impossible, to answer. Why did he save the evidence of his wrongdoing and donate his academic papers to Boston University? Why didn't his professors notice and object to the numerous passages copied almost verbatim from well-known theological texts? Were expectations and standards for theology students lower than for students in other fields? Were they lower for black students than for white students?

I suspected that King's professors saw him as a skilled black preacher able to synthesize theological scholarship but not likely to contribute to it. His plagiaries also may have escaped notice because he wove them together with his own words to present a convincing and consistent theological identity. Crozer professor Morton Enslin, who predicted King would "probably become a big, strong man among his people," probably revealed more than he intended when he described King as a "very able" student who "rarely misses anything which he can subsequently use" and observed, "All is grist that comes to his mill." Even a professor at Boston University who noticed that King had "inaccurately quoted" Tillich in an early dissertation draft later praised the "expository chapters" of King's final manuscript for presenting an "accurate, objective, and clear...portrayal of the views of Tillich and Wieman."

I later discovered that King's doctoral advisor, the late Harold DeWolf, remained enthusiastic about his student's abilities as a theologian, though he also once observed that "all modern theology which is competent is essentially derivative," a

comment that suggests that he did not demand or expect originality. DeWolf lav-
ished praise on King for translating "theology into action" and took pride that he
was the source for his most famous student's "system of positive theological belief."
DeWolf even expressed pride that King's language followed "closely the special
terms of my own lectures and writings."

The statements of King's mentors helped to explain why he got away with plagiary, but I could find nothing in King's papers to explain why he consistently did
it. Although King's plagiaries delayed our other research, his unoriginal academic
writings nonetheless contributed to my understanding of his ideas. They showed
that he became remarkably adept at mining theological texts for nuggets of insight
that would prove useful both as a minister and as a civil rights leader. In my article,
I argued that his seriously flawed writings increased his awareness of modern theological and philosophical ideas and prepared him for his subsequent role as a black
leader capable of influencing white as well as black Americans:

> His characteristic compositional methods contributed to the rhetorical
> skills that became widely admired when King was called unexpectedly
> to national leadership. His...use of political, philosophical, and liter-
> ary texts—particularly those expressing the nation's democratic ideals—
> inspired and mobilized many Americans, thereby advancing the cause of
> social justice.

As I sent drafts of the article to the board members for their comments, it
became clear that the plagiarism discovery could not be kept under wraps for long.
Fortunately, in this pre-Internet period of the last century, no American reporter
noticed when a *London Telegraph* columnist revealed that King had plagiarized part
of an earlier dissertation by another Boston University student. I suspected that
the leak came from the Atlanta office, which was pursuing this line of research.
Washington Post reporter Dan Bolz later came by my office at American University
to ask me about similar rumors, but I put him off with a promise to let him know
when we were prepared to publish our findings. Soon afterward, several scholars
told me that Dave Garrow had discussed the plagiarism discovery with them. When
I called him to point out that this disclosure violated the confidentiality of Advisory
Board discussions, he responded by insisting that I was suppressing his right to
speak freely with other scholars.

After I submitted the article manuscript to *The Journal of American History*, my
hope for a prompt publication date ran into a snag when David Thelen resumed his
role as the journal's regular editor. Although Thelen obtained quick, mostly positive

reviews of my manuscript, he disputed my argument about the larger implications of King's "compositional methods," feeling that this obscured the ethical issues relating to plagiary. I pointed out that King's habitual practice of appropriating the words of others hardly excused his plagiaries. I was willing to revise the article, but I was disturbed that Thelen seemed to be pushing his own interpretation of the King Project's discovery. I objected strongly when he said he would publish the article but only as part of a forum that would include a summary of our plagiarism findings followed by a collection of reaction pieces by me and other scholars. Thelen's plan meant delaying publication until the following June, making it almost impossible for me to prevent the plagiarism discovery from reaching the media.

By early October, my fears materialized when someone at the project's Atlanta office leaked news—inadvertently at a party, I was told—of our discovery. Peter Waldman, a *Wall Street Journal* reporter, began investigating King's textual appropriations from the Jack Boozer dissertation. Waldman told me that he had already done enough research to publish a story, so I decided it was best to cooperate with him by providing accurate information about our research. At least we would have time to prepare for the storm of controversy that I expected would follow the appearance of the *Journal* article. Through Mrs. King's chief aide, Dr. Cleveland Dennard, I informed her about the impending article. Fearing that reporters would jump on any King Center statement that was misleading or inconsistent with the King Project's findings, I suggested to Dennard that all statements to the press about the plagiarism issue should come from me.

Waldman's front-page article appeared on Friday, November 9, 1990. After skimming through it, I was relieved that it was mostly a matter-of-fact account of how we had, with some regret, made the discovery. The article prompted a one-day media storm at the project's Stanford office, with more than seventy requests for interviews. Staff members spent the day answering phones. ABC television news parked in front of our office to broadcast my comments for the evening national newscast. Mixed in with the reporters' queries was an angry call from San Francisco clergyman Amos C. Brown berating me for damaging the reputation of a person who had once been his teacher at Morehouse College.

I tried to limit my comments to the factual detail we had already released to the *Wall Street Journal*, but many reporters wanted me to describe the anguish I felt about a discovery that damaged the reputation of a revered African American. Resisting the temptation to judge King publicly, my inner thoughts that day nonetheless turned to Ella Baker's observation about "prophetic leaders" with "heavy feet of clay." I wondered if my equanimity concerning the project's discovery was rooted in SNCC's skepticism about King and other charismatic leaders. Although I worried that the plagiarism controversy would have a negative impact on King's leg-acy and the celebration of the national King Holiday, but I found it reassuring that King's admirers would have to celebrate him as an exceptional yet flawed human being rather than a saint.

Keeping such thoughts to myself, I felt relieved after fielding the final press inquiry. I vowed to say no more to the press about the issue and retreated with Susan to recover during a weekend in the small town of Inverness, north of San Francisco. Exhausted by my day at the center of the news frenzy, I was, nonetheless, pleased that two years of secrecy had ended.

Time magazine would later label our discovery as one of the year's top educa-tional stories. *Newsweek* devoted a full page to it. The controversy soon left the front pages and subsided once reporters realized there was nothing more to be revealed. For the most part, the initial spate of articles reflected our findings, although some subtleties were obscured by the use of the term "plagiarism." I suspected that many readers and even some scholars assumed that King's plagiaries involved submitting entire papers of others as if they were his own. This practice that would have been more readily detected by his professors than his habit of weaving together his words with those of others to express his views.

When I traveled to Atlanta in January 1991 to deliver a King Holiday lecture at Morehouse College's King International Chapel, the large audience at King's alma mater gave me a cordial reception, and there were no hostile questions. During a dinner that evening hosted by Lawrence Carter, the chapel's dean, several of the guests—including former King aide Andrew Young and Joseph Roberts, pastor of Ebenezer Church, where King had once been co-pastor—questioned me about the controversy. I was glad that most of the evening was devoted to discussing how King would have reacted to news reports that American military forces had just attacked Iraq in response to its invasion of Kuwait. We talked about the substance of King's inspiring ideas rather than the sources of his academic papers.

Many scholars applauded my handling of the issue, but, in January 1991, a con-servative journal, *Chronicles*, published a piece blasting the Papers Project for sup-pressing the plagiarism story to protect King's reputation. Although the allegation was baseless, I appreciated the irony that it would have been more credible if we had waited for *The Journal of American History* to publish our findings.

The *Chronicles* article attracted little attention, and I hoped that the contro-versy would die down. When the King Federal Holiday Commission asked me to give a briefing on the controversy at its April 1991 planning meeting in Santa Fe, I was at first reluctant to accept the invitation. Nonetheless, I wondered whether it would be better for me rather than someone else to explain the King Project's discovery to representatives of the states that celebrated the King Holiday. I also knew that Mrs. King, who was the Commission's chair, would attend the gathering. I had talked only infrequently with her since the plagiarism story broke in the *Wall Street Journal*, in part because I wanted to handle the issue without any involvement by her or King Center spokespersons. Concerned that reporters might ask whether Mrs. King had talked to me about the controversy, I had instead communicated with her through Dr. Dennard. After accepting the invitation, I thought of calling her but found it difficult to initiate a discussion about my handling of the controversy. I concluded it was best to see her in person at the Commission meeting rather than talk by telephone, and I asked Dennard to arrange time for us to meet.

Because the Commission meeting took place not far from my hometown, so I invited my mother to drive down from Los Alamos to attend Mrs. King's address at the Commission's opening session. After her speech, I introduced the two women to each other for the first time. Mom still bore a grudge against Mrs. King for her initial "high-handed" treatment of me in 1985, but was nonetheless eager to meet the woman who had become so much a part of her son's life. My only concern was that she might interpret Mrs. King's sometimes reserved manner at public gatherings as condescension. The impromptu encounter nonetheless went well, especially after they realized that their birthplaces were not far apart and that both had once lived in Montgomery. I regretted that they did not have more time to become acquainted.

Later that afternoon, I met privately with Mrs. King in her suite at the Hotel Plaza Real next to Santa Fe's historic Plaza. I saw at once that she was in a somber mood. She asked why I hadn't called her in recent months. I knew that each of us could have called the other, but we hadn't. I had never been comfortable making unsolicited telephone calls to her. I pointed out that I had stayed in touch with Dennard and assumed that he kept her informed about our conversations.

"But you've talked to plenty of reporters."

"Only when they've contacted me, Mrs. King, and mostly on the day of the *Wall Street Journal* article," I responded.

"But that doesn't explain why you didn't contact me afterwards."

I was reluctant to say that it was easier for her to contact me than vice versa, that I had been busy getting *Volume 1* through the publication process, and mostly that I had wanted to handle the plagiarism controversy without any suggestion that I was following her instructions. Unwilling to say any of this, I felt like a child being chastened for not calling home.

"In retrospect, how would you have wanted me to handle the situation differently?" I asked.

"Better communication would have helped," she observed.

The tension between us dissipated only after I admitted that it was difficult for me to initiate conversations with her about contentious issues, but conceded that I should have reached out to her more often. As I came close to apologizing, her tone became less accusative. I promised to do better in the future.

As we gradually moved on to less weighty matters, I proposed that we take a walk around Santa Fe's central Plaza during the pleasantly sunny afternoon. I suspected that she had probably seen little of the scenic area outside her hotel. She was reluctant at first, not wanting to be recognized, but she finally gave in to my assurance that in Santa Fe even movie stars attracted little attention. (I didn't add that such stars gain anonymity by adopting the very informal local dress norms.) We wandered slowly past the seventeenth-century Palace of the Governors, with its native artisans selling their wares in front, and then across the Plaza toward the historic La Fonda Hotel. She appeared relaxed as I related bits of Santa Fe's rich history and my childhood experiences there. The Plaza was crowded, but no one seemed to recognize her.

During the months after the Santa Fe meeting, it seemed that the plagiarism controversy had finally run its course. King's critics had another reason to question whether he deserved a national holiday, and his admirers recognized that his deficiencies as a scholar—like his infidelities—should not detract from his achievement as an advocate for global peace and human rights. For a brief moment, the story fed the nation's insatiable appetite for scandal, but a story that centered on footnotes could not keep the public's attention. When the *Journal* finally published Thelen's forum of articles in its June 1991 issue, the media paid almost no attention.

I did not have any more talks with Mrs. King about the plagiarism issue, but it placed a strain on our relationship that was not readily eased. Since the summer of 1985, when I had contemplated making a graceful exit from the King Papers Project, I had still not established a strong collaborative relationship between the King Project at Stanford and the King Center in Atlanta. Even before the controversy, I wondered why she had turned not to me and my King Project colleagues, but instead to theologian James M. Washington, to prepare the recently published anthology, *A Testament of Hope: The Essential Writings and Speeches of Martin Luther King Jr.*, a volume I knew would reach a much larger readership than *The Papers*. As a scholar, I needed editorial independence, but I also needed Mrs. King's support to achieve my goal of making the Papers Project a financially secure research center capable of helping her disseminate King's ideas. I recognized the unique importance of our comprehensive, annotated edition of *The Papers*, but I also believed that the King Papers Project should become a multifaceted research center able to bring King's ideas to students and the general public rather than just to scholars and researchers. Part of my goal of broadening the scope of the King Papers Project involved inviting civil rights veterans such as Dorothy Cotton to our yearly open house and King Holiday celebrations, which local media sometimes covered. I hoped these celebrations would allow our young staff to feel more a part of the ongoing effort to preserve the legacy of the struggle.

The plagiarism controversy not only strained my relationship with Mrs. King, but it also weakened morale within the King Papers Project. Project staff members and student researchers were motivated mostly by the notion that they were contributing to King's legacy. Yet many of these idealistic students spent countless hours checking King's sources for his academic papers rather than studying his positive contributions to the Southern freedom struggle. There was little sense of satisfaction that a staff comprised mainly of students had discovered something that had eluded previous King scholars.

I generally maintained good relationships with staff members at Stanford during the early years of the project; however, there were tensions and sometimes serious problems. My relationship with Ralph Luker had also frayed, in part due to the tensions surrounding the plagiarism issue. Eventually, I decided not to renew his contract. My respect for his skills remained considerable and he later returned to the King Project, working briefly at the Stanford office as a consulting editor. At the Stanford office, I found it difficult to provide adequate supervision for as many as a dozen undergraduate researchers, and I delegated day-to-day supervision to other slightly more experienced young staff members. I initially tried to recruit a scholar with a doctorate to supervise the student workers, but some candidates understandably viewed the non-tenured position as temporary while continuing to seek a teaching position.

Although the overall quality of the students' research was high, it was also uneven. My sometimes lax supervision placed severe burdens on senior staff members who found it difficult to balance their devotion to the King Papers Project with their own career ambitions. I would especially regret that Penny Russell and Peter Holloran, who became assistant editors with title page credit on the initial volumes of *The Papers*, would in the 1990s be among those who concluded that they had to leave the project to pursue their careers.

Despite these problems, the King Papers Project provided an opportunity for dedicated students to acquire research skills. I enjoyed working with the youthful researchers, especially those who were affiliated with the project during much of their time at Stanford. During the 1990s, external funding enabled us to offer summer fellowships designed to encourage students to consider academic careers in the field of history. We eventually attracted applicants from dozens of other colleges and universities. Our summer program provided an enriching experience for the interns who participated, and benefitted visits by civil rights veterans and field trips to local sights. One group of interns made T-shirts calling themselves "Clay's Kids." For many of the other undergraduate and graduate students who worked part time or during summers, the experience provided encouragement to pursue or continue graduate studies. Two won Rhodes scholarships, and at least a dozen of the student researchers during the project's first decade would become faculty members at various colleges and universities.

Chapter 12

Atlanta Roots

*E*arly in 1992 the King Papers Project published *The Papers of Martin Luther King, Jr. Volume 1: Called to Serve, January 1929–June 1951*. I finally had something tangible to show for the project's seven years of work. My colleagues—many of them students—and I had completed the daunting task of assembling thousands of documents from dozens of archives and personal collections, preparing a detailed chronology of King family history extending back to 1810, completing the introductory essay, and drafting meticulous headnotes and footnotes for the documents (from thirty-four archives and personal collections) selected and transcribed for publication. Once that was completed, we had to check and recheck the final manuscript to verify the accuracy of the transcriptions. Studying the documents in the first volume was like peering through windows into King's formative years, bringing me closer to the man I had first seen on a speaker's platform.

With the book in print, I hoped to finally distance myself from the initial dispute with Mrs. King over her insistence that I move to Atlanta, the difficulty of photocopying the King papers at Boston University while the King Estate was suing them, and the plagiarism controversy. More generally, I was looking for a reprieve from disruptive staff turnover as well as the challenges of securing sufficient funding and staying on schedule when many vital aspects of the project's work were beyond my control.

As advance copies of the first volume reached leading newspapers and magazines, interview requests poured into the Stanford office, although the volume of calls was considerably less than after the *Wall Street Journal*'s plagiarism article. During the King Holiday period, I appeared on several local radio and television stations, and on King's birthday Terry Gross interviewed me about the volume on her NPR program, *Fresh Air*. On January 29, 1992, I flew to New York for a day of radio and television appearances arranged by the University of California Press, the volume's publisher. Interviewers typically drew attention to the volume's disclosures about King's family roots and asked mercifully few questions about plagiarism.

On February 20, the official publication date, I returned to New York to appear on *Good Morning America* and various morning radio shows, and then I flew to Washington for a Capitol Hill reception at noon, hosted by the National Historical Publications and Records Commission. King Center administrator Cleveland Dennard had warned me that Mrs. King was "livid" because she hadn't been adequately involved in the planning of this event, but NHPRC director Roger Bruns repaired the damage and convinced Mrs. King to participate. I was relieved to see her chatting amiably with the other invited guests, including Atlanta congressman and former SNCC chair John Lewis and Harris Wofford, the King Project board member who had recently been elected to the U.S. Senate by Pennsylvania. After the reception, I flew to Atlanta for a book signing that also featured Mrs. King and King's older sister Christine King Farris. Hundreds of customers stood in line; I knew that few of them were seeking my autograph. The eventful day in three cities left me exhausted but exhilarated.

The Papers of Martin Luther King, Jr. received overwhelmingly positive reviews. The *Atlanta Constitution*'s glowing assessment especially pleased me, given the likelihood that King family members would read or hear about it. The *San Francisco Chronicle* book critic described *Volume I* as "superb, meticulously researched" and "the most intimate and authoritative glimpse of the civil rights leader yet." *Ebony* magazine lauded it as "one of those rare publishing events that generate as much excitement in the cloistered confines of the academy as they do in the general public." The *New York Times* reviewer praised our annotations as "painstaking and impressive," applauded the introductory essay for its findings about King's ancestral roots, but oddly faulted us for not including in King's papers the speeches we had discovered by his father and grandfather. I accepted that the prominently featured reviews would not make the scholarly book a best seller (except, perhaps, in the category of multivolume documentary editions), but it was nice to see the Papers Project praised for the broad range of its research rather than merely for its revelations about King's academic writings.

Apart from our encounters at publication events, I rarely talked with Mrs. King during the months after our meeting in Santa Fe. Despite my promise of better communication, I made only a few trips to Atlanta during the summer and fall of 1991, and these mostly involved consultations with Virginia Shadron, who had succeeded Ralph Luker as director of the King Papers Project's office at Emory. My wife and I were experiencing transitions in our family life that made it difficult for me to travel as much as I had during the King Project's initial years. Our daughter Temie had graduated from high school, but was uncertain about her future. Her teenage years had been troubled by a rebellious streak that was exacerbated by my frequent travels. Hers reminded me of my own adolescence (the saying is that children are the punishment we get for how we mistreated our parents). She became pregnant in 1992 and raised her daughter, Dalila, as a single parent while successfully working her way through college with our help. Fortunately we were able to repair our relationship, and she went on to earn her master's degree in social work, becoming a specialist in child welfare.

Our son Malcolm was back from Howard University to begin his studies at Stanford Law School. He left at the end of the first semester, but, after a stint learning Spanish in Mexico, transferred to the University of California's Boalt School of Law. He would earn degrees in law and urban planning and gain a lucrative law firm job before eventually becoming a downwardly mobile but highly principled attorney for the Legal Aid Foundation.

To help pay Malcolm's law school expenses, Susan and I rented out our home and moved into Potter House, one of Stanford's residence halls, as Resident Fellows. Among our responsibilities included developing programs on our chosen theme: the 1960s. The arrangement allowed Malcolm and Temie to have their own dorm rooms, giving them considerable independence, and our apartment was a convenient short walk from the project's offices. For the next four years, we served as "dorm parents" for about a hundred students even as our own children navigated adulthood.

My lone attempt during the fall of 1991 to arrange a meeting with Mrs. King did not turn out well. This meeting was intended to get her support for a nationally televised broadcast in which prominent actors, including Ruby Dee and Ossie Davis, would perform dramatic readings of passages from documents tracing King's life. Los Angeles producer Marilyn Solomon, who had helped the University of California Press raise funds to support publication of *The Papers*, had proposed that the reading take place during the 1992 celebration of the King Holiday. I reminded Solomon that she would have to get permission from the King Estate, and she assured me that this would not be a problem once she garnered corporate support for the venture. Believing the broadcast would draw attention to *The Papers* and also attract financial support for the Papers Project, I agreed to write a script based on King's autobiographical statements and the recollections of his relatives and movement colleagues.

In October 1991 Solomon and her corporate sponsors came with me to the King Center to present the idea. I was surprised that Mrs. King did not attend the meeting and instead sent her thirty-year-old son, Dexter, and Mrs. Farris's son, Isaac Jr. Two years earlier, Dexter had briefly replaced his mother as the King Center's president but resigned when it became clear that he did not have the support of certain board members. The two men listened briefly to Solomon's proposal before Dexter King summarily rejected it. I was stunned and embarrassed that I had misjudged the situation and had failed to determine beforehand whether the King family would give the proposal serious consideration. I also should have known about Dexter King's growing influence over King Estate matters.

A short time later, I learned from Dennard that Mrs. King wanted to have a discussion with me that would include her four children. I agreed to fly to Atlanta for the April 22 meeting. It was the first time I had seen Mrs. King with all of her offspring, although I had met briefly with Dexter the previous fall and once had lunch with Yolanda when she performed a theatrical piece at Stanford with Attallah Shabazz, one of Malcolm X's daughters. My contacts with Bernice and Martin III were limited to greetings at King Center events. It was daunting to face five family members, but I knew I needed to address their concerns and thought I might as well do it all at once.

Rather than meeting in the more formal King Center boardroom, we gathered close together on chairs in Mrs. King's office. She explained that all the family members had been affected by the plagiarism controversy, but they also felt left out of the discussions about how to handle the issue. Sensing that she wanted the siblings to hear what I had told her a year earlier in Santa Fe, I noted how difficult it would have been to keep everyone informed during the busy days before the *Wall Street Journal* article appeared. I did concede that I should have communicated directly with Mrs. King, especially once the controversy abated.

When asked why I had used the term "plagiarism," I explained that there was no question that Dr. King had violated academic rules, but added that it didn't imply that he had simply copied the writings of someone else. I went on to reiterate much of what I had argued in the *Journal of American History* article about King's compositional habits before realizing that they were not comforted by my suggestion that their father habitually "borrowed" passages for his speeches and sermons as well as his academic papers. I emphasized that my forthright response to press queries had quenched press interest in the story, and judged that the controversy had done little lasting damage to their father's reputation as a great leader.

As the interrogation continued, it became clear that at least some of the siblings believed I had brought attention to myself at their father's expense. By then I had come to see that this was at least partly true. I did not enjoy talking in public about the plagiarism issue, but the controversy had enhanced my reputation as an independent editor. I had isolated myself from Mrs. King in part to ensure that she would not influence my handling of the plagiarism discovery.

By the time everyone had an opportunity to speak and ask questions, the meeting had already lasted two hours. I was then caught off guard when Dexter asked why I had recently published *Malcolm X: The FBI File* while serving as editor of King's papers. His tone suggested that I had contributed to the growing popular interest in Malcolm X—especially among young black men. Spike Lee had written an introduction for my book, and the forthcoming release of Lee's film *Malcolm X* would likely call attention to the lack of a comparable major Hollywood film about King. I noted that I still had scholarly interests apart from editing the King papers. I added that I would like to write a popular book about Martin Luther King Jr. and mentioned the proposal I had already sent to Mrs. King.

As I flew back to California, I felt assured that the meeting at least allowed the King family's concerns to be voiced but regretted that my first extended encounter with King's children was focused on their father's plagiaries. I hoped that I had convinced them that our goals were compatible. They were responsible for preserving and disseminating the ideas that were the most valuable part of their inheritance, and I had signed on to help them carry out their mission. I thought privately that the legal battle with Boston University had been a mistaken over-reach by Mrs. King and her lawyers, but knew that I too had made mistakes in sometimes failing to recognize their prerogatives. It had been seven years since I became editor of King's papers, but my conversations with the King family still skirted around the issue of how much independence I should have as head of the project.

After the meeting at the King Center, I was concerned that the King children did not seem to share my pride in the King Project's research. I wanted them to appreciate the importance of the project's findings about their family's deep roots in Atlanta's black community and in the black Baptist church. I also hoped that they would see that the project's discoveries about their father's formative years had enhanced understanding of his historical significance. Certainly the project's research had affected my own appreciation of King's legacy. In 1963, I saw him as a charismatic orator and an inspiring leader. Three decades later, I had begun to understand that King's oratorical brilliance and his swift rise to a preeminent role in the modern African American freedom struggle resulted from his deep connections to the black community and the rhetorical traditions of black Baptist preachers.

Perhaps because I grew up in was one of the few black families in a New Mexico town isolated from the main currents of African American life, King's rootedness in Atlanta fascinated me. With no memories of my birthplace, I lived in a rented home in a neighborhood with no history before my family moved there and in a town hardly older than I was. In contrast, many of the key events of King's life took place near his birth home on Atlanta's Auburn Avenue, and he spent the first eleven years of his life in the house that his grandparents had purchased early in the twentieth century. I never saw two of my grandparents, have few memories of the other two, and had never attended a predominantly black church until my college years. King on the other hand grew up amid constant reminders of his family's proud past, and throughout most of his life he would remain connected to Ebenezer Baptist Church, just a block from his birth home. From 1894 until after his assassination, a member of King's extended family would serve as Ebenezer's pastor.

While studying the King papers, I became aware of the profound impact of King's formative experiences on his leadership qualities that I witnessed at the March on Washington. The biblical references that I had not fully understood in his "I Have a Dream" speech became clearer to me after studying the preaching careers of his grandfather and father, as well as the religious documents from his nearly years. As I considered the sources of his identity and his worldview, a comment in an article King wrote in 1965 stuck in my mind. I used it as the epigram for *Volume 1*'s introductory essay:

> [In] the quiet recesses of my heart, I am fundamentally a clergyman, a Baptist preacher. This is my being and my heritage for I am also the son of a Baptist preacher, the grandson of a Baptist preacher and the great-grandson of a Baptist preacher.

During my visits to the King Center, I often tried to imagine how the surrounding predominantly black Auburn Avenue neighborhood looked during King's childhood. This was before more affluent blacks and eventually the King family moved to newer and larger houses elsewhere, especially on the city's west side and later its suburbs. I talked to older residents who recalled the vibrancy that once characterized "Sweet Auburn." I generally stayed in a downtown hotel, but sometimes walked along Auburn from Peachtree to the King Center and frequented the restaurants and other businesses that still survived from the avenue's heyday in the 1930s and 1940s. On several occasions I had my hair trimmed at the same barber shop that King did.

Because of my acquaintance with pastor Joseph Roberts and other church staff, I was able to explore inside Ebenezer Church, and stand in the sanctuary and the pulpit where Martin Luther King Jr., his father, and, before them, his grandfather had preached. My study of African American history had made me aware of the importance of black churches such as Ebenezer in the long struggle of black Americans to overcome slavery and advance in a white-dominated world.

On one visit, I convinced a National Park Service ranger to accompany me as I walked slowly through King's birth home at 501 Auburn, a block from Ebenezer. Not much larger than the Los Alamos duplex where I had grown up, the two-story home exemplified the Queen Anne architectural style that was fashionable during the Victorian age. It reflected the social stature that King's father and grandfather attained after each had migrated from rural Georgia to Atlanta. Recalling the documents I had studied about King's childhood, I realized that the youthful preacher's son would have acquired his understanding of African American history largely through his daily experiences rather than through the kind of research I had done as an adult.

King was only two years old when his grandfather died, but he remembered the "interesting stories" his grandmother told him. He learned that his maternal great-grandfather's ties to the Baptist church extended back to the Great Awakening that stirred the religious feelings of millions of Americans during the decades before the Civil War. We reported in *Volume 1* that in 1846, "Willis, servant boy of William N. Williams, came forward" to join Shiloh Baptist Church in Greene County, Georgia, and then became an "exhorter," convincing other slaves to join the predominantly white congregation. He would later marry Lucrecia (or Creecy) Daniel, who would bear five children, including Adam Daniel Williams (A.D.), the grandfather of Martin Luther King Jr.

A. D. Williams would never know the exact date of his birth, but he chose to celebrate it as January 2, 1863, the day after the Emancipation Proclamation became effective. After his father died in 1874, his mother moved A. D. and his four siblings from the Williams plantation to nearby Scull Shoals, where they became sharecroppers. Early in his life, A. D. Williams decided that preaching was his calling. He would remember preaching as a child at the funerals of farm animals: "The children of the community would call him to preach the funeral and they would have a big shout." Williams came of age during the period after Reconstruction when black Baptists throughout the South formed their own self-governing congregations and sought religious leadership from members of their own race. With help from his pastor, he gained the rudiments of literacy and earned his preaching license in 1888. He made a precarious living as an itinerant preacher, serving several small congregations, while supplementing his income with other work. A sawmill accident left him with only the nub of a thumb.

In 1893 Williams joined the black migration from rural Georgia to Atlanta—"with a dime and a five dollar gold piece," he recalled. A year later, he became pastor of the thirteen-member Ebenezer Baptist Church. Initially preaching in a private home, Williams gradually attracted new members while also overcoming his educational shortcomings by earning his ministerial certificate at Atlanta Baptist College (later Morehouse). He attended the founding meeting in Atlanta of the National Baptist Convention, which became the largest black-led organization in the United States. During the 1890s, he married Jennie Celeste Parks, a carpenter's daughter who had attended high school at Spelman Seminary (later Spelman College). The couple's only surviving child, Alberta Christine Williams, the mother of Martin Luther King Jr., was born in 1903.

Williams was one of the black ministers in Atlanta and elsewhere who connected biblical teachings with civil rights advocacy, creating a black variant of the social gospel movement that also attracted widespread support among white clergymen during the early twentieth century. In 1906 he was among the five hundred black Georgians—including Atlanta University professor W. E. B. Du Bois and Atlanta Baptist College's newly selected president, John Hope—who organized the Georgia Equal Rights League to mobilize resistance to lynching and the Jim Crow laws that had been passed in Southern states to reverse Reconstruction-era racial gains. Soon after the gathering, a major race riot erupted in Atlanta, resulting in one white and twenty-six black deaths, setting back hopes for racial progress.

Despite the riot, Reverend Williams continued to thrive as a minister and purchased the Auburn Avenue home where he and Jennie would spend the rest of their lives. A few years later, Williams led the effort to acquire a nearby lot on the corner of Auburn and Jackson where Ebenezer would build its new home. With a growing congregation, Williams solidified his position as a religious leader in black Atlanta and expanded his political involvement. In February 1917 he was one of the "fifty or so…leading colored men" of Atlanta who organized the Atlanta branch of the NAACP, which became the nation's largest and most enduring civil rights organization. Williams later served as branch president, building its membership, hosting the NAACP's national convention in 1920, and launching a voter registration drive that pressured white leaders in Atlanta to build new schools for black children— including the Booker T. Washington High School that Martin Luther King Jr. later attended. Although Williams's influence had waned by the time his grandson was born, he served as role model for Mike King, a young black preacher who arrived in Atlanta soon after World War I.

The new migrant would remember the spacious front porch of the Williams home as the place where Alberta Williams caught his eye as she sat in a rocking chair. King was there to visit his older sister, Woody, who had come to Atlanta a few years earlier and rented one of the Williamses' upstairs bedrooms. King knew at once that Alberta was the woman he wanted to marry. The barely literate, twenty-two-year-old itinerant preacher at first found it hard to attract Alberta's interest and, even more, to convince her father of his suitability as a match for his sixteen-year-old daughter. She had grown up in relative comfort as the only daughter of a successful minister, while King was the child of sharecroppers in rural Greene County, Georgia, near Stockbridge. His father, Jim King, had little interest in religion and often turned to alcohol as a refuge from poverty and racial oppression. On one occasion, Mike King wrote in his memoirs, he had to rescue his mother Delia from one of Jim King's drunken assaults. Attending church with his mother became "a way to ease the harsh tone of farm life, a way to keep from descending into bitterness."

Alberta was attending high school at Spelman Seminary and later studied at Hampton Institute to become a teacher, but Mike King had only been able to attend the poorly equipped Stockbridge Colored School a few months per year. He decided early that his future lay in preaching rather than farming and honed his skills singing in an a cappella group that toured local churches. After years of studying the Bible and practicing eulogies on his family's chickens, he convinced the pastor and deacons of his church to license him to preach. He arrived in Atlanta with, according to his own account, only "a smattering of education."

Reverend Williams probably empathized with King, seeing the younger man as an earlier version of himself, since he had also migrated to Atlanta without formal education but with a strong ambition to succeed as a Baptist minister. He encouraged King to overcome some of his educational deficiencies by studying with students half his age at Bryant Preparatory School. Seeking admission to Morehouse College's School of Religion, he was not dissuaded when he failed the entrance exam. Williams interceded with Morehouse president John Hope to gain admission for his future son-in-law. On Thanksgiving Day 1926, a few months after King started his studies at the Morehouse School of Religion he married Alberta in a well-attended ceremony at Ebenezer Church and moved his new bride into an upstairs bedroom at the Williams home. It was in that home that Alberta gave birth on September 11, 1927, to Willie Christine King, and later, on January 15, 1929, to her first son, Michael King Jr. By the time King Sr. earned his bachelor's degree in theology from Morehouse in the spring of 1930, he was awaiting the birth of his second son, A. D., named after his grandfather.

After A. D. Williams died in 1931, his widow, Jennie Celeste Williams, lobbied successfully for her son-in-law to become Ebenezer's new pastor. Like other social gospel ministers of the 1930s, King Sr. expanded his congregation by creating programs designed to help less fortunate neighborhood residents; yet he also expected that the expanding Ebenezer congregation would compensate him generously. In 1934 he was able to tour the Holy Land and Europe while traveling to the World Baptist Alliance meeting in Berlin. After returning in 1934 from the homeland of the founder of Protestantism, he reinforced his growing stature by changing his name—and that of his son—from Michael to Martin Luther King. Close acquaintances came to know him as Daddy King.

Because my own mother had sometimes expressed resentment about the ways her in-laws treated her, I wondered whether Daddy King found it difficult to live in such close quarters with his mother-in-law. King Jr. experienced his grandmother's death in 1941 as his first major trauma—"because of the extreme love I had for her"—but soon after her passing, the elder King moved his family to a more imposing house that he purchased three blocks away.

He tried to shield his children from the harsher aspects of his personality and of the surrounding world. "To prepare a child for a world where death and violence are always near drains a lot of energy from the soul," he recounted. "Inside you, there is always a fist balled up to protect them. And a constant sense of the hard line between maintaining self-respect and getting along with the enemy all around you." His own difficult relationship with his embittered, violence-prone father led him to see strict discipline as necessary preparation for the often cruel world his children would enter. He believed that the "switch was usually quicker and more persuasive" in disciplining his boys but increasingly deferred to his wife's less stern but effective approaches to child rearing. He recalled that his wife "insisted... as the children grew older, that any form of discipline used on them by either of us had to be agreed upon by both parents," and only Alberta could "investigate and soothe" his oldest son's "sensitivities."

During King Jr.'s childhood, Daddy King organized meetings to encourage black people to register to vote. In 1939, he proposed, to the opposition of more cautious clergy and lay leaders, a massive voter registration drive to be initiated by a march to City Hall. At a rally of more than a thousand activists, he urged black residents toward greater militancy. "I ain't gonna plow no more mules," he shouted. "I'll never step off the road again to let white folks pass. I am going to move forward toward freedom, and I'm hoping everybody here today is going right along with me!" A year later King Sr. braved racist threats when he became chair of the Committee on the Equalization of Teachers' Salaries, which protested discriminatory policies that paid higher salaries to white teachers than to black teachers with equivalent qualifications and experience. King Jr. later wrote that he and his siblings wondered how their father avoided being physically attacked during the "tension packed atmosphere" of their childhood years.

Along with other "progressive" black Baptist preachers, King Sr. stressed the need for an educated, politically active ministry. In a 1940 speech on "the true mission of the Church" delivered to the Atlanta Missionary Baptist Association, he referred to a biblical passage that his son would later cite on many occasions when he told his fellow clergymen that the church must touch every phase of community life.

> Quite often we say the church has no place in politics, forgetting the words of the Lord, "The spirit of the Lord is upon me, because he hath anointed me to preach the Gospel to the poor; he hath sent me to heal the broken-hearted, to preach deliverance to the captives, and the recovering of sight to the blind, to set at liberty them that are bruised."... God hasten the time when every minister will become a registered voter and a part of every movement for the betterment of our people. Again and again has it been said we cannot lead where we do not go, and we cannot teach what we do not know.

In King Jr.'s retelling, love pervaded the King home. In a revealing paper written in the fall of 1950 for a first-year class at Crozer Theological Seminary, the younger King would remember the "very congenial home situation" he experienced at the family's Auburn Avenue house. His fourteen-page, handwritten essay, entitled "An Autobiography of Religious Development," was the most comprehensive personal statement he would prepare in the years before acquiring his public persona as a civil rights leader. King recalled that his parents "were very intimate and they always maintained an intimate relationship with us." He added, "I can hardly remember a time that they ever argued (My father happens to be the kind who just won't argue)." He describes his mother as "behind the scene setting forth those mother cares, the lack of which leaves a missing link in life" and remembered that his "saintly grand-mother" was "dear to each of us, but especially to me." He considered himself her "favorite grandchild" and remembered "very vividly how she spent many evenings" recalling the family's past. King saw his childhood experiences as sources of his religious beliefs as an adult. Although his studies at Crozer and Boston University added layers of theological sophistication to these beliefs, his enduring optimism was an outgrowth of his early experiences.

It is quite easy for me to think of a God of love mainly because I grew up in a family where love was central and where lovely relationships were ever present. It is quite easy for me to think of the universe as basically friendly mainly because of my uplifting hereditary and environmental circumstances. It is quite easy for me to lean more toward optimism than pessimism about human nature mainly because of my childhood experiences.

King may have glossed over his childhood with nostalgia, but his autobiographical sketch also revealed his growing awareness of the world outside his comfortable home. He painted his Auburn Avenue community as "wholesome" with people of "average income." But he also recalled that his infancy coincided with the Great Depression that was spreading "its disastrous arms into every corner of this nation." At five he asked his parents about "the numerous people standing in breadlines," a memory that he saw as the source of the "anti-capitalistic" feelings that he took with him to Crozer. He appreciated that his father was able to send all of his children to college—"although it has been somewhat a burden from a financial angle, he has done it with a smile." The younger King saw his father's "noble example" as something he "didn't mind following" and later cited his admiration for his father as "the great moving factor" in his decision to enter the ministry. Nonetheless, once he left his childhood home and entered his teenage years, King Jr. became increasingly skeptical of the lessons he learned at Ebenezer's Sunday school. "I guess I accepted Biblical studies uncritically until I was about twelve years old," he wrote in his autobiographical sketch.

At the age of 14 I shocked my Sunday school class by denying the bodily resurrection of Jesus. From the age of thirteen on doubts began to spring forth unrelentingly. At the age of fifteen I entered college and more and more could I see a gap between what I had learned in Sunday school and what I was learning in college. This conflict continued until I studied a course in Bible in which I came to see that behind the legends and myths of the Book were many profound truths which one could not escape.

At Morehouse, under the tutelage of religion professor George Kelsey, he was able to remove "the shackles of fundamentalism" and accept the "liberal interpretation" of the Bible "with relative ease." I too remember undergoing a similar religious transformation as a teenager but King was a preacher's kid questioning basic aspects of his father's Baptist beliefs. As he came of age, he struggled to reconcile his inherited calling with his awareness that he did not share his father's unquestioning faith. He often recalled the importance of weekly chapel talks by Morehouse president Benjamin Mays, who showed King that religious faith could be consistent with intellectual rigor. During childhood King Jr. was largely sheltered from the Jim Crow system, but he remembered times when even his forceful, successful father could not shield his children from Southern racism. When a white clerk at a shoe store insisted that King and his dad must go to the back of the store for service, his father stormed out muttering, "I don't care how long I have to live with this system, I will never accept it." On another occasion, a white woman in a store slapped the young King after saying he stepped on her foot. In high school, King had to give up his bus seat to a white passenger while returning to Atlanta from an oratory contest. Ironically he spoke on the topic, "The Negro and the Constitution," and he remembered feeling "the angriest I have ever been in my life." At Crozer, a Southern white student pointed a gun at him in the mistaken belief that King had pulled a prank on him. On another occasion, a tavern owner refused to serve Martin, his date, and another couple, and then threatened the group with a gun. That encounter led King to join his friends in a legal suit against the owner for violating state civil rights law (the case was later dropped, perhaps because King recognized that his late-night attempt to gain service at a tavern might damage his ministerial career).

Studying Martin's formative experiences made me more aware of the central importance of Daddy King in shaping his son's religious worldview while at the same time serving as a point of departure for his son's religious development. Daddy King wanted his sons to become ministers and recognized the special promise of the elder one. He hoped that his sons would benefit from his Baptist connections, "family ties, school and fraternal relationships, the so-called hometown connections that kept phones ringing and letters moving in consideration of help requested and granted, favors offered and accepted. The world is too tough for anyone to think of challenging it alone."

King Jr. had long "felt the urge" to follow his father's calling, despite his "accumulated doubts." Only as he finished his undergraduate studies did the impulse return "with an inescapable drive." Even as a first-year seminary student, he would admit that he had "never experienced the so called 'crisis moment'" that would supplant doubt with faith. His call to the ministry "was not a miraculous or supernatural something; on the contrary it was an inner urge calling me to serve humanity." His family and childhood experiences infused him with his father's "noble ideals" and "noble example." He admitted that this intaking has been largely unconscious."

Recognizing that he differed "a great deal" theologically from his father, King still felt the effects

> of the noble moral and ethical ideals that I grew up under. They have been real and precious to me, and even in moments of theological doubt I could never turn away from them. Even though I have never had an abrupt conversion experience, religion has been real to me and closely knitted to life. In fact the two cannot be separated; religion for me is life.

Chapter 13

Passages

*E*arly in 1992, I invited playwright-actress Anna Deavere Smith, a recent addition to Stanford's Drama Department faculty, to visit my office at the King Papers Project. I had just seen her bravura performance (she played all the roles) in *Fires in the Mirror*, the docudrama she had written based on her interviews about a violent black-Jewish clash in Brooklyn's Crown Heights section. After I mentioned the ill-fated televised dramatic reading about King's life, she suggested that I use my script for the reading as a starting point for a play. The idea of writing a docudrama intrigued me. I was uncertain whether the King Estate would approve the play's use of King's words, but I didn't want the script to be wasted. After attending a fundraiser in Berkeley featuring a dramatic reading—staged by Candace Falk, editor of the papers of anarchist-feminist Emma Goldman—I thought that a similar reading based on King's papers might at least draw attention to our work and perhaps attract some donations. Smith made clear that she couldn't help me while she was readying *Fires* for its Broadway opening, but she introduced me to Victor Walker, a younger African American colleague in her department, who expressed interest in collaborating with me on a King play. I agreed to work with him to revise the script.

The insights I had gained from *Volume 1* research about King's family background and formative experiences led me to envision a play about his personal as well as public life. I knew that I was unlikely—at least in the near future—to attempt a major King biography rivaling David Garrow's or Taylor Branch's Pulitzer Prize-winning books, but I hoped at least to craft a play that was compelling enough to be performed publicly. Neither Victor nor I had ever written a play, but he had acted, done some directing, and was finishing work on his doctorate in drama. His expertise certainly exceeded my own. I was flattered that he was willing to devote time to the experiment. I thought that a successful production at Stanford might convince

Dexter King to approve a future televised reading or perhaps even authorize additional productions of the play.

Once the Drama Department added the play to its spring 1993 schedule, my collaboration with Victor became an accelerated course in dramatic writing. In addition to offering general advice, he recruited student actors for readings that helped me transform historical documents into convincing dialogue and scenes. I gradually became better at creating opportunities for characters to reveal crucial aspects of themselves not only through their words but also through their reactions to other characters. During the readings, I gained an appreciation for the skills of actors, even inexperienced ones, who could give unexpected meanings to the script.

Writing the play became my hobby (in addition to pick-up basketball and photography), providing a kind of intellectual stimulation unlike anything I had experienced editing the first two volumes of *The Papers of Martin Luther King, Jr.* More than a decade had passed since I had published *In Struggle*, and my writings about King had been limited to scholarly articles—several of them about his plagiaries—and book reviews. Yet I had long envied creative writers, such as Richard Wright and James Baldwin, whose works spoke to political issues and bridged genres. When I worked for Audience Studies on the Columbia Pictures lot, I imagined becoming a screenwriter, even to the point of taking drama and screenwriting classes at UCLA. The play became a way to bring "Martin" to life for people who would never read *The Papers* or my scholarly writings.

Early in the process, I decided that the play would focus on Martin's complex relationship with his father, the protective patriarch I had come to know through the King Project's research. Martin's early writings revealed that he saw Daddy King as both the "noble example" he wanted to follow and the theological conservative he wanted to transcend. Having read the elder King's memoir, *Daddy King*, as well as another never-published autobiographical manuscript, I knew that he was thrilled that his eldest son followed him into the Baptist ministry and took paternal pride in "M. L.'s" rise to prominence. But he was also initially wary about his son's attraction to modern theological scholarship that diverged from his own religious teachings. In one of Daddy King's few recorded sermons, he pronounced his son—by then his assistant pastor at Ebenezer Church—"a great preacher," but added, "He's a mystery to me, and I'm his father."

Martin's mother—Daddy King called her "Bunch"—also exerted enormous influence in the King household, but I had less material on which to construct the character of a mother Martin remembered as largely "behind the scenes." King Sr.'s references to his negotiations with Bunch about parenting suggested that she exerted her influence with the subtlety and tact she acquired as the daughter as well as the wife of a Baptist preacher. Because King's parents played roles that were a reversal of my own parents' relationship—Dad usually deferring to Mom's forceful will—I was fascinated by a kind of black patriarchy that I had not experienced as a child. While Martin hardly remembered times when his parents argued, my childhood memories were colored by the gradual deterioration of my parents' marriage.

Although Martin, like his father, expected to marry a dutiful pastor's wife, I wanted to portray "Coretta" as the strong-willed, independent leader I had known since accepting her offer to direct the King Papers Project. She had devoted herself to raising four children while her husband rose to national prominence, but I imagined scenes in which Coretta conveyed her strong convictions and her irrepressible determination to be part of the freedom struggle. Unfortunately, my initial portrayal of Coretta could not take account of the politically infused love letters that she and Martin exchanged during their courtship. I would not learn about this correspondence until later in the decade, when I edited *The Autobiography of Martin Luther King Jr.*

As for Martin, I was determined to avoid portraying him simply as the charismatic civil rights leader who delivered the "I Have a Dream" speech. Despite Victor's urgings, I didn't even include a passage from the speech in the initial script, although I would eventually give in a bit by including references to it. Mostly, I wanted to portray a preacher's son defining his own identity, distinct from his father's, even while modeling his father's example. I also wanted to call attention to the difficulties Martin faced as he tried to balance his roles as husband, father, and son after being unexpectedly called upon to lead a movement he had not started and could never control.

The religious convictions of Daddy King, Coretta, and Martin became another element in the evolving script. Victor and I agreed that many of the play's key scenes should take place in Ebenezer Baptist Church—Martin's "second home" and the setting where he sometimes sermonized with exceptional candor about his limitations and self-doubts. Though many Americans had heard the Dream speech, far fewer had ever heard one of Martin's sermons at Montgomery's Dexter Avenue Baptist Church or at Ebenezer. It was in the pulpit that he displayed his sense of being "fundamentally a clergyman, a Baptist preacher."

I also added a gospel choir to the play to provide an emotional backdrop for the church scenes. Sacred songs and the freedom songs were essential elements of the Southern struggle, and church music was one of the areas where Coretta, Bunch, and Bunch's mother, could exhibit confidence rather than spousal deference. The choir would also serve as a kind of Greek chorus, not only commenting on the action but also eliciting responses from the main characters. Although adding music to the play pushed me beyond the limits of my expertise, I had become familiar with these aspects of African American culture through participation in numerous programs featuring gospel music and freedom songs. The play gained new creative energy when Victor and I recruited members of the Stanford Gospel Choir to participate and convinced Stanford staff member Michael Britt, a keyboard specialist and choir leader, to become its musical director.

The choir became an animated audience for the scenes in which SNCC activists questioned Martin's leadership as too cautious. When Malcolm and later Stokely openly challenge Martin's nonviolent principles, choir members also portrayed activists who were torn between King and his black critics during the tumultuous middle years of the 1960s. Some of Martin's most compelling speeches, I felt, came during the period after passage of the 1964 Civil Rights Act when his words were sometimes met with indifference or derision rather than enthusiastic applause. Especially for young people growing up in the era of King Holiday celebrations, I wanted to show that Martin was far less popular during his final years than he would become after his death.

Malcolm X only met Martin once and then only briefly, but I saw him as one of Martin's key antagonists in the play. Just as I sought to humanize Martin, I felt that Malcolm's often harsh criticisms of King obscured the fact that Malcolm also recognized his own limitations as a leader. During the 1960s, many observers exaggerated Martin's leadership role, and young black people familiar with Alex Haley's *Autobiography of Malcolm X* did the same for Malcolm, mistakenly viewing his influence as comparable to Martin's when both were alive. Malcolm's posthumous impact on Woody Coleman and other N-VAC activists was evident in the days before the Los Angeles rebellion, but no activist I knew then would have doubted—even if they preferred otherwise—that Martin was the preeminent spokesperson of the black freedom struggle. Moreover, research for my edition of *Malcolm X: The FBI Files* had revealed that the Bureau was less concerned about Malcolm than about Martin. Malcolm only belatedly recognized the need to connect with the mass protests in black communities during 1963 and 1964.

While working on the script, I recalled my mild disappointment with Spike Lee's film biography of Malcolm, which I first saw at a preview showing in Oakland (where incidentally I also met Rodney King, whose beating by Los Angeles police was depicted in the film). I greatly admired Lee's previous films and applauded his uphill battle to secure sufficient backing for his most ambitious project, however, I felt that he did not give sufficient attention to the political reasons for Malcolm's split with Elijah Muhammad. (My critical appraisal of *Malcolm X* later appeared in the anthology *Past Imperfect: History According to the Movies*.) In his *Autobiography*, Malcolm himself had acknowledged the failure of the Nation of Islam to become involved in the expanding freedom struggle: "I felt that, wherever black people committed themselves, in the Little Rocks and the Birminghams and other places, militantly disciplined Muslims should also be there, for all the world to see, and respect, and discuss. It could be heard increasingly in the Negro communities: 'Those Muslims talk tough, but they never do anything, unless somebody bothers Muslims.'"

Lee's film had shown Malcolm watching televised scenes of black protest activities but regrettably had not mentioned his efforts, during the last months of his life, to forge ties with grassroots activists, including SNCC's John Lewis and Fannie Lou Hamer. For example, he might have included a scene showing Malcolm traveling to Alabama early in February 1965, just days before his death, to speak to young protesters and express support for the voting rights struggle. Malcolm missed meeting Martin, who was in jail at the time, but this trip led to a cordial meeting in Selma with Coretta. To suggest that relations between the two men might have taken a more productive direction if Malcolm's life had not been cut short by assassination, I included in the script the message Malcolm conveyed to Martin through Coretta—"I want Dr. King to know that I didn't come to Selma to make his job difficult; I really did come here thinking that I could make it easier."

I also welcomed the chance to create a "Stokely" character, although I knew that Stokely Carmichael would be an unfamiliar name to audiences in the 1990s. Unlike Malcolm, Stokely knew Martin personally. My interviews with him for *In Struggle* provided a striking contrast to King's own recollections about their discussions over the Black Power slogan. Even as they clashed in public, I knew that the two men respected each other. Through Stokely's words, I could express my own initial skepticism about Martin's often cautious leadership, and through Martin I could express my more mature understanding of the limitations of SNCC's sometimes rash rebelliousness.

At an early stage, I decided that *Passages of Martin Luther King* would be an appropriate title for a play that explored varied meanings of the term "passages"— texts, pathways, and transitions as they applied to the play's two central characters. I was struck by the ways in which some of the crucial events of Daddy King's life—and A. D. Williams's life before him—became templates that guided his son's choices, despite the many differences in their class and educational backgrounds. Both father and son were called to the ministry as teenagers, both ardently courted women they identified as suitable minister's wives, both preached social gospel Christianity, and both would also struggled to keep pace with the rapidly changing political world around them. *Passages* would show that Martin's religious convictions and political activism were closely intertwined, because, at crucial points in his public ministry, his religious faith enabled him to overcome his fears and self-doubts.

The initial script ambitiously surveyed the years from Daddy King's arrival in Atlanta in 1920 to Martin's death in 1968. Starting with a scene depicting Bunch and Daddy King's reaction to hearing the news of their son's assassination, I used flashbacks to trace the elder King's efforts to realize his ambition, both through his own remarkable rise from poverty to prominence in black Atlanta and then through his son's even more remarkable assent to international renown. The script concluded with a scene in which Martin discusses his premonitions of his death with his parents once his optimistic Dream gave way to a realization that global peace with social justice would not be achieved during his lifetime.

By early 1993, even as I continued to revise the script, Victor invited not only students but also the entire Stanford community to try out for the play. Fortunately, we attracted the interest of the dynamic Stanford campus minister Floyd Thompkins. Although he had never acted before, his moving sermons had gained attention on campus. Based on his powerful recitation of one of King's orations, we decided he was the best choice for Martin, although Victor realized that he would need considerable preparation to convey other aspects of Martin's personality. Because he would be onstage for practically the entire play, Floyd faced an enormous challenge for a novice actor, but he immersed himself in the role, and we never regretted our decision.

Another key to the play's success was our recruitment of Tony Haney, a professional actor with the local TheaterWorks Company, for the role of Daddy King. Because of Floyd's inexperience, Tony's assured acting skills made him the glue that held the cast together. He brilliantly conveyed Daddy King's mixture of bombast and charm, providing touches of humor to balance the overall somber context. Victor also selected Janice Edwards, a local television personality with some acting experience, for the role of Coretta. The other roles, including the choir, were filled by Stanford staff and students. For the role of Malcolm X, we chose Thom Massey, an assistant dean at Stanford who had never acted before. He had appeared at a tryout made up to resemble Malcolm and read the black leader's lines with force and conviction.

Victor had difficulty coordinating everyone to attend all the rehearsals, and the large cast, including the gospel choir, proved unwieldy. With the abundance of

With my parents in post–World War II Seattle.

Photo taken a year before I participated in the March on Washingon.

A portrait of the Carson family during late 1950s, with me on the far right.

MARCH ON WASHINGTON FOR JOBS AND FREEDOM
AUGUST 28, 1963

The March on Washington program, August 28, 1963.

LINCOLN MEMORIAL PROGRAM

1.	The National Anthem	*Led by* Marian Anderson.
2.	Invocation	The Very Rev. Patrick O'Boyle, *Archbishop of Washington.*
3.	Opening Remarks	A. Philip Randolph, *Director March on Washington for Jobs and Freedom.*
4.	Remarks	Dr. Eugene Carson Blake, *Stated Clerk, United Presbyterian Church of the U.S.A.; Vice Chairman, Commission on Race Relations of the National Council of Churches of Christ in America.*
5.	Tribute to Negro Women Fighters for Freedom Daisy Bates Diane Nash Bevel Mrs. Medgar Evers Mrs. Herbert Lee Rosa Parks Gloria Richardson	Mrs. Medgar Evers
6.	Remarks	John Lewis, *National Chairman, Student Nonviolent Coordinating Committee.*
7.	Remarks	Walter Reuther, *President, United Automobile, Aerospace and Agricultural Implement Wokers of America, AFL-CIO; Chairman, Industrial Union Department, AFL-CIO.*
8.	Remarks	James Farmer, *National Director, Congress of Racial Equality.*
9.	Selection	Eva Jessye *Choir*
10.	Prayer	Rabbi Uri Miller, *President Synagogue Council of America.*
11.	Remarks	Whitney M. Young, Jr., *Executive Director, National Urban League.*
12.	Remarks	Mathew Ahmann, *Executive Director, National Catholic Conference for Interracial Justice.*
13.	Remarks	Roy Wilkins, *Executive Secretary, National Association for the Advancement of Colored People.*
14.	Selection	Miss Mahalia Jackson
15.	Remarks	Rabbi Joachim Prinz, *President American Jewish Congress.*
16.	Remarks	The Rev. Dr. Martin Luther King, Jr., *President, Southern Christian Leadership Conference.*
17.	The Pledge	A Philip Randolph
18.	Benediction	Dr. Benjamin E. Mays, *President, Morehouse College.*

"WE SHALL OVERCOME"

My arrest during an antiwar protest brought me to the attention of the FBI. The Bureau supplied me with an alias: "Clyde Carson."

UNITED STATES GO␣RNMENT

Memorandum

TO : DIRECTOR, FBI DATE: 10/28/66

FROM : SAC, LOS ANGELES (100-68784) (P)

SUBJECT: CLAYBORNE CARSON, Jr., aka
Clyde Carson
SM-C

OO: Los Angeles

On 9/5/66, CLYDE CARSON, born 6/15/44, New York, was one of eight individuals that was arrested by the Los Angeles, California Police Department on the charge of loitering. CARSON and those other youths who were arrested were distributing leaflets which were opposed to the war in Vietnam in front of Union Station, Los Angeles, California, which is private property. His address is 115½ Vista, Venice, California.

On 10/17/66, ▓▓▓▓▓▓▓▓▓▓▓▓ furnished the following information:

CLAYBORNE CARSON, JR., born 6/15/44, Buffalo, New York, was enrolled as a history major at UCLA from January, 1965 to the present time. He was enrolled as a student at Los Alamos High School from 1957 to 1962 and the University of New Mexico at Albuquerque, New Mexico from 1962 to 1964. His mother was shown as LOUISE CARSON, nee Lee, and his father was shown as CLAYBORNE CARSON, Security Inspector, 4408A Sycamore Street, Los Alamos, New Mexico.

On 8/17/66 ▓▓▓▓▓▓ furnished information which disclosed that CLYDE CARSON was identified from a photograph as a participant at a demonstration which was held in opposition to the war in Vietnam on 8/6/66. This demonstration was sponsored by the Peace Action Council of Southern California which took place at the Federal Building, Los

3 - Bureau (RM)
2 - Albuquerque (RM)
3 - Los Angeles
(1 - 25-73940) (CLAYBORNE CARSON)
LOB/rns
(8)

446596

OCT 31 1966

55 NOV 9 1966

I took this photo of Stokely Carmichael/ Kwame Toure during a visit to Stanford in the 1970s.

During our self-imposed exile in Europe, Susan and I posed for a street photographer in Madrid on February 19, 1968.

With former SNCC organizer Bob Moses during a visit to the King Papers Project at Stanford in the late 1980s.

King Papers Project staff members and student researchers at Stanford enjoy Coretta Scott King's visit on November 6, 1986.

Susan and I attended Coretta Scott King's seventy-fifth birthday celebration, held in Atlanta on April 29, 2002.

Former football star Ronnie Lott after announcing a $1 million pledge to the King Research and Education Institute, January 14, 2005.

With his Holiness, the 14th Dalai Lama, during his visit to the King Institute at Stanford, November 4, 2005.

A scene depicting King's 1963 arrest in Birmingham, from the National Theatre of China's production of my play, Passages of Martin Luther King.

The closing night of the National Theatre of China's production of Passages of Martin Luther King.

A group photo taken during the 2007 King Holiday celebration at the King Research and Education Institute at Stanford. From left to right: Clarence Jones, Isaiah Washington, Dorothy Cotton, Tavis Smiley, myself, and Cornel West.

With Andrew Young and John Lewis in Washington, DC, January 2009.

At the King National Memorial, August 26, 2011.

Actor Ramzi Maqdisi portrays King leading a protest in the Palestinian National Theatre's production of Passages of Martin Luther King.

scenes I had written and the additional audio-visual material that Victor wanted to add, the rehearsals indicated that the play would run well over two hours. I had naïvely thought that a play covering more than half a century and with numerous set changes could be condensed into one act. After Victor advised that the play needed an intermission, I feared that many audience members would simply lose interest, but it was then too late for major script revisions.

While rehearsals were taking place, I was still waiting for approval from the King Estate. I had considered writing a script only loosely based on King's words, but I felt that it would result in a less compelling presentation. Moreover, a major reason I had decided to write the play was to call attention to the King Papers Project by using actual passages from documents. After some further wrangling with Estate representative Michelle Clarke Jenkins, we won approval for the Stanford production only weeks before the opening night.

Uncertain how the play would be received, I could hardly contain my emotions when I attended the *Passages* premiere on April 2, 1993. Family members, including my new three-month-old granddaughter, Dalila, and close friends were among the approximately four hundred people who filled more than half of the seats in Dinkelspiel Auditorium, a venue normally used as a concert stage. The final rehearsal did not go smoothly, and I imagined the worst, knowing that Walker had arranged to videotape the initial performances. What if the audience didn't laugh when my script intended humor or laughed when it was supposed to be serious? What if a significant portion of the audience left before the performance ended? If it flopped, how could I justify the time I had invested?

The opening scene with Daddy King and Bunch entering Ebenezer and reacting to news of their son's assassination in Memphis grabbed the audience's attention, but I allowed myself to breathe deeply only during the initial flashback when Daddy King first encounters Alberta Williams on her front porch and bluntly expresses his intentions:

DADDY KING: Well, let me take you out for a ride sometime.

BUNCH: Father would never allow that!

DADDY KING: The truth is that I'm preaching pretty good along in here, and I was wonderin' if you ever thought about courting. I'd like it if you'd consider it.

BUNCH: Court? But I don't know you, Reverend King.

DADDY KING: No better'n I know you. Difference is that I'm interested in knowin' more about you 'cause you seem to me such a fine person, very gracious and all.

Tony Haney's performance was a highlight of the premiere. His depiction of Daddy King verged on caricature, but I could see that his occasional overacting relaxed the other performers and engaged the audience. The spirited singing of the gospel choir prompted enthusiastic applause, although the mechanics of moving the singers on and off the stage interrupted the flow of the play.

A few scenes later, the audience seemed amused by a scene showing Martin's similar eagerness in courting Coretta Scott, when both were students in Boston during the early 1950s. My depiction of their first meeting was based on Coretta's account in *My Life with Martin*:

CORETTA: Actually, Martin, I feared you would be like the preachers I've known: fundamentalist, overly pious, wearing that look of sanctity all of you put on like your black suits.

MARTIN: Well, perhaps you've met the wrong kind of ministers. I see you have a mind of your own, and it's wonderful that you can do something else besides sing. I've met quite a few girls in Boston, but none that I'm that interested in. I want a wife...

CORETTA: What's that?

MARTIN: You have everything I have ever wanted in a wife. There are only four things, and you have them all.

CORETTA: I don't see how you can say that. You don't even know me.

MARTIN: Yes, I can tell. The four things that I look for in a wife are character, intelligence, personality, and beauty. And you have them all. I want to see you again. When can I?

As the performance continued, I was relieved that the opening night audience enjoyed the play. Yet I could also see many things I wished I had changed. The Narrator role that I had inserted was not really needed to provide transitions between scenes, and choir members had difficulty shifting from ensemble singing to their acting roles. I realized that many more rehearsals would have been necessary to orchestrate the interactions of the choir and the major characters. Some parts of the play, especially the scenes depicting relations between Martin and militant SNCC protesters of the early 1960s, moved slowly. Although this part of the play dealt with a period I knew well, I could see that audience members had little interest in these tactical arguments.

The play skipped over the March on Washington to focus on its violent aftermath—the Birmingham church bombing a few weeks later that took the lives of four black girls. I liked Victor's staging of Martin's brief subsequent White House meeting with President Kennedy, when Martin forcefully pleads for action while Kennedy complacently sits in a rocking chair. The dialogue came almost verbatim from a recording of the meeting:

MARTIN: The Negro community is reaching a breaking point. We have been consistent in standing up for nonviolence. But more and more our people are saying, "What's the use?"

KENNEDY: It is because you Negro leaders have conducted yourselves in the way you have that public opinion is with you, but if your people start going for their guns, then that will just wipe away the support that you have built up. I can't do very much, and Congress can't do very much unless we keep the support of white communities throughout the country. Tell your people that this is a very hard price which they have to pay to get this job done...

MARTIN: (interrupts) I am convinced, Mr. President, that if something isn't done to give the Negro a new sense of hope and a sense of protection, there is a danger we will face the worst race riot we have ever seen in this country.

At the end of the scene, the stage goes briefly black and then Kennedy's rocking chair is empty, signaling his assassination, which happened two months after the meeting. Martin then comments to Coretta that "Kennedy's death exposed America to itself. Americans tolerated the hate that killed him. They tolerated the violence. It was the same climate that murdered Medgar Evers."

Malcolm's appearance onstage predictably captured the audience's attention. While watching rehearsals, I could see that Malcolm's sharp verbal jabs pushed Martin to become more animated and interesting as a character. With Walker's help, I created a scene based on my conversations with Dorothy Cotton. During a visit to the Papers Project, she had mentioned seeing Malcolm at the New York rally held in Martin's honor after returning from the Nobel Peace Prize ceremony in Oslo. Martin was probably not aware of Malcolm's presence, but the close proximity of the two men provided a way for me to show them competing for the choir's support. After choir members loudly cheer Martin's determination to leave "the mountain" of Nobel fame to return to "the valley" of the Southern voting rights struggle, Malcolm appears in back of the crowd and quickly redirects their attention:

MALCOLM X: King got the prize! We got the problem! I don't want the white
    man giving me awards. If I'm following a General, and he's leading me into
    battle, and the enemy tends to give him medals, I get suspicious of him.

A later exchange between Martin and Coretta suggests that Malcolm's barbs hit
home:

MARTIN: Remember, Corrie, that time Malcolm told people in Harlem that
    I was soft, always talking about love, saying that I approved of black chil-
    dren being bitten by dogs, that I was just a polished Uncle Tom? They
    actually threw eggs at me!
CORETTA: But that was when Malcolm still preached that black separatism
    stuff, Martin. Before he left the Nation of Islam, before they shot him, he
    wanted to reach out to you, but he just couldn't bring himself to do it.

When Stokely replaces Malcolm as Martin's main antagonist, the play conveys
some of the verbal warfare that I remembered from my political activism in Los
Angeles. When Stokely admits that he used the march as an opportunity to force
Martin to "take a stand for Black Power," Martin responds by gently putting his hand
on the younger man's shoulder: "Well, Stokely, I've been used before. One more time
won't hurt." Unable to reconcile their differences, Martin and Stokely walk to separate sides of the stage. Martin explains why Stokely had become embittered: "You've
seen that the death of a white civil rights worker gets more attention than the death
of a black one, but we can't become bitter. Hate is too great a burden to bear."

When Stokely hears his supporters—played by choir members—harshly remark,
"King's outlived his usefulness to the struggle," he rebukes them with a soliloquy
taken from one of my interviews with him:

STOKELY: I have a great deal of respect for Martin. He taught us to confront the
    enemy without fear. He was the number one target for every racist with a
    rifle, shotgun, or stick of dynamite. The brother has lived with that every day.
    Yet he never backed down. I've seen his courage. I've seen him when every-
    body was shivering with fear. I've seen him making you think ain't nothing
    goin' on when the Man was tryin' to kill us. He loves his people, and the
    people love him. I've seen people climb over each other just to say, "I touched
    him! I touched him!" The old people especially saw him like a God! These
    were the people we were working with who didn't even know what Snick
    was. They just said, You one of Dr. King's men? I'd say, Yes, Ma'am, I am.

The last part of the play moves along at a brisk pace as Martin faces an increasing crescendo of criticism from both blacks and whites (represented by the choir) as he opposes the war in Vietnam and calls for a war against poverty. While mobilizing support for the Poor People's Campaign, he returns to Atlanta to be with his family. When he announces to his parents that he has something they have to hear, Daddy King and Bunch recognize the dangers facing their son:

MARTIN: Mother, there are some things I want you to know.

BUNCH: No, we don't need to talk about that now.

DADDY KING: Martin, Bunch's right. We don't need…

MARTIN: There's a chance, Mother, that someone is going to try to kill me, and it could happen without warning at all. I have to go on with my work, no matter what happens now. My involvement is too complete to stop. Sometimes I do want to get away for a while, go some place with Coretta and the kids and be Reverend King and family, having a few quiet days like any other Americans. But I know it's too late for any of that now. I've been to the mountaintop. And if mine isn't to be a long life, Mother, Dad, well then I respect that, as you've always taught us to respect it as God's will.

The play's fantasized concluding scene was adapted from a King sermon delivered late in 1967. Stressing common commitment rather than ideological differences, it brought together on the stage the main characters—Martin, Daddy King, and Coretta—as well as Martin's antagonists, Malcolm—returned to life—and Stokely:

CORETTA: (to audience)

Martin often quoted the phrase, "If you have not found something worth dying for,…

MARTIN: (walking down stage to hold hands with Coretta)

…then you aren't fit to live. You may be thirty-nine years old, as I happen to be.

(expresses surprise as Malcolm X walks toward him)

MALCOLM: You may be thirty-nine years old, as I happen to be.

MARTIN AND MALCOLM: And one day, some great opportunity stands before you and calls upon you to stand up for some great principle, some great issue, some great cause.

(*Daddy King and Bunch walk forward to hold hands with Martin, Coretta, and, with some awkwardness, Malcolm.*)

DADDY KING AND BUNCH: And you refuse to take a stand because you are afraid that you will lose your job, that you will be criticized, that you will lose your popularity.

MARTIN AND MALCOLM: Or you're afraid that somebody will stab you or shoot at you or bomb your house.

(*Stokely steps forward to offer Martin a "soul" handshake that becomes a hug.*)

STOKELY: So you refuse to take the stand.

MARTIN: Well, you may go on and live until you are ninety, but you are just as dead at thirty-nine as you would be at ninety, for the cessation of breathing in your life is but the belated announcement of an earlier death of the spirit.

CAST AND CHORUS: You died when you refused to stand up for right. You died when you refused to stand up for truth. You died when you refused to stand up for justice. Don't ever think that you're by yourself. Take a stand for what you think is right.

MARTIN: The world may misunderstand you

CAST AND CHORUS: But you never go alone.

After the opening night performance, I was pleased that the audience gave warm, sustained applause to the cast. The following three performances attracted crowds of similar size and responsiveness. Victor later told me that the play attracted more people than any of the other Drama Department productions that year.

Despite the positive feedback about my play, I wished that there had been more time to refine the script and more time for rehearsals. Creating a play had been an instructive departure from the work of editing. I had come closer to understanding Martin's Dream and his legacy. But performances of plays are always ephemeral. I knew that I had to get back to my day job, and the student actors needed to get back to their classwork.

During the next few years, I tried unsuccessfully to get approval from the King Estate for additional productions of *Passages*. My requests were not turned down; they were simply ignored as the King Center and the King family entered a period of rapid transition. Nonetheless, I continued to tinker with the *Passages* script. I arranged dramatic readings—usually during the King Holiday period—based on revised scripts. In January 1994 Floyd Thompkins and Tony Haney reprised their roles in a reading before a large crowd at Stanford Memorial Church. Stanford provost Condoleezza Rice delivered a convincing reading of the Coretta part. After Victor left Stanford for Dartmouth, we presented a reading there in January 1996. During the next decade, there were other readings at Willamette University (with Oregon's governor performing Kennedy), at Princeton Theological Seminary, and at the University of Washington, Tacoma (followed by a spirited performance in a Tacoma church).

In 2003, in response to the invasion of Iraq, I drafted a script featuring King's antiwar statements. Danny Glover performed King for a large, receptive audience at Oakland's Lakeshore Avenue Baptist Church and Aldo Billingslea later played the role at Stanford. In subsequent years, Billingslea, a superbly talented Bay Area actor, gave powerful readings of my script at various events. But it would be fourteen years after the original Stanford production before I would witness another full-scale production of *Passages*. On that occasion, gifted Chinese actors would perform Martin and the other characters at the play's international premiere in Beijing.

Chapter 14

Dexter's Vision

On April 14, 1994, Dexter King arranged to meet with me while I was attending an Organization of American Historians convention at the downtown Atlanta Hilton. I was participating in a roundtable with Julian Bond, Cornel West, and others addressing Martin Luther King Jr.'s enduring question—"Where do we go from here?" I readily agreed to set aside time to meet before the convention's opening evening session, and Dexter arrived with Philip Madison Jones, a close friend from their undergraduate days at Morehouse College. Jones was head of Intellectual Properties Management (IPM), the company the two had formed to manage the King Estate. Two years earlier, about the time of my meeting with all of the King siblings, Mrs. King had given her youngest son, then thirty-three years old, control over the Martin Luther King Jr. Estate. The King Estate consisted mainly of King's intellectual property, especially his writings and speeches, and it controlled depictions of him for commercial purposes. I sensed that there was some urgency that compelled Dexter and Phil to come to me. After some brief greetings, Dexter, who was taller than his father but resembled him, came to the point: "We think it is necessary for you to move to Atlanta."

My mind raced back to 1985 during the first weeks of my tenure as editor of King's papers when Coretta King had made the same demand. Even as I struggled to determine his intentions, I knew I had to take his words seriously. Dexter was not the head of the King Center, but he now controlled the King Estate. It was the King Estate that had authorized the King Papers Project to publish its fourteen-volume edition of *The Papers of Martin Luther King, Jr.* Moreover, five years earlier, Dexter had served a brief term as the Center's president, and I saw him as Mrs. King's likely successor when she retired.

"There are many things that I want to do with my father's legacy, and we need the King Papers Project to be headed by someone who lives here," Dexter explained. Caught off guard, I considered how to respond. Was I being fired or simply being tested? Was he showing that he would be a stronger executive than his mother had been? Struggling to control my emotions, I carefully formulated a response: "I don't think I can move here. I agreed to direct the Papers Project with the understanding that I would stay at Stanford."

I went on to explain that the researchers I had hired at Stanford did most of the work on *The Papers*. After an awkward moment of silence, I asked what they had in mind for the future of the King Papers Project. Not really answering my question, Dexter and Phil became increasingly animated as they described an ambitious plan for an entertainment company "to bring the King legacy into the twenty-first century." They envisioned building a multimedia King theme park across the street from the King Center featuring computerized interactive displays and holographic images of King. They predicted that such a high-tech center would appeal to young people who had little understanding of King's ideas. They were dismayed that Malcolm X's life story had been turned into a major Hollywood film, but there were no plans for a comparable King film. Appreciating that the issue of my future status had been temporarily set aside, I listened quietly.

I inwardly winced when Phil insisted that both the King Center and the King Estate should be run more like businesses. I was aware of the King Center's inefficiencies, but I hoped they realized that its mission was to preserve a legacy and disseminate ideas rather than make a profit. I found myself agreeing that new approaches were needed to bring King's legacy to a younger generation that had not experienced the freedom struggles of the 1960s. I couldn't ignore the fact that King Holiday events in which I participated usually featured gray-haired speakers, like I was becoming. Most young people came with their parents rather than on their own.

The two mentioned plans for mass dissemination of Martin's ideas through deals with major publishers who could reach a much larger audience than we did with our scholarly edition of King's papers. I mentioned that I had proposed to Mrs. King that King's speeches, sermons, and autobiographical writings should be published in books for general audiences, but she had not responded. They seemed interested as I described possibilities for reprinting King's "great speeches" or "great sermons" in audio as well as print editions. I also told them that an edited King "autobiography" could provide a counterpart to Alex Haley's narrative of Malcolm X's life. Leaving the issue of my future residence unresolved, we ended the meeting with polite promises to continue our discussions by phone or mail once I returned to California.

Somewhat in a daze, I returned to the convention plenary session where I spied Vincent Harding, a historian who had become acquainted with the Kings when they all lived in Atlanta during the early 1960s. During the early 1970s, Mrs. King had forced Vincent to resign as the King Center's first research director due to his reputed black nationalist leanings. I found it difficult to imagine anyone mistaking Vincent—a longtime advocate of nonviolence—for a black nationalist firebrand, but Mrs. King had reconciled with him and named him to the King Project's National Advisory Board. I tapped him on the shoulder and whispered, "I think I've just been fired."

Sensing my distress, he suggested that we go elsewhere to talk. After I quickly reviewed the conversation with Dexter and Phil, Vincent calmly reassured me and urged against any precipitous response. As we discussed my options, I realized that Dexter couldn't actually fire me, because I was not employed by him or even by the King Center, and the Stanford office was independently funded. At most, Dexter could remove me as editor of his father's papers, but he could not easily move the Stanford office of the King Papers Project and find a scholar to replace me. It occurred to me that perhaps he didn't care whether the project's edition of *The Papers* was completed.

When I returned to California, I wrote to Mrs. King, offering to step aside as editor of King's papers but only after wrapping up work on the third volume, which would document the Montgomery bus boycott movement. I knew that Dexter would resent my going around him to his mother, but I needed to determine whether he was acting in concert with her. Mrs. King had selected me to undertake the King Papers Project, and I thought she should be aware of the negative consequences that would result from my abrupt departure. I was also concerned about the project's staff. If I simply quit, I could return to my tenured faculty position and resume a more normal academic career, but my colleagues would have to find new jobs. After devoting almost a decade of my professional life to the Papers Project, I wanted to leave only on my own terms. After writing the letter, I waited in vain for a response. As was the case during the summer of 1985, I was in limbo, but this time I could go on with my King Project activities as if the meeting with Dexter and Phil had never happened.

When I returned to the Center in the fall, I had brief and uneventful meetings with Mrs. King, who said nothing about my letter. For the most part, the discussions concerned the forthcoming publication of the second volume of *The Papers*. I predicted—rightly, it turned out—that the volume's extensive documentation of King's plagiaries would receive little attention in the press because the issue was already old news.

Unfortunately, this also meant that little attention would be given to the project's most impressive discovery to date: King's first recorded sermon, "Rediscovering Lost Values," delivered in February 1954 at Detroit's Second Baptist Church while he was still a graduate student at Boston University. The transcript of this sermon that appeared in the volume was an important addition to the documentary record about King's early development as a minister in the years before he led the Montgomery bus boycott movement. I had treasured the experience of listening for the first time to the voice of twenty-five-year-old Martin Luther King Jr. confidently expressing his worldview:

> The great problem facing modern man is that the means by which we live have outdistanced the spiritual ends for which we live. So we find ourselves caught in a messed-up world. The problem is with man himself and man's soul. We haven't learned how to be just and honest and kind and true and loving. And that is the basis of our problem. The real problem is that through our scientific genius we've made of the world a neighborhood, but through our moral and spiritual genius we've failed to make of it a brotherhood.

I suspected that Dexter dropped his insistence that I move to Atlanta not only because I resisted but because he had more pressing matters absorbing his attention. Just a week after my visit, the King Center's board accepted Mrs. King's nomination of Dexter as her successor. The *New York Times* account indicated that Mrs. King's "strong support and even insistence" on behalf of her son had "won the board members over," but it also quoted a skeptical, anonymous board member: "This is probably the last shot at the King Center being a family treasure. I support Dexter, but if this doesn't work, they can't keep playing musical chairs with the center's leadership."

Dexter's subsequent public announcement of the planned theme park set off a storm of controversy. Most Atlanta civic and political leaders supported the U.S. Park Service's plan to build a King Visitor Center on the land Dexter and Phil wanted for the theme park. Critics denounced the King family for failing to back this federally funded venture, and derided the theme park as a Disney-style "I Have a Dreamland." The *Atlanta Constitution*'s editor Cynthia Tucker bluntly accused the King family of seeking to profit from the King legacy. Atlanta congressman John Lewis was quoted as saying, "Dr. King's legacy shouldn't be up for sale like soap."

These criticisms intensified after Dexter officially became the Center's president in January of the following year. By then, Phil had sent me a copy of the theme park proposal. I saw that the two had worked with a design firm to develop a serious plan, but I also knew that the plan would be ignored due to doubts about Dexter's leadership abilities and about his motives. I didn't question that he and King's other children should benefit financially from their inheritance. Their father had left them little material wealth, and many other people were profiting from King's legacy. I often heard suggestions that the King intellectual property should be in the public domain but suspected that this would lead to more commercialization of his legacy rather than less. It was, perhaps, too much to expect that King's children would forgo the material benefits of their inheritance, but I hoped that they would be discreet about it.

Dexter, however, seemed unconcerned about the serious cumulative damage the King family's reputation had sustained from the unsuccessful legal battle with Boston University, lawsuits against *USA Today* and CBS News for reprinting the "I Have a Dream" speech without permission, and the dispute with the Park Service. This damage could not easily be undone. I feared that the tendency of Dexter and Phil to define King's legacy as the family's private property and the King Estate as a profit-seeking business would continue to fuel controversy.

On February 13, 1995, a month after Dexter became head of the King Center, my thoughts turned to personal matters when I heard from my brother Chris that my father had died in his sleep of heart failure. He was seventy-nine and had been living alone in an Albuquerque apartment. His divorce from Mom was about to be finalized. When I saw him during the previous few years, he appeared happy to be retired and able to travel to many places that he had always wanted to visit such as Europe and Mexico. He even came to Atlanta once when I was giving a talk at Emory, and on another occasion showed up unexpectedly at our dorm apartment on the Stanford campus.

I wish I had known him better. I understood, however, that he was part of a generation of fathers who were reticent about expressing their aspirations and their disappointments. Was I like him in my emotional reserve? I realized that I loved him and he loved me but could not remember a time when we admitted that to one another. I would miss him most because of the conversations that we could now never have. I wondered what more he might have revealed if I had asked him about his life—especially about his experiences as a soldier during World War II, a returning black veteran during the postwar period, and perhaps the first black man to work in Los Alamos.

Together with Susan, our children, and our two-year-old granddaughter, we went to his funeral in Santa Fe and his interment at the National Cemetery where my brother Michael was also buried. I tried to comfort Mom, while trying to imagine her thoughts. Did she blame herself for driving him away? Their marriage had long been troubled but remarkably endured. I knew they had stuck together for our happiness and then out of habit.

A few weeks after Dad's funeral, I returned to Atlanta to meet with Dexter for the first time in his role as King Center president. I noticed that much had changed inside the building. Dexter had moved into Mrs. King's second-floor office, and her mementos had been removed. It took me a while to realize that Mrs. King no longer had an office anywhere in the institution she had founded. Her absence effectively conveyed the message that no one could circumvent Dexter's authority by appealing to his mother. I was saddened that an era had passed and wondered when or if I would see her again. I also wondered what lay ahead as I dealt with the King Center's new leader, a man fifteen years younger than I, who had been two years old when I listened to his father at the March on Washington.

It did not take long to determine that Dexter and Phil wanted my help. Leaving behind the issue of where I would live, they made clear that their plans included me. They exhibited little interest in *The Papers of Martin Luther King, Jr.*, but they grasped the importance of the Papers Project's effort to copy and catalog all of King's papers, including those that might still be in Mrs. King's home. Although Dexter controlled the King Estate, he recognized that there was no inventory of the several hundred thousand historical documents and audio-visual items that constituted his inheritance. Many of these materials had been seen only by a handful of scholars, and no single scholar had seen them all. Even the King Papers Project had cataloged only a small portion of the materials that King and his close acquaintances had left behind.

In contrast to his mother, who viewed the King papers mainly as a collection of physical documents, Dexter appreciated that these documents were also valuable as intangible intellectual property that could be disseminated digitally as well as in print form. My background as a computer programmer and his as an aspiring music producer led us to see the untapped potential for disseminating the King legacy using modern communications technology. Although the development of the Internet was only in its early stages during the mid-1990s, the project office at Stanford was located in Silicon Valley at the center of this new technology. Stanford students would found companies such as Yahoo and Google. Envisioning a time when people throughout the world would readily access thousands of King-related documents and audio-visual materials, I tapped into the expertise of my undergraduate student researchers and secured funding from the black-owned Woodside Summit Group to create a project website.

As we continued our meeting, Dexter took me up to the King Center's third-floor archive and talked about his plan to digitize all the materials stored there. Walking through the archive, I could see that many King recordings were still on large reel-to-reel tapes that were slowly deteriorating. Fragile film footage had been stored for decades in metal canisters vulnerable to fire damage. I knew that the audio-visual materials would have to be converted to digital formats before it became impossible to find appropriate equipment to hear the recordings or view the footage.

Dexter also took me inside a locked vault—the size of a small closet—where particularly important documents and artifacts were stored. I had been in the vault before for short periods but had never been given a key to it. I knew, however, that it contained original documents that Louise Cook had culled from the King collection during the late 1980s. She explained to me at the time that documents with King's handwriting on them and letters from major historical figures had become targets for theft as the value of King-related historical artifacts escalated during the decade. She replaced these documents with photocopies to be used by researchers unless there was a special need to see the original.

As I looked around the vault, I saw that there were also artifacts and mementos. "Has anyone done a complete inventory of everything in here?" I ventured. "Well, that's what we need to work on," Dexter replied. After we left the vault, he told me, without elaborating, "There are many more important documents that have not even been moved here, yet." I wondered what surprises lay ahead.

Because of the intense local opposition, nothing came of the theme park proposal, and Dexter eventually dropped his public opposition to the King Visitor Center. I consulted with the design firm selected by the Park Service to create the exhibit there, and for many years thereafter, my recorded comments about King's early years greeted the thousands of visitors who came there. The plan to preserve and catalog the King Center's historical documents did move forward, at least in halting steps. I was enthusiastic about the idea of digitizing all of King's writings and statements, including all recordings of his voice, into a single online database.

After consulting with a Stanford expert on audio preservation to assess the condition of the reel-to-reel recordings, I convinced Dexter to allow the King Papers Project to begin preserving and digitizing them. During the spring of 1996, with the help of associate editor Virginia Shadron, who supervised the student researchers at the project's Emory office, a local recording studio began making preservation-quality copies as well as cassettes for use by researchers. Additional copies of these recordings were then sent to the Stanford office to be cataloged and later transcribed for possible inclusion in *The Papers*. I knew that the task of transcribing these record-ings and determining their historical value would take many years.

Once this effort was under way, I reconsidered an idea that I had firmly rejected. Susan and I decided to relocate for a semester to Emory University in Atlanta. This plan only became feasible once William Chase became Emory's president. I knew Bill when he was a dean at Stanford and both of us were involved in the Western Culture controversy during the 1980s. Although we were on opposing sides of that debate, the two of us had arranged a compromise that led to the establishment of a new program of required undergraduate courses on Culture, Ideas, and Values. With support from Emory historian Dan Carter, Bill arranged for me to become a "Distinguished Visiting Professor," teaching a lecture course on the modern African American freedom struggle and a seminar on King.

I was already familiar with the Emory campus, having often visited the King Project office that had been established there in 1989. From the early 1990s, associ-ate editor Virginia Shadron directed the team of student researchers working on the fourth volume of *The Papers*. I hoped to use my visiting professorship as an oppor-tunity to begin the copying effort at the King Center. Shortly before Susan and I arrived in August 1996, however, this plan ran into a snag. Virginia Shadron and her most experienced co-worker unexpectedly resigned. I was disturbed not only that they had suddenly left the project, but that the Emory dean responsible for the project had hired the two to work in her own office. After complaining to no avail to the dean and to Chase, I was forced to spend several weeks finding a replacement to supervise the Emory student researchers. I soon realized that progress on the volume was not as far along as I had expected.

While dealing with this setback, I started teaching a lecture class while also trying to initiate the King Center photocopying effort. Although I knew that few of the King Center documents would be included in the initial volumes of *The Papers*, I decided that the Papers Project might never again have an opportunity to pho-tocopy the entire King Papers collection at one time. After renting photocopying machines to replace the inadequate equipment in the archive, I hired a Kenyan stu-dent, Nducu Ngugi, who was willing to spend much of the next year copying tens of thousands of documents. We also continued the effort to make digital cassettes of the reel-to-reel recordings at the King Center. I often personally transported recordings from the King Center to the studio and then brought the cassettes back to the King Center.

I felt certain that the documents and recordings we were copying would greatly benefit the King Papers Project over the long term. The massive photocopying effort at the King Center continued, and the King Papers Project acquired many thousands of documents that are still being cataloged and studied by me and my colleagues. The digitization of recordings was constrained due to funding limitations, but continued and allowed hundreds of King's speeches, sermons, interviews, and public statements to be available to the project.

Nonetheless, Susan and I also suffered under the strain of administering the project's Emory office while also supervising the work at the King Center. I remember days spent leaving our apartment in the morning to drive to the King Center or to Crawford Media Services, rushing back to teach a class at Emory, and then leaving immediately afterward to open the project office in Candler Library for the student researchers. While I enjoyed strengthening my Atlanta friendships during the fall, Susan barely tolerated being away from our adult children, grandchild, and other relatives in the Bay Area. When December arrived, we were glad that the exhausting months had finally ended.

We soon learned, however, that our work in Atlanta had hardly begun. Early in 1997, Dexter and Phil informed me that they intended to sell the King papers through Sotheby's auction house. I was uncertain exactly which of King's papers they intended to sell, but feared that many of them would be dispersed, perhaps displayed on the wall of a billionaire's home and never again available to scholars. They mentioned Stanford once again as a possible buyer. Sotheby's had suggested that the selling price for the collection might be as high as $30 million. I was relieved when Dexter said that the King Papers Project would be able to make copies and prepare an item-by-item inventory of all of the documents to be sold. Although reassured, I also realized Dexter and Phil were not asking for my permission. My King Project colleagues and I would have only a limited amount of time to go through the documents before Sotheby's began transporting them to New York. The information contained in King's papers would be preserved, but I feared that a public announcement that the King family was selling King's papers would undoubtedly generate more negative press coverage. I asked how long we had before the papers would be moved. They told me that they intended to move ahead as soon as possible.

I was confident that the photocopying effort would be completed within a few months but thought about Dexter's reference to other papers that still needed to be moved to the King Center. I asked whether the sale would include documents still in Mrs. King's home. "Yes, we're going to move all of my father's papers out of Mother's home," Dexter said.

I was concerned, but not entirely surprised by the news of the sale. While teaching at Emory the previous fall, I had urged Dexter to consider moving the King collection—and other collections, including the SNCC papers—from the King Center to another local archive with greater staff resources and long-term stability. The

King Estate's unsuccessful legal battle against Boston University had been based on the claim that King's papers deserved better care, but I could see that the King Center's archive was no longer in the condition it had been when I first visited it in 1985. News articles had criticized the Center's failure to repair the archive's roof so that it would not leak during rainstorms.

I expected that auctioning King's papers to the highest bidder would prompt renewed criticism of Dexter but I was also excited that I would finally discover whether historically important documents were still stored in Mrs. King's home. The possibility that the papers might end up at Stanford was an intriguing development. Although much of the photocopying of the King collection at the King Center had been completed by the spring of 1997, bringing the originals to the Stanford campus would make it easier for the King Papers Project. We could consult originals when photocopies were unclear or incomplete and could make facsimiles for the published volumes of *The Papers*. After experiencing the difficulties of working for years with documents in dispersed archives, I welcomed the prospect of having a large portion of King's papers close to my Stanford office.

After first contacting Stanford president Gerhard Casper to determine his interest in the idea, I prepared a proposal for Michael Keller, the head of Stanford Libraries. I had worked with him during the early 1990s to purchase the papers of Huey P. Newton, the late former leader of the Black Panther Party. Keller agreed during the spring of 1997 to send an appraiser to Atlanta to assess the collection. By this time, I had begun examining the documents in Mrs. King's home and soon realized that they were far more significant and revealing than I had imagined.

Chapter 15

In Coretta's Basement

During the early years of the King Papers Project, King Center librarian Louise Cook told me that a collection of documents remained in Mrs. King's modest brick home on Sunset Avenue, the house that she had shared with her late husband during his final years. The King Center's collection of papers did not include these documents, because, at the time of his death, they were in his home study rather than his SCLC office and therefore deemed personal. Louise also mentioned that Mrs. King kept a box of Martin's letters stored under her bed. I accepted that Mrs. King might want to keep private some of the letters written to her but was of course interested in determining which documents in her home were historically important and should be included in *The Papers of Martin Luther King, Jr.*

I suspected that Mrs. King was too busy to go through the documents in question and make this assessment. Soon after becoming the Papers Project's editor, I warned her that withholding or even belatedly releasing historically important documents would seriously undermine the project's credibility. In 1987, she agreed to allow us to inventory the files in Martin's home study. When I came to Atlanta to do the inventory, I found to my dismay that she wanted it done by two King Center employees, Louise and Dr. Lillian Ashcraft-Eason, a recently hired King Project assistant editor. Disturbed that I had been barred from examining the files in her house, I was nonetheless pleased that the inventory was completed and that I had gained access to the documents that were transferred to the vault in the King Center's archive. Afterward, I periodically asked Mrs. King whether there were other important documents in her home, but she assured me that the historically important documents were already in the vault or had been moved to Boston University during the mid-1960s.

Although my curiosity did not diminish during the 1990s, I became resigned to the fact that Mrs. King would not take time to search through all the materials stored in her home and would never allow me to do it for her. I assumed that some documents in her possession would become available only after her death and perhaps not even then. I held these assumptions until Dexter offered me the opportunity to inventory the documents before their sale. (I discovered later that Mrs. King had signed a legal agreement assigning all her papers, as well as those of her late husband, to a trust under Dexter's control.)

Whether the remaining documents were historically important or not was unclear, but I knew that I might never again have the chance to examine such a large, previously unavailable collection. While director of the King Papers Project, I had not yet felt the exhilaration that had accompanied my SNCC research when I had discovered documents in basements and attics that no other scholar had seen. In contrast to the organized and well-used collections at the King Center or at Boston University, I imagined that the documents in the King home would be similarly untouched—or perhaps last touched by Martin Luther King Jr. himself.

Furthermore, it was personally satisfying to get past the experience of being barred from taking part in the 1987 inventory. Since Mrs. King's phone call in 1985, my quest to understand Martin Luther King Jr.'s legacy had encountered unexpected obstacles, some due to the King family's desire to control my access to their inheritance. I had only gradually gained the kind of special knowledge of King that I initially hoped would result from editing his papers. The King Papers Project had already made important discoveries about his early years, but I still had not discovered a significant body of previously unavailable documents that enhanced my understanding of King.

I wanted my most experienced staff members to assist me when I went inside the house that Mrs. King had shared with Martin and still lived in. I knew that Susan would want to be involved, even though it would mean taking her away from pressing work at the Stanford office. I would have to make certain that everyone took proper care to avoid damaging or misplacing irreplaceable items. Aware that some documents might sell for hundreds, perhaps thousands, of dollars, I knew that the inventory had to record every page of every document.

In March 1997, Susan, her assistant Elizabeth Baez, and I made our first visit to Mrs. King's home, a modest brick house in a declining black neighborhood near Morehouse. Mrs. King's personal aide, Patricia Lattimore, greeted us at the door in a low voice that suggested that her employer was still sleeping. As we walked quietly past the unlighted living room and kitchen, I glanced at the numerous old photographs on the walls and found myself wishing that we could also make copies of them. When we arrived at the small study toward the back of the house, Lattimore pointed to a photocopy machine on a table and indicated that we could use it but would have to bring our own supplies.

In the study, there was a large desk surrounded on two sides by wall shelves filled with books. I noticed the file cabinets that Louise had gone through a decade earlier. From the large number of books with religious titles, we knew that the Rev. Martin Luther King Jr. had used the study when he was assisting his father as co-pastor of Ebenezer Baptist Church. We later noticed that many of the books were autographed by authors acquainted with King or contained marginal notes by him. I concluded that our inventory should include the library books that may have influenced the development of King's religious and political ideas.

Lattimore then took us down to the large basement. Across from the stairs we saw a storeroom filled with boxes. I looked inside to see if the boxes had been opened, but they appeared to have been undisturbed for decades. I worried that their contents had been damaged by humidity or water seepage in the basement, but I was thankful that no one had tried to move or organize the materials inside the boxes. I knew that much could be learned from the proximity of documents to one another, because nearby items might offer clues about undated or unsigned ones.

Even my first glimpse at the piled-up boxes suggested that it would take weeks to create even a rudimentary inventory of their contents, months to identify each individual item, and years to determine the historical significance of the collection. I reflected ruefully that the work should have been done years earlier, when the King Papers Project had offices and staff at the King Center. Nonetheless, we were eager to get started.

After numbering the boxes, we began pulling them out of the storeroom and onto the basement floor where we could examine their contents. I wanted to keep the documents in their original containers, but noticed that an especially large olive green box, about the size of two normal banker's boxes, was in flimsy condition and could not be moved without the file folders inside spilling out. After a quick trip to buy storage boxes, we began transferring the folders and recording the order of the folders and documents inside.

I recognized King's handwriting on the labels describing the contents of each folder that had been in the green box. We could see that the folders contained outlines, drafts, and texts of familiar King sermons. One folder, called "Loving Your Enemies," contained a handwritten outline and text of the "Love Your Enemies" sermon that King had delivered at Howard University's Andrew Rankins Memorial Chapel in November 1957. The "Our God Is Able" folder contained outlines, handwritten drafts, as well as the text of a sermon of the same name by Boston minister

Frederick M. Meek. We determined that there were more than two hundred such folders.

Even without taking time to study the contents of each folder, the three of us became increasingly excited as we recognized the importance of the documents we had discovered in the box. We had found the files that Martin Luther King Jr. used when preparing his sermons. The folders contained the source materials he had consulted while composing or revising the handwritten early outlines or drafts. King had dated many of the folders that detailed his evolution as a preacher from his years at Crozer Theological Seminary through the period of his public ministry and political activism. Because these files provided revealing new evidence regarding this crucial aspect of King's life, the "Sermon Box," as we began to call it, was the King Papers Project's most important discovery.

Although King had become known mostly as a civil rights leader, our early volumes had shown that he saw himself as "fundamentally a clergyman, a Baptist preacher." His views regarding nonviolence and social justice were rooted in his religious beliefs. Some religious scholars had studied King's published sermons, but these folders provided an abundance of new information regarding the interplay between his public ministry and his life as a pastor. Apart from the historical value of the sermon folders, we knew that these documents had considerable potential monetary value, because many were handwritten or contained textual revisions in King's hand.

My elation was mixed with dismay that the project did not previously have access to these folders. Many of the sermon drafts and texts would certainly have been included in the three volumes of King's papers that had already been published. Why had Mrs. King withheld them? Had she believed that King's sermons were unconnected with his role as a civil rights leader? Because we were so excitedly busy during our first few days in the basement we couldn't dwell on these questions.

As we examined the contents of other boxes, we discovered that there were indeed many personal letters to Mrs. King, as well as financial receipts and Christmas and birthday cards, the kind of items that are stored in the basements or attics of many families. There were also printed materials—SCLC newsletters, press releases, pamphlets, texts of King's speeches, newspaper clippings, church programs—that were available elsewhere or were already included in the King collections used by researchers.

Interspersed with this miscellany, we also found fascinating correspondence with King's SCLC colleagues—including James Orange, Stanley Levison, Andrew Young, William Rutherford, Chauncey Eskridge, and Clarence Jones—and with other notable figures, such as Cesar Chavez, leader of the National Farm Workers

Association. One box contained correspondence with King's literary agent, Joan Daves, and with his various editors and publishers. In another box, we found the handwritten diary that King wrote during the 1962 Albany campaign.

Going through one of the last boxes pulled from the storeroom, I saw several folders relating to King's receipt of the 1964 Nobel Peace Prize. A yellow legal pad inside one of them with King's handwriting on it caused me to struggle to control my emotions as I grasped the significance of what I read:

> I accept the Nobel Prize for Peace at a moment when 22 million Negroes of the United States of America are engaged in a creative battle to end the long night of racial injustice. I accept this award on behalf of a civil rights movement which is moving with determination and a majestic scorn for risk and danger to establish a reign of freedom and a rule of justice.

I realized that the pages of the legal pad probably were the only existing handwritten draft of the acceptance speech that King delivered in Oslo on December 10, 1964. Although I was familiar with the text of his acceptance address, seeing it in King's handwriting somehow brought me nearer to him at one of the mountaintop moments of his life. Why had this extraordinary document been kept in a box in a basement? What was going to happen to it? I could not help thinking about the monetary value of what I was holding: It was perhaps worth hundreds of thousands of dollars, maybe even millions. "We better find something to protect this," I told Susan. We slid it inside a plastic protector until we could transfer it to an acid-free archival folder.

During our initial days in the basement, we did not encounter Mrs. King in her home when we left the basement to photocopy documents or when we went to lunch or left at the end of our workdays. I understood from Lattimore that she rarely came out of her bedroom until about noon. As we spent more of our time in the study photocopying the inscriptions and annotations on the books, we occasionally saw her as she was having lunch or was preparing to leave for an event with her assistant Lynn Cothren. I spoke to her and expressed our gratitude for letting us into her home, and she responded graciously. She sometimes asked Susan about our children and also seemed genuinely interested in Elizabeth, Tenisha Armstrong, and other young researchers who would accompany us during our visits to her home.

I gave Mrs. King updates about what we were discovering. She occasionally gave us useful background information about particular items that perked her interest. I knew that she was the person most responsible for preserving the historical records about Martin's life. Sometimes our questions about the documents would prompt discussions that would extend into our work time, but, despite feeling pressed to complete our work, we never considered interrupting our impromptu talks. During an especially extended talk, she mentioned that Martin had not wanted to buy the Sunset Avenue house and had wanted the deed to be in her name—"he never wanted to own anything." She attributed this to the influence of Gandhi. I thought of the irony of King's antimaterialistic ideas becoming such valuable intellectual property.

Despite her increasing openness, I found it difficult to gauge her feelings about our work. It was not clear whether she wanted the documents to be taken away. Unwilling to ask the obvious question, I never learned why she had not previously given the Papers Project access to the sermon files or the other historically important documents in the basement. She once suggested that she intended the sermon files for her daughter Bernice's use in her ministry—her book of sermons and speeches, *Hard Questions, Heart Answers,* had been published in 1996—but this did not explain why these files had not at least been transferred out of old boxes into acid-free archival containers.

As we prepared our inventory of the basement materials and photocopied the documents of greatest historical interest, an appraiser retained by Stanford came to Atlanta to help library head Michael Keller determine whether the university should purchase the King papers. I realized by then, however, that "the King papers" had come to mean several different collections. Would the appraised value be based on the King Center collection already available to researchers? Would it include the originals stored in the Center's vault or would it include the materials we were finding in Coretta's basement? I knew that Keller would have little interest in a King collection with only photocopies of key documents, but, if the vault and basement documents were included, I was not sure whether Stanford would be willing to pay what the collection was worth.

When I returned to Stanford in April, I urged Keller to make a comprehensive offer to purchase all the documents that the King Estate possessed. I was excited by the possibility that a King Papers collection at Stanford might include documents that had never before been available to scholars. However, this brief window of opportunity closed when officials at Emory University leaked news of Stanford's possible raid on Atlanta's historical heritage in order to strengthen Emory's own unsuccessful bid to buy the papers. "The papers belong in the South," former SNCC worker Julian Bond told the *New York Times.* Rudolph Byrd, director of Emory's African American studies program, went further, claiming that removing the papers "would create a rupture in our collective memory that would have unknown and far-reaching consequences."

The statement was certainly hyperbole, given that King himself had instructed that his papers be given to Boston University, but the squabbling lessened the likelihood that the King papers in Atlanta would be kept together in a university archive. Instead, the most valuable documents were taken to New York to be sold to the highest bidder. Even as we finished our inventory, Sotheby's representatives began to work in the basement, preparing a less detailed inventory as part of their appraisal of the collection's value.

From my meetings with Sotheby's executive David Reddin, I realized that our time was limited, although I was not certain which documents he intended to transfer to New York. Late in May 1997, I wrote to Dexter and Phil expressing my concern about whether Sotheby's had moved "documents that had not been photocopied or even catalogued." I suggested that they "should set a maximum number of items (1,000 might be a reasonable figure) to be included in the sale." By this time, however, Sotheby's was clearly in charge of determining what documents they wanted to move. Aware that we might never again have unfettered access to the basement documents, we worked through one night in a hotel room to finish our inventory.

Fortunately, Dexter and Phil reached an agreement with Reddin that gave the King Papers Project limited access to the collection after it was transferred to New York. I arranged to travel to New York at the end of June 1997 to clarify what items had been transferred. During the next few years, I would make additional trips and establish a cooperative relationship with the archival staff. Although I was eventually assured that historically important information in the documents would not be lost, I still worried about the consequences of the sale. Dexter and Reddin reiterated to me that the collection would remain intact, but I feared that future researchers would have difficulty understanding the significance of the materials in the basement and the vault if some were eventually sold separately from the rest of King's papers at the Center.

It would take many years to assess the importance of the materials we found in Mrs. King's basement, and I knew that the discovery would alter the work of the King Papers Project. After discussions with my colleagues, I decided that we would begin work on a new thematic volume documenting King's religious development and featuring documents from the "Sermon file." To some extent, this new volume would overlap coverage in the chronologically arranged volumes, but it seemed obvious that the sermon files would shed new light on King's years as a seminary student at Crozer and as a graduate student at Boston University. I would later ask

Gerald Smith, a minister and professor at the University of Kentucky, to co-edit the volume with the help of his graduate student Troy Jackson, also a minister.

King had preserved the evidence of how his homiletic ideas evolved from notes into a completed sermon. The folders contained the books, poems, statistics, Christian hymns, stories, and contemporary news events he used to create his homilies. The documents illustrated his ability to weave together biblical texts and ideas drawn from other sources into a coherent, persuasive presentation.

Most importantly, I began to see the basic continuity of King's life—the ways in which his early seminary papers on social gospel Christianity foreshadowed the Poor People's Campaign two decades later. "Above all I see the preaching ministry as a dual process," he had confidently written in 1948 during his first semester at Crozer.

> On the one hand I must attempt to change the soul of individuals so that their societies may be changed. On the other I must attempt to change the societies so that the individual soul will have a chance. Therefore, I must be concerned about unemployment, slums and economic insecurity. I am a profound advocator of the social gospel.

Rather than viewing King as moving from civil rights issues to economic concerns after the passage of the 1965 Voting Rights Act, the sermon files suggested that he was returning to the social gospel concerns that were always central to his ministry.

I could also see, more clearly than ever, the continuity between King's social gospel beliefs and those of his father—and, more generally, those of an earlier generation of black activist preachers. In his 1952 sermon outline, "Communism's Challenge to Christianity," King had cited the biblical source of the social gospel: "We must never forget the words of Jesus: 'The spirit of the Lord is upon me. He hath anointed me to preach the gospel to the poor; he hath sent me to heal the brokenhearted, to preach deliverance to the captives, and recovering of sight to the blind.'" (Jesus was himself adapting the words of the prophet Isaiah.) King was also adapting his father's similar social gospel admonition urging clergymen to become "part of every movement for the betterment of our people."

The early sermons revealed that King's wide-ranging social justice concerns were evident years before Rosa Parks transformed him from a social gospel minister into a civil rights leader. In addition his notes for the series of 1953 sermons—delivered at Ebenezer and broadcast on Atlanta's WERD radio station—on the "false gods" of the modern era shed light on the views he held before he was called the following year to Dexter Avenue Baptist Church. He warned his listeners that "the god of science which we so devoutly worship has brought about the possibility of universal annihilation." In one sermon he derided the "False God of Nationalism," which he suggested was the source of both white supremacy and imperialism. "If we are to avoid the drudgery of war; if we are to avoid being plunged across the abyss of atomic destruction, we must transcend the narrow confines of nationalism. Nationalism must give way to internationalism." He also condemned the elevation of the dollar "to the status of a god. It becomes a power that corrupts and an instrument of exploitation."

The newly found documents revealed that once King arrived in Montgomery and was thrust into his leadership role, his religious convictions served as a foundation for his civil rights activism. The King Papers Project had previously published many of the speeches King had delivered at mass meetings, but the basement documents illuminated the interplay between his Dexter sermons and his public statements and between his faith and his courage and confidence as a leader. In a sermon entitled "Our God Is Able," delivered four weeks into the boycott, King could confide his uncertainties to his congregation: "Much of my ministry has been given to fighting against social evil. There are times that I get despondent, and wonder if it is worth it. But then something says to me deep down within God is able." Responding to criticism that the bus boycott was disrupting peaceful race relations in Montgomery, he remarked in a March 1956 sermon, "Yes it is true that if the Negro accepts his place, accepts exploitation, and injustice, there will be peace. But it would be an obnoxious peace." As the boycott dragged on through the spring and summer of 1956, his sermons continued to strengthen his resilience and give hope to his followers. "We can do it because we know that as we walk, God walks with us," he affirmed in a September sermon on "Living Under the Tension of Modern Life."

By the time we published the thematic *Volume 6: Advocate of the Social Gospel, September 1948–March 1963*, the sermon box and the basement materials as a whole had given substance to a fuller interpretation of King's life—both as a clergyman and as a civil rights leader. These insights would not have surprised Mrs. King, who was a deeply spiritual person. Nonetheless, I felt that the spring of 1997 marked the beginning of a new stage in my relationship with her, partly because she no longer ran the King Center or the King Estate, and also, perhaps, because I had grown older. Our conversations during the next few years became increasingly informal and open ended, if not completely unguarded. I returned to her home on a number of occasions during the next three years as I wrapped up the research based on the basement documents and the materials in the study. We would talk from time to time over the telephone about the projects that would result from Dexter's new vision for disseminating his father's legacy. Over time, my encounters with Coretta in her home gave me a new understanding of her.

I recorded a few of our talks, but I remember a specific conversation we had in April 1999—this may have been my last visit to the Sunset Avenue house. I wanted to ask her about her early years before she met Martin. I had, of course, read *My Life with Martin Luther King Jr.,* which she had published in the aftermath of his assassination, and this memoir formed the basis of the Coretta character I crafted for *Passages.* I had never been quite satisfied with the book's depiction of her early political evolution. Given my knowledge of her onetime sympathy for the Progressive Party's challenge to the Cold War liberalism of the Truman administration, I sensed that she played down the extent to which her beliefs were unconventional.

I was pleased that she was willing to expand on what she had revealed in her memoir. She told me that her parents talked about the controversial 1930s Scottsboro case involving nine black teenagers convicted on bogus rape charges who would have been executed before the Communist Party rallied support for them. She added that her parents didn't have the educational background to become politically active. She talked about her years at Lincoln School, the "oasis in the desert" middle and high school she attended during the early 1940s. It was at this Deep South outpost of liberation where she encountered white teachers for the first time and forged enduring ties with pacifists Fran and Cecil Thomas. She recalled the time that they invited Bayard Rustin, the son of a Quaker, erstwhile Communist, and longtime civil rights activist, to lecture about Gandhi. He was the first black pacifist she had ever met, and their paths would cross again when she attended Antioch College and later when she was involved in the Montgomery bus boycott.

She described meeting Progressive Party activist and singer Paul Robeson while at Antioch. Robeson's ability to combine singing with political commentary, she said, served as a model for the "Freedom Concerts" she would help to organize in the 1960s. She added that "three of my favorite teachers were progressive party members" and that she had been a student delegate to the party's convention in Philadelphia. She recalled participating in campus peace rallies and becoming convinced that peace and justice were indivisible. She talked about a "steady" relationship with Walter, a white music student, but insisted it was not "romantic."

The information she conveyed was only somewhat more revealing than her memoir, but the conversation helped me to understand the political attitudes that drew her to her future husband and he to her. By the time of my interview I had greatly increased my understanding of the earlier years of their relationship. This understanding resulted not only from Mrs. King's growing openness about her past, but also from her youngest son's efforts to involve her in his ambitious plans for the legacy of Martin Luther King Jr.

Chapter 16

Autobiographer

Shortly before I finished teaching my course at Emory in the fall of 1996, Dexter and Phil told me that they were negotiating a major book deal with Warner Books, the publishing arm of Time Warner Corporation. As I learned more about their intentions, I realized that they had incorporated the publishing ideas I had discussed with them into a five-book proposal. In addition to a new memoir by Mrs. King that would update *My Life with Martin Luther King Jr.*, and a memoir by Dexter—which became *Growing Up King*—they had proposed three additional books: an anthology of King's speeches, one of sermons, and *The Autobiography of Martin Luther King Jr.* compiled from his autobiographical writings. Excited that my ideas for books intended for general rather than academic readers would finally be realized, I was also uncertain how this book deal would affect my life. Three years earlier, I had been unsure whether I would remain editor of King's papers; now I faced the challenge of editing three of five new books about his life.

Early in January 1997, I flew to New York to participate in the press conference announcing the agreement between Warner Books and the King Estate. Realizing that the deal had been arranged with only minor involvement from me, I couldn't help wondering when I would have a chance to discuss my role. Dexter and Phil rightly assumed that I wanted to edit the books, but they had never mentioned essential details. How much would I be paid? When would the anthologies be published? I thought about the impact of the deal on the King Papers Project's effort to finish the fourth volume of *The Papers*. Would the project receive compensation for the use of its resources or would I have to hire researchers to help me prepare the three books? As I mulled over these questions, the saying "Be careful what you wish for" came to mind.

At the Warner Books offices, I greeted Mrs. King, as well as Dexter and Phil, and was introduced to the Time Warner executives. We assembled at the site of the press conference where a dozen or so reporters waited. Time Warner CEO Gerald Levin introduced Mrs. King, who announced that the publishing agreement was "a great day for the legacy of Martin Luther King Jr." Warner Books head Laurence J. Kirshbaum told reporters that the King Estate would earn $5 to $10 million from the deal, an amount that took me by surprise. King's own books had never been best sellers. Had he gained a posthumous popularity that he had not enjoyed during his life? Or did they expect Mrs. King's memoir to reach a vast audience? I couldn't imagine the anthologies earning millions of dollars in royalties.

When it was my turn to speak, I described plans for the autobiography, offering examples to illustrate how I would use King's papers to stitch together a comprehensive narrative of his life. I had outlined this plan in my earlier book proposal, but I was not certain that I could pull it off. King had written full accounts of his involvement in the Montgomery bus boycott movement, the 1963 Birmingham campaign, and the 1966 Mississippi voting rights march, but I wasn't sure that there was sufficient autobiographical material about other periods of his life. I kept these doubts to myself, however, as I responded to a few questions from reporters.

After the press conference, I chatted informally with Mrs. King, Dexter, Phil, and the Time Warner executives. Despite the celebratory mood, I remained concerned about my role in this ambitious undertaking. If the King Estate was slated to earn millions, what would I receive and how would this affect the King Project? I hoped that the project would benefit from publications that would draw attention to its scholarly work, but this was by no means certain. When I had a private moment with Levin, I asked whether Time Warner had a charitable arm that might support the Papers Project, but he said he had no control over that. Kirshbaum later said he would be contacting my literary agent—I didn't have one at the time—to work out an arrangement.

News accounts of the Warner Books agreement confirmed my fear that it would be seen as additional evidence of the King family's profiteering. Although several articles mentioned the proposal for a posthumously edited King autobiography, their principal focus was on the deal's financial aspects. The *New York Times* observed that the King Estate's "unusual partnership" in a "multimillion-dollar joint venture" could be viewed "as crass commercialism, a media conglomerate's effort to cash in on a popular public figure." I remained distressed to know so little about the details of the publishing agreement or about its potential impact on the ongoing effort to publish *The Papers of Martin Luther King, Jr.*

Soon after I returned to California, Phil called me at home to berate me for asking Levin about a charitable donation to the King Papers Project. I realized that the informal gathering was probably not the proper time for my query, but insisted that I was only asking for information. After he accused me of trying to "screw up" the Warner deal, my own pent-up resentments came to the surface.

"Time Warner can help the project," I blurted out. "Why shouldn't I ask? Your million-dollar deal won't get done without the research support of the King Project."

"You should have raised that with me, not with the Time Warner people."

"What are you and Dexter going to pay me for editing the books?"

"If you aren't careful," he warned, "we might just get someone else to do them." The conversation didn't resolve anything, but I felt good that he had not been able to intimidate me. I didn't take seriously his threat to hire someone else to do the King autobiography, which was a key element of the deal. I felt confident that Warner Books would not agree to involve another scholar, even in the unlikely event that Phil had someone else in mind.

Soon after the New York meeting I contacted Sandra Dijkstra, a California-based agent, who had previously offered her services as I considered new book projects following the publication of *In Struggle*. She enthusiastically agreed to represent me in negotiations with Warner Books, and during the next few weeks, she secured a large advance against royalties for *The Autobiography*. Although the advance was considerably more than the royalties I had received for *In Struggle*, I knew that much of it would go to taxes, my agent's fees, and the salaries of researchers assisting me with the book.

Sandra also arranged for smaller royalties for the other two books—which became *Knock at Midnight: Inspiration from the Great Sermons of Reverend Martin Luther King Jr.* and *A Call to Conscience: The Landmark Speeches of Dr. Martin Luther King Jr.* I decided that these royalties should go to the King Papers Project. I wanted to separate, as much as possible, work on the Warner books from the King Papers Project, but I also knew that editing the books would inevitably draw upon the project's staff and document resources.

I was eager to begin work on *The Autobiography*, but far from pleased when Warner executives insisted that it become the first of the five books to be published and that it would be in bookstores by the end of 1998. It didn't make sense to me to publish *The Autobiography*, which required searching through all of King's autobiographical statements, before publishing the anthologies of sermons and speeches, which required much less research. The Papers Project's research had hardly reached into the 1960s, when most of the events to be covered in *The Autobiography* took place. In addition, the Papers Project had not yet organized the photocopies we had made of King Center documents covering the period after 1962.

Despite my pleas, I soon realized that none of the Warner Books executives—and certainly not Dexter and Phil—understood or cared about the difficulties I faced. The executives were not going to wait for Mrs. King to complete her memoir (she never did), and they concluded that *The Autobiography* would be the best option for launching the publishing venture. Despite my misgivings about completing the book in less than two years, I looked forward to immersing myself in King's auto-biographical writings and statements. As was the case with my play about King, I expected that editing his autobiography would be another way to expand my under-standing of him and convey that understanding to others.

The Time Warner deal connected my work to the King Estate even as I arranged to sever the King Project's financial ties to the King Center. I had also become con-vinced that the Emory office should be closed. Dexter decided to reduce the number of programs that the King Center sponsored and agreed to shift all of the King Papers Project's federal funding to Stanford. Because Dexter had little interest in administrating the project's federal grants, he accepted the obvious reality that it was now connected to Stanford more than the King Center. My decision to spend time in Atlanta ironically led to an outcome that contradicted Mrs. King's initial desire to have the project based at the King Center.

After returning to Stanford, I soon realized that the Stanford office had suffered as a result of our stay in Atlanta. It was evident that I had mistakenly placed too many responsibilities in the hands of young people, many of them recent college graduates with little work experience. As a result of staff turnover, recent college graduates had stepped into roles as *de facto* assistant editors, supervising even less experienced research assistants. Pete Holloran, the Stanford alum who had helped to launch the Stanford office in 1985, returned on a part-time basis to help Howard University graduate Dana Powell and Stanford graduate Katrina Nusum complete the third volume of *The Papers* on schedule, but all of them would soon leave to pursue graduate studies.

Susan and I were now faced with the task of taking over work on the fourth volume that had been started at Emory without any staff member having more than a year of experience. This volume was due to the press by the end of 1998 for publication early in 2000. Fortunately, we were able to hire several exception-ally talented and energetic young researchers, including Kerry Taylor, who had just completed course work for his master's degree in southern studies at the University of Mississippi, and Adrienne Clay, a Colby College graduate and participant in our summer intern program. Both quickly assumed increased editorial responsibilities, eventually becoming volume editors.

Susan's role as the project's managing editor expanded considerably during this period. Initially a part-time consultant, she had become the most experienced researcher and editor apart from me. She became involved in every aspect of the King Project's work, from preparation of grant proposals and database management to document annotations and manuscript preparation. Burnout and rapid turnover in the mostly young staff would remain a problem during the late 1990s, but the situation stabilized enough to allow work on *The Papers* to regain momentum.

Even as I turned my attention to *The Autobiography*, I sought to maintain the high standard of the first three volumes, which I thought were major contributions to the historical understanding of King. Nonetheless, despite the hoopla surrounding the first volume and the controversy preceding publication of the second, I realized that each subsequent volume would attract little public notice. Even the first volume sold less than ten thousand copies, and these sales would exceed the combined sales of the next five volumes. Although the Papers Project had published many previously unavailable documents and made important discoveries, *The Papers* and other such documentary editions are too specialized to attract the interest of general readers and are rarely considered for major book prizes.

When I began work on the manuscript for *The Autobiography*, I imagined myself being asked by King during the last year of his life to help him write an autobiography even while he was preoccupied with mobilizing the Poor People's Campaign. My task would be to organize everything he had previously written or said about his life into a coherent narrative so that he could make the final—hopefully minimal—revisions. And of course, in my imagining, he dies before he is able to make the revisions and I am left with the task of finishing the manuscript. The book would be his, not mine, but I would use my historical and editorial skills to give readers the best possible approximation of the autobiography that King might have written had his life not suddenly ended.

I knew that some parts would be relatively easy to edit. King had written three autobiographical books covering periods of his life: *Stride toward Freedom: The Montgomery Story*, *Why We Can't Wait*, and *Where Do We Go from Here: Chaos or Community?* I would abridge the narrative sections of these books to trace King's involvement in his principal protest campaigns. King's "Autobiography of Religious Development," written at Crozer, provided a starting point for a narrative about his formative years, and his 1960 *Christian Century* essay, "Pilgrimage to Nonviolence," surveyed his intellectual and theological development.

My challenge was to cobble together these published narratives with chapters drawn from a miscellany of sources to depict other periods of his life, including his trips to Ghana, India, and Oslo (where he received the Nobel Peace Prize) as well as his participation in the March on Washington, the Chicago Campaign, and the Poor People's Campaign. In some instances, I would rely on letters, sermon recordings, interviews, and statements that were not intended for publication. I took full advantage of the research I had done for *Passages of Martin Luther King*, utilizing the revealing sermons King delivered at Ebenezer Church during the difficult period after 1965.

Most important, I had to blend together all of these disparate source materials into a seamless narrative, so that readers would not notice where one source ended and the next one began. I recognized the limitations inherent in trying to reconstruct King's perspective at the end of his life. If he had written his own autobiography, would he have revised his earlier judgments about phases of his life? Would he have been more revealing or less revealing about his private life, his relationship with Coretta and his parents? More candid or less candid about colleagues and critics? I couldn't definitively answer these questions, but I assumed that he would not have disclosed personal information in an autobiography that he had never disclosed elsewhere. He would not have written a tell-all book.

As I constructed the chronologically arranged chapters of the book, I found myself becoming increasingly enveloped in King's worldview. Although I had read numerous books about him, I began to see him as he saw himself or at least as he presented himself to the world. By limiting myself to his own words, I gained an intimate, close-up view of the man I had seen from a distance at the March on Washington. Shaping his words into a life story allowed me to appreciate King's unique metaphorical diction, especially his ability to depict the key events of his life with vivid imagery. I learned to distinguish passages in his writings that were ghostwritten from those he wrote for himself. I began to notice the central themes of his life, the dreams he wanted to realize and those that were unfulfilled, his mountaintop experiences and the valleys in between.

I started to understand that autobiography is a kind of fiction, but even the stories we make up about ourselves can be revealing—sometimes inadvertently so. The consistencies or inconsistencies in the recollections he offered at various points in his life offered clues about the consistencies and contradictions in his personality and character.

I was frustrated that some pieces were missing from King's autobiographical narratives, especially his failure to say much about some of his closest associates, such as Ralph Abernathy and his other colleagues in the Southern Christian Leadership Conference. Having utilized Daddy King's reflections about his son to define their onstage relationship in *Passages*, I found myself wishing that King Jr. had said more about his parents beyond the idealized way he had described them in the sketch he wrote while a student at Crozer. Nevertheless, one of his concise and cogent reflections about his parents that particularly intrigued me became part of *The Autobiography*:

> In my own life and in the life of a person who is seeking to be strong, you combine in your character antitheses strongly marked. You are both militant and moderate; you are both idealistic and realistic. And I think that my strong determination for justice comes from the very strong, dynamic personality of my father, and I would hope that the gentle aspect comes from a mother who is very gentle and sweet.

Expecting that Mrs. King would read my manuscript carefully, I took particular care to find every available source regarding Martin's feelings about her. I could not find any evidence in King's papers of serious tensions in their marriage and certainly no hints of extramarital affairs or the marital conflicts during the late 1960s that David Garrow claimed. Instead I gained a clearer sense of the qualities that brought them together during the early 1950s and that sustained their marriage during a turbulent time. Martin's portrait of Coretta when he first met her and before he became a public figure helped me understand the public figure she became after his death.

I had of course known Mrs. King as the founder and president of the King Center, but King's description of her illuminated the extraordinary qualities she brought to the marriage and then doubtless suppressed as the wife of the Rev. Martin Luther King Jr. Ironically, after she resigned as president of the King Center, I came to know her as Coretta, a woman who had accomplished much in her own right. I witnessed her fierce determination to shape her late husband's legacy, and I was impressed that she continued to live in the same modest house she had shared with Martin.

Through Martin's writings it was clear that he felt fortunate to have found a wife who had all the qualities he sought—"I had to have a wife who would be as dedicated as I was." He appreciated that Coretta "never became panicky or overemotional" and never allowed her fears to "hamper my active participation in the movement."

He could remember times "when I sent her away for safety" only to "look up a few days later, and she was back home, because she wanted to be there." Yet he conceded: "Basically she has been a pastor's wife and mother of our four children, Martin Luther III, Dexter Scott, Yolanda Denise, and Bernice Albertine." Reflecting on her commitment to the Southern struggle, he commented: "I wish I could say that I led her down this path, but I must say we went down it together because she was as actively involved and concerned when we met as she is now."

As I pieced together Martin's account of the March on Washington, I relived the moment when our paths briefly converged. However, this time I could experience the event and his speech as he did rather than through the eyes of a nineteen-year-old. I understood the larger historical context in which Martin was placed that summer: "The heroic but spasmodic and isolated slave revolts of the antebellum South had fused, more than a century later, into a simultaneous, massive assault against segregation." I found that he disputed the notion that the march consisted merely of "heroism" and "drama."

> It is true that these elements have meaning, but to ignore the concrete and specific gains in dismantling the structure of segregation is like noticing the beauty of the rain, but failing to see that it has enriched the soil. A social movement that only moves people is merely a revolt. A movement that changes both people and institutions is a revolution.

He recalled the "many dignitaries and many celebrities" who came to the march, "but the stirring emotion came from the mass of ordinary people who stood in majestic dignity as witnesses to their single-minded determination to achieve democracy in their time." I thought of the teenage version of myself when he referred to those who "came in every form of transportation," who "were good-humored and relaxed, yet disciplined and thoughtful." The marchers, he recalled,

> applauded their leaders generously, but the leaders, in their own hearts, applauded their audience. Many a Negro speaker that day had his respect for his own people deepened as he felt the strength of their dedication. The enormous multitude was the living, beating heart of an infinitely noble movement.

I learned that while I was beginning my overnight bus trip from Indianapolis to Washington, D. C., King was traveling from New York to Washington, D. C., arriving at Washington's Willard Hotel at about 10:00 P.M. that evening. While I was up most of the night talking, he was preparing his speech. "I thought through what I would say, and that took an hour or so," he remembered. "Then I put the outline together, and I guess I finished it about midnight. I did not finish the complete text of my speech until 4:00 A.M. on the morning of August 28."

He was supposed to provide the press with at least a summary of his text by the previous evening. "But, inasmuch as I had not completed my speech by the evening before the march," he recalled, "I did not forward any portion of my remarks which I had prepared until the morning of August 28." I realized that he must have been at least as exhausted as I had been that morning.

His speech at the march resonated with my own experiences. The march had been the beginning of my activism: "Nineteen sixty-three is not an end but a beginning." Two years later, I had witnessed the "whirlwinds of revolt" in Los Angeles. I had seen mobs satisfying their "thirst for freedom by drinking from the cup of bitterness and hatred." I had applauded Black Power politics and lamented the "distrust of all white people" that came afterward. My SNCC research increased my familiarity with the grassroots activists who had been "battered by the storms of persecutions and staggered by the winds of police brutality."

By the time I edited King's *Autobiography*, I was familiar with the story of how he had departed from his prepared text to deliver the extemporaneous remarks about his Dream. His prepared remarks, which were intended to assess the historical significance of the African American freedom struggle, had been modeled on Lincoln's Gettysburg Address—"five score years ago, a great American, in whose symbolic shadow we stand today, signed the Emancipation Proclamation." A century later, King had continued, this "great beacon light of hope to millions of Negro slaves" had left their descendants "still sadly crippled by the manacles of segregation and the chains of discrimination," still living "on a lonely island of poverty in the midst of a vast ocean of material prosperity."

In the years since becoming a historian, I had learned about "the architects of our republic" that King described as signing "a promissory note" when they "wrote the magnificent words of the Constitution and the Declaration of Independence." King insisted that the nation's founders had made "a promise that all men, yes, black men as well as white men, would be guaranteed the unalienable rights of 'Life, Liberty, and the pursuit of Happiness.'" I now understood that King was part of an African American oratorical tradition asserting that white American leaders were not living up to their nation's democratic ideals. "Instead of honoring this sacred obligation," he continued, "America has given the Negro people a bad check, a check which has come back marked 'insufficient funds.' But we refused to believe that the bank of justice is bankrupt." (I would later learn that Clarence Jones, one of King's legal advisors, helped to draft this section of King's speech.)

King's prepared remarks were thoughtful and forceful, but he must have sensed that something more was needed for the extraordinary occasion. "I started out reading the speech, and read it down to a point," he recalled. "The audience's response was wonderful that day, and all of a sudden this thing came to me." He remembered a speech he had delivered the previous June at a massive rally in downtown Detroit

in which I used the phrase "I have a dream." I had used it many times before, and I just felt that I wanted to use it here. I don't know why. I hadn't thought about it before the speech. I used the phrase, and at that point I just turned aside from the manuscript altogether and didn't come back to it.

My years of research had revealed the gradual process of intellectual development that had enabled King to have this sudden, timely burst of inspiration. Long before the 1963 march, he had begun formulating the Dream theme in his speeches and sermons, often using the phrase "The American Dream." In 1959 he spoke of the need "to bring into full realization the dream of our American democracy—a dream yet unfulfilled...a dream of a land where men do not argue that the color of man's a skin determines the content of his character."

By the fall of 1962, the American Dream had become King's own dream. King probably first used the phrase "I have a dream" in public in Rocky Mount, North Carolina, on November 27 of that year. References to his Dream soon became one of his favorite riffs—to be adapted and utilized whenever he sensed his audience needed special stimulation. When he delivered a major address at Detroit's Cobo Hall on June 23, he had refined the passage he would perfect two months later in Washington:

Yes, I have a dream this afternoon that one day in this land the words of Amos will become real and "justice will roll down like waters, and righteousness like a mighty stream." I have a dream this evening that one day we will recognize the words of Jefferson that "all men are created equal, that they are endowed by their Creator with certain unalienable Rights that among these are Life, Liberty and the pursuit of Happiness."

And then, just as he reached the end of his prepared remarks at the Washington march, King recognized that there was still more to be said, that it was not enough to sustain a massive freedom struggle unless participants could imagine a future that made the sacrifices worthwhile:

> Let us not wallow in the valley of despair. I say to you today, my friends, that even though we face the difficulties of today and tomorrow, I still have a dream. It is a dream deeply rooted in the American dream. I have a dream that one day this nation will rise up and live out the true meaning of its creed—we hold these truths to be self-evident that all men are created equal.

I realized that there had been times—especially during my voluntary exile in Europe—when I lost sight of my own dreams, my own hopes for the future, only to realize even more extraordinary dreams in the changed America of the years after King's death.

As King approached the conclusion of his extemporaneous remarks, he once again called upon his memory to provide an appropriate conclusion. He adapted a passage that had been initially honed by his friend, the Chicago preacher and politico Archibald J. Carey Jr. Speaking at the 1952 Republican convention, Carey passionately called for equal rights by adapting the patriotic song, "My Country 'Tis of Thee": "…from every mountain side, let freedom ring. Not only from the Green Mountains and the White Mountains of Vermont and New Hampshire; not only from the Catskills of New York; but from the Ozarks in Arkansas, from the Stone Mountain in Georgia." Carey's influence was evident by the time King spoke at an Emancipation Day Rally in Atlanta on New Year's Day, 1957. After quoting the lyrics of the anthem, King continued: "As I heard a great orator say some time ago…Freedom must ring from every mountainside."

In subsequent speeches, King continually improved on Carey's use of the mountain metaphor, adding to his already vast oratorical repertoire. By the time of the Washington march, he was able to supplement his Dream by drawing upon the symbolic importance of the Liberty Bell as a key element of the nation's heritage. "From every mountain side, let freedom ring." King then moved to his conclusion: "And when this happens…we will be able to speed up that day when all of God's children…will be able to join hands and sing in the words of the old Negro spiritual, 'Free at last! Free at last! Thank God Almighty, we are free at last!'"

King's address at the march was a great oration because it brought together in new ways source materials rooted in American political and religious traditions. Beginning with the Gettysburg Address and ending with a slave spiritual, he made his own contribution to a continuing dialogue about the meaning of freedom.

Martin's ethical lapses when he was a graduate student had contributed to his ability to adapt more Christian scripture and the great documents of the American political tradition—the Gettysburg Address and the Declaration of Independence—for his own purposes. In an instant of inspiration, he assembled a cogent, coherent, and colloquial conclusion to a speech delivered before the largest audience he would ever face.

As I traveled on to New York after the March on Washington, Martin and other civil rights leaders were meeting with President Kennedy. For me, getting to the march had been an adventure marking the end of my childhood and the beginning of my activism. I had simply been an anonymous teenager among the multitudes. For him, it

> was the first organized Negro operation that was accorded respect and coverage commensurate with its importance. The millions who viewed it on television were seeing an event historic not only because of the subject but because it was being brought into their homes. Millions of white Americans, for the first time, had a clear, long look at Negroes engaged in a serious occupation. For the first time millions listened to the informed and thoughtful words of Negro spokesmen from all walks of life.

I didn't expect that *The Autobiography* would attract scholarly praise, but I hoped that reviewers would at least see it as a new and innovative way of reformulating the project's research in order to reshape the public's understanding of King's life and ideas. I was aware, however, that it would attract some criticism from those who suspected that the King family had authorized the book only to make money. In addition, I expected that the provocative title would provide an invitation to critics. I had rejected the idea of using a safer, blander title such as *An Anthology of the Autobiographical Writings and Statements of Martin Luther King Jr.* Because I was using King's papers as sources, I believed that my edition would be closer to King's intentions than was Alex Haley's *Autobiography of Malcolm X,* which was extensively edited by Haley and others with little input from the "author," who died before the book was published.

By the time I finished editing King's autobiographical narrative late in the summer of 1998, questions about how it would be received had given way to thankfulness that it was done. Although I hoped that Warner Books would help promote interest, the publisher seemed more intent on getting it into bookstores by December. Having become used to the University of California Press's more extended publication process, I was amazed that a book could be in print a few months after the manuscript was completed.

Warner Books arranged for *Time* magazine, a Time Warner publication, to prepare an advance review of *The Autobiography*, but this review would be the most negative that the book would receive (so much for corporate synergy). The reviewer dismissed the book as "a cut-and-paste job," authorized by "his family." Although I had prepared myself for negative coverage, I was still disturbed that the book was criticized for failing to discuss King's relationship with the Kennedys, because I had included everything King had said, publicly or privately, about them.

Subsequent reviews were more positive. The *New York Times* reviewer called the book a "mistitled but otherwise worthy compilation" that was "a valuable reminder that on those subjects and occasions when he could not have borrowed his words, King was consistently eloquent and polished, a master of word and effect, possessed of a voice that was unmistakable and true." A piece in *The New Yorker* praised me for creating "an exceptionally successful posthumous autobiography" but observed that "while his selection deserves credit, King's own shining direct language makes the impression."

During the next few years, I also completed work on the two anthologies I had promised for Warner Books. With Pete Holloran, who had helped me begin the King Papers Project, I co-edited *Knock at Midnight: Inspiration from the Great Sermons of Reverend Martin Luther King Jr.* With help from Mrs. King, we assembled introductions to the sermons from former King colleagues Wyatt T. Walker, C. T. Vivian, and Vincent Harding, as well as luminaries such as Billy Graham and Archbishop Desmond Tutu. With Kris Sheppard, former staffer at the Emory office, I co-edited *A Call to Conscience: The Landmark Speeches of Dr. Martin Luther King Jr.* with introductions by Rosa Parks, Congressman John Lewis, Senator Edward M. Kennedy, Ambassador Andrew Young, His Holiness the Dalai Lama, and others.

The books did not meet the publisher's expectations, although my prediction of steady sales over time proved to be true. *The Autobiography* would be published in more than a dozen languages, and the audio version of it would win the 2000 Grammy Award for Best Spoken-Word Album, with LeVar Burton reading King's words. I was proud that I had enabled King posthumously to tell his own life story and pleased that the three new anthologies made King's ideas more widely available throughout the world.

Chapter 17

A Dream Deferred

*I*n March 1998, while completing the manuscript for my edition of *The Autobiography of Martin Luther King Jr.*, I obtained the love letters Martin wrote to Coretta Scott in Boston during the summer of 1952. Having heard Louise Cook's gossip about the box of letters under Mrs. King's bed, I was pleasantly surprised to learn that they existed. When Dexter unexpectedly sent copies of them to me, I wondered whether he or his mother had made the decision to make them available for *The Autobiography*. Had she finally opened this window into her private life or had Dexter's desire for a successful publishing venture with Time Warner prompted him to persuade his mother? I wanted to believe that she wished to make public the letters, which provided important insights into her relationship with Martin. After swiftly examining their contents, I realized that they were unlike any other documents I had seen in Martin's papers. Although Coretta's side of the correspondence was missing, the letters exposed intimate emotions that lovers share only with one another. I saw that Martin fell quickly and deeply in love with Coretta after their first meeting in late January 1952, during his first year of graduate studies at Boston University's School of Theology and her first year at the New England Conservatory of Music. I also saw that Martin confided his anticapitalist sentiments more forthrightly in the letters than in any of his other writings and public statements. I understood immediately why Coretta had kept them from public view for almost half a century.

My thoughts returned to the period a year earlier when my colleagues and I had spent weeks in her basement exploring the revealing documents there. On certain days when our paths crossed, Mrs. King seemed eager to talk about her years with Martin. Now that she was approaching her seventieth birthday, she had perhaps reached a stage in her life when secrets were easier to disclose or when seemingly forgotten events were unexpectedly remembered.

Although Martin had acknowledged in the "Autobiography of Religious Development" that his Depression-era experience of seeing "numerous people standing in bread lines" had produced "anti-capitalistic feelings," his published writings were more circumspect. In his 1958 memoir, *Stride toward Freedom: The Montgomery Story*, King acknowledged that he "carefully scrutinized" *Das Kapital* and *The Communist Manifesto* during his Crozer years but also assured readers that he rejected communism's "materialistic interpretation of history" and its "ethical relativism." His letters to Coretta, however, were written with the confidence that they would remain private. Before he was a public figure, he explained to her his political and economic views with a remarkable frankness amid the anticommunist hysteria of the Cold War. Public revelation of these early views would certainly have seriously damaged his standing as a civil rights leader. Once Martin and Coretta had erected the shields required for their future roles as the nation's most prominent African American couple, she had decided those views should remain private.

The letters also revealed aspects of Martin's romantic relationship with Coretta that were only hinted at in her memoir. Coretta's account reveals Martin's eagerness to find a wife who met his exacting standards while also being able to be the supportive wife of a Baptist minister. The letters showed that their compatible political views strengthened their mutual attraction and enabled them to bridge significant differences in their backgrounds. Even though Coretta was not a Baptist, Martin pursued her, and Coretta overcame her reluctance to marry a minister because she shared Martin's strong commitment to peace and social justice. He struggled to reconcile her ambition to become a professional singer with his own—and his parents'—expectations that she would be a conventional minister's wife. The conflicts that threatened their relationship were eventually resolved, but the letters shed light on the inner feelings of Coretta and Martin as they continued their romance despite the opposition of Martin's father.

At the time they met in Boston, Coretta Scott was more of an activist than Martin. Two years older than her future husband, she had lived through the harsh racism and class inequities that her working-class family suffered in rural Alabama. At Lincoln Normal School in Marion, Alabama, she had been exposed to pacifist and leftist ideas and met visiting black Gandhian activist Bayard Rustin, who later became Martin's advisor. One of only three black students in her class at Ohio's Antioch College, she "took to heart" the admonition of Antioch's first president, nineteenth-century abolitionist reformer Horace Mann: "Be ashamed to die until you have won some victory for humanity." When her application to teach music at a local public school was turned down on racial grounds, the experience left her "more motivated than before," and she became active in the campus branch of the NAACP as well as a "Civil Liberties Committee."

At Antioch, Coretta met black leftist singer-actor Paul Robeson, who encouraged her to continue her voice studies after they both performed on campus. Robeson was then a Progressive Party activist rallying opposition to the Cold War. A fetching photograph in the second volume of *The Papers* shows Coretta as a student delegate at the 1948 Progressive Party convention in Philadelphia carrying a "Wallace/Taylor" banner.

In contrast, Martin grew up in relative comfort, shielded by his protective father from the harsh realities of the Jim Crow system. His social and political awareness increased as he reached his teenage years and ventured into the white-dominated world outside his Auburn Avenue neighborhood. During his late teens he had witnessed "economic injustice firsthand" after accepting a summer job—against his father's wishes—at an Atlanta factory. Martin's political activism was negligible, perhaps because he entered Morehouse at fifteen and attended a small seminary rather than a college like Antioch, where student activism was the norm. Nonetheless, Martin's experiences at Crozer shaped his subsequent attitudes just as surely as did Coretta's at Antioch. For example, his 1950 encounter with a gun-wielding New Jersey tavern owner would surely have pushed him toward a greater readiness to participate in civil rights activism, although at the time he refrained from pursuing a legal case over the incident.

When Martin met Coretta, he was feeling increasing pressure from his parents to transition from going out with women who attracted his interest to choosing a suitable wife. Daddy King knew that his son had no difficulty finding women to date. Martin informed his mother, "the girls are running me down" after J. Pius Barbour, a family friend who pastored a church in Chester, Pennsylvania, told his congregation that the young student at nearby Crozer came from a rich family. W. T. Handy, his friend at the time, later told me that Martin "wasn't running after the girls; the girls were running after him." The elder King knew that his son's advanced degrees would mean little in terms of finding a pastorate if he remained unmarried, given that most congregations would associate his bachelor state with a lack of maturity and stability. Martin could not have missed the import of a teasing letter from his mother: "Remember M. L., we are expecting great things from you." Only he, she added, could "restrain our expectations from bearing fruit."

Just after Martin arrived at Boston University, Daddy King suggested that his son call Jewelle Taylor, a Radcliffe freshman who was also the daughter of a fellow Baptist minister. Their dates, she later told me, consisted mainly of going to a Boston-area church where he was preaching. Taylor soon advised the seminarian that she was not pleased: "If you want to keep dating me, we're going to have to do something like go to a movie or something. This is not my idea of fun."

The two students did go to a few movies together, but the prospect of marriage to a minister did not appeal to Jewelle. "I decided my mother had sacrificed a lot of herself for my father and being the perfect wife and opening up her home all the time," she recalled. "I didn't want to do that. I wanted to have a life of my own, plus I didn't want to live in the South. And he made it very clear to me very early on that he wanted to go back South, and he had these ideas of changing the South; he didn't know how, but he had some very strong ideas." Taylor later became a professor at the UC Berkeley, and the wife of one of my Stanford colleagues.

As Martin's relationship with Taylor was ending, he called Coretta at the suggestion of their mutual friend, Mary Powell, who, like Coretta, was a student at the New England Conservatory of Music. Coretta's description of the initial phone call conveyed the eagerness of Martin's courtship: "He quickly said, 'a mutual friend of ours told me about you and gave me your telephone number. She said some very wonderful things about you and I'd like very much to meet you and talk to you.'" Coretta remembered that Martin began "talking, very easily and smoothly. I had never heard such talk in all my life. He said, 'You know every Napoleon has his Waterloo. I'm like Napoleon. I'm at my Waterloo, and I'm on my knees.'"

On their first date at Sharaf's restaurant, Coretta recalled quickly overcoming her initial misgivings about the height of her suitor. After hearing him talk, her five-foot, seven-inch date "grew in stature." He exhibited "very masculine self-possession, he seemed to know exactly where he was going and how he was going to get there." Martin was similarly impressed that Coretta knew "about things other than music." According to Coretta's account, "he quickly laid his cards on the table," observing that the "qualities of character, intelligence, personality, and beauty" comprised "everything I have ever wanted in a wife." Coretta would later recall that Martin talked of marriage "much of the time from that very first day" of their courtship. Their intellectual and political compatibility helped deepen their relationship. Coretta recalled that Martin would say, "I don't want a wife I can't communicate with." Some of their talks were "quite serious," touching on philosophical matters. Martin had, of course, read the writings of Karl Marx, who, he said, had convinced him that neither Marxism nor traditional capitalism held the whole truth, but he told Coretta that each contained partial truths. "I could never be a Communist," he said. "My father is a thoroughgoing capitalist, but I could not be that either. I think a society based on making all the money you can and ignoring people's needs is wrong. I don't want to *own* a lot of things."

Martin made clear that he expected Coretta's values would have to be compatible with her role as the wife of a minister in a Southern black community. She would have to share his sense of dedication to the needs of his congregation. He asked whether she could adjust to "Aunt Jane"—"Martin meant the good but uneducated parishioner who does not know the differences between 'you does' and 'you don't.'" Coretta assured him that she had grown up among women like "Aunt Jane" and "would never forget my origins to look down upon the kind of people who were my own." She became confident that she and Martin did not have "serious differences of opinion about racial matters or economics."

While Coretta continued to pass Martin's suitability tests, her desire to have a career of her own caused her to retreat from his effusive talk of marriage. "I was not a young girl," she later explained. "I had thought myself in love before, but things did not work out, and I had resolved not to become emotionally entangled again until I was absolutely certain." She was also uninterested in dating ministers "who went around wearing a look of sanctity that they put on like their black suits." Having drifted away from her childhood roots in the African Methodist Episcopal Zion Church, she was considering becoming a Quaker or a Unitarian and rejected the Baptist doctrine that immersion was necessary. Martin reassured her—"You would not have to be immersed. There is no saving efficacy in water." Nonetheless, she recognized that his attitudes about the role of a wife would never coincide with her own.

> On the one hand, he believed that women are just as intelligent and capable as men and that they should hold positions of authority and influence. But when it came to his own situation, he thought in terms of his wife being a homemaker and a mother for his children. He was very definite that he would expect whoever he married to be home waiting for him.

Coretta's doubts about Martin also revolved around his continued close ties to his family and their Atlanta social network. She learned from Mary Powell that, although Martin was seriously seeking a wife, "he was in an ambivalent position" because he had already proposed marriage to the daughter of a longtime family

friend in Atlanta. Martin explained that the engagement was not a formal arrangement but merely an assumption on the part of the families: "My father wants me to
marry, and he will help me to take care of my wife as long as I'm in School. But I am
going to make my own decisions. I will choose my own wife."

Even as their romance blossomed during the spring of 1952, Coretta remained
unsure whether she could adjust to being a minister's wife even if she could convince herself that it was another way to fulfill her commitment to service. "I knew
this was the most important decision of my life, that it had to be the right one," she
later wrote. "The process of careful thought and prayerful meditation went on for
about two or three months." She also continued to worry about Daddy King's influence over his son. "I wondered whether, if his father said no, Martin would give in
to him." Gaining the approval of her sister Edythe, who visited Boston during the
summer, made her more willing to consider forgoing her career plans in order to
marry. Yet, despite her realization that she was twenty-four years old at a time when
most American women were married by the age of twenty, she was not yet convinced that she should marry, until she had a dream: "In my dream Martin's father,
whom I had never met was there, and the girl in Atlanta was also there. Martin's
father was smiling at me, and somehow I knew he approved of me. I woke up with
a great feeling of relief."

Marriage plans were threatened, however, when Martin asked Coretta to visit
him after he returned to Atlanta in July to serve as pastor-in-charge of Ebenezer
during his father's summer vacation. Coretta realized that she would pass through
Atlanta on her own trip back home to Alabama but was still uncertain whether she
was sufficiently committed to Martin to endure the critical scrutiny of his parents.
She declined his invitation "to test him, to see if he really wanted me or not." In her
memoir, Coretta recounts that Martin became "very upset. He said, 'If you don't
want to come—just forget everything. Forget it. Forget the whole thing.'"

The letters revealed new details about this crucial turning point in their relationship. They suggest that Coretta's memoir of her life with Martin, written more than
sixteen years after these events, did not fully convey the emotional force of Martin's
ultimatum. Moreover, the letters show that Martin was willing to use the threat of
breaking up with Coretta to emphasize the importance he placed on having a wife
suited to be both a minister's wife and the daughter-in-law of his religiously conservative parents. The letters also demonstrate how the political views they held in
common helped to heal their wounds resulting from this conflict.

A letter Martin sent to Coretta on July 14 indicates a dramatic chilling of the
relationship after Coretta apparently suggested during a phone call that Martin

also visit her parents. Coolly addressing his letter "Dear Miss Scott," Martin asserts that he is still "angry" about Coretta's reluctance to meet his parents. Describing her invitation as an "insult," he blames her friends for advising her to insist they visit one another's parents. "Either you are under the influence of some frustrated women and men or you just don't give a damn."

After Coretta reacted to his outburst with her own letter, Martin wrote again on July 18. Returning to the "Dearest" salutation, he reports, "Fortunately, I am in a better mood today. Your letter was sweet and refreshing to my heart, which had well-nigh grown cold toward you." Martin chose to soften the impact of their disagreement by digressing to mention the copy of Edward Bellamy's utopian socialist novel *Looking Backward* that Coretta had sent him the previous April to solicit his reaction to Bellamy's predictions, which included the transformation of the United States into a socialist society. "In some ways it is rather encouraging to see how our social order has changed since Bellamy's time," she added in an inscription to Martin. "There's still hope for the future...Lest we become too impatient."

Coretta's assumption that Martin would be interested in Bellamy's utopian socialist novel reflected the unconventional political leanings of the two during a period when accusations of communist sympathies damaged many careers. Few anticommunist zealots would have distinguished between communists and socialists. Just a year earlier, the anticommunist campaign of Wisconsin senator Joseph McCarthy had intensified after Ethel and Julius Rosenberg were convicted and sentenced to death for their alleged roles in helping Los Alamos scientist David Greenglass transfer scientific secrets to the Soviet Union, thereby speeding its development of atomic weapons. (My father had assured me that this happened before he began his security job at the Los Alamos lab.)

Mentioning Coretta's gift did not indicate that he had healed his bruised feelings over parental visits, but in his letter Martin assures Coretta that the "solid foundation" of their love can survive "the stormy winds of anger." After a "poetical and romantic flight" on the power of love—"the most inexplicable and yet the most beautiful force in life"—he continues:

> Darling I miss you so much. In fact much to[o] much for my own good. I never realized that you were such an intimate part of my life. My life without you is like a year without a spring time which comes to give illumination and heat to the atmosphere which was been saturated by the dark cold breeze of winter.

Martin follows this conciliatory gesture with an extended affirmation that Bellamy's socialist views were "in line with my basic ideas." Although Martin admits not having previously read *Looking Backward*, he had already worked out his views on communism in writings and sermons, including one titled "Christianity and Communism" that he would deliver the following month at Ebenezer. He would preach several later versions of this sermon, but Martin's letter addressed the topic with a frankness he would never replicate in public:

> I imagine you already know that I am much more socialistic in my economic theory than capitalistic. And yet I am not so opposed to capitalism that I have failed to see its relative merits. It started out with a noble and high motive, viz, to block the trade monopolies of nobles, but like most human systems it [fell] victim to the very thing it was revolting against. So today capitalism has outlived its usefulness. It has brought about a system that takes necessities from the masses to give luxuries to the classes.

He applauded Bellamy for emphasizing "that the change would be evolutionary rather than revolutionary." "This, it seems to me, is the most sane and ethical way for social change to take place. This, it will be remembered, is one of the points at which socialism differs from communism, the former emphasizing evolution and the latter revolution. Communist[s] would insist that the means justify the end." Martin expresses agreement with Bellamy's prediction of the ultimate demise of capitalism, but chides him for failing to recognize its staying durability.

> I don't think he gave capitalism long enough time to die. It is probably true that capitalism is on its death bed, but social systems have a way of developing a long and powerful death bed breathing capacity. Remember it took feudalism more than 500 years to pass out from its death bed. Capitalism will be in America quite a few more years my dear.

The concluding passage of Martin's political digression begins with a sentence that would surely have gravely damaged his reputation as a black leader:

> I would certainly welcome the day to come when there will be a nationalization of industry. Let us continue to hope, work, and pray that in the future we will live to see a warless world, a better distribution of wealth,

and a brotherhood that transcends race or color. This is the gospel that I will preach to the world. At this point I must thank you a million times for introducing me to such a stimulating book. You are sweet and thoughtful indeed.

After this heady discussion of communism and socialism, Martin might well have concluded on a positive note that emphasized the political values they shared, but his festering resentments were too close to the surface to suppress. "It hurt me very much to know that you believe that I would invite you to Atlanta and then mistreat you, especially as nice as I've been to you in the past. Oh well I guess all of us have a little of the unappreciative attitude in us." After requesting that Coretta confirm her arrival, Martin delivers one more jab: "Of course if you don't come I will know that you have no confidence in me and I will proceed to think out our courtship in those lines. I hope we won't have to break up about this trip." He ends with a reminder "that daddy still loves you."

By the time of Martin's next letter on July 29, they had resolved the crisis in their relationship. He writes that he was "overjoyed to know that you are coming to Atlanta. I'm sure that you will not regret a minute of the visit." He concluded warmly—"your darling Martin." Despite Martin's upbeat tone, Coretta's assessment of her subsequent visit with the Kings on August 9 was that it "was not an unqualified success." She found Martin's mother, Alberta Williams King, "a little hard to know, at first" and described her greeting as "polite but casual." Daddy King was "gentle and courteous" but also "casual"—a description that was more positive than the senior King would suggest: "I wanted Martin to marry another girl, and I wanted him to get married soon. There were so many girls who liked him. They were pushing him. I was afraid he would get tied up with one we did not like."

When Coretta observed Martin's sermon at Ebenezer the next day on "The Challenge of Communism to Christianity," she probably noticed the similarities between it and Martin's earlier description of his political views. She would describe the homily in her memoir only vaguely as "interesting and moving." After her departure to her parents' home in Alabama, Martin sent an upbeat letter: "I could hardly adjust myself to your leaving, but somehow these things must be faced. I am very glad to know that you had an enjoyable stay even if it was very short." He related that his parents "were very impressed" and that his father "thinks you are darling"—although he added that his father and his sister Christine "take to people very slow."

Martin also reported that he would not be visiting the Scott family, insisting that a doctor had confined him to bed with a virus infection: "The doctor contends that I have been going so much that I have no resistance at all." He closed, "Martin still loves Coco, so what else is there to be desired." After recovering from his illness, he wrote an even more comforting note to "Dearest" in response to "a sweet letter" from Coretta, who was now at her parents' home. "Darling you are so inspirational," he added. "A word from you comes as spiritual food to a soul that is well-nigh starved." King reiterated his strong feelings toward Coretta: "When lonesome moments come just remember that I am at your side every day in the week, every hour in the day, every minute in the hour, and every second in the moment." Suggesting that Coretta join him in driving back to Boston together in September, he mentioned the possibility of her staying at the King home but added that, because his parents would be away at the time, "I don't think it will be too appropriate." Martin closed with, "Your Lover 'M. L.'"

Coretta's visit by no means allayed the concerns of Daddy King. A trip to New York to attend a meeting of the Morehouse Board of Trustees gave him and Alberta an opportunity to "drop in" on their son, who was then sharing an apartment with fellow Morehouse alum Philip Lenud. After the Kings arrived, Daddy King wrote in his memoirs that he noticed the neatness of the apartment—"I wasn't so sure that these two fellows were responsible for the touches of housework so evident throughout the place." He also observed that Martin "was so much in love, stars were just glittering in his eyes." Although he conceded that Coretta "seemed extremely level-headed and serious," after Coretta stopped by to greet him, his doubts resurfaced—"as I watched them make eyes at each other across the room, they seemed even younger and less mature than I knew they were." When he found a brief opportunity to talk privately with Coretta, he indicated that he was still concerned about her goal of a professional career as a singer—"Perhaps, I suggested, she'd find much more in common with someone from her own field of interest, music." He hinted that she and Martin were "experiencing a little infatuation that probably wouldn't last out the school term."

After this bit of fencing failed to ruffle Coretta, Daddy King bluntly asked: "Do you take my son seriously, Coretta?" Coretta responded, "No," thinking, she recalled, that he was referring to something Martin had said. Daddy King later recounted what followed:

I felt myself turn warm under the collar. I was too angry to say anything right away, but as M. L. rejoined us, I found myself speaking very rapidly to Coretta. I told her I was glad she had no serious intentions as far as M. L. was concerned. Well, naturally, upon hearing this, M. L.'s jaw dropped almost to his belt buckle.

Daddy King then mentioned that his son had "gone out with the daughters of some fine, solid Atlanta families, folks we've known for many years, people we respect, and whose feelings we'd never trample on. I'm talking, Coretta, about people who have much to share and much to offer." At this point, as Daddy King recalled, Coretta lashed out: "Anger flashed briefly through her eyes, but I could also see that Coretta Scott was determined not to lose control of herself. Her voice was very full and confident when she spoke. 'I have something to offer, Reverend King.'"

Coretta recalled that Martin was silent during the confrontation. "He just sat there grinning like an embarrassed schoolboy. He did not want to hurt his father by going against him." Still uncertain about Coretta's suitability as a minister's wife, Daddy King realized "that she wasn't a giggly little girl with no substance or sense or spirit." He also knew that his son's mind "was already made up." Coretta recalled that Martin told his mother, "Coretta is going to be my wife," while Daddy King remembered his son telling him, "I must marry Coretta....I know you don't really approve, but this is what I have to do." After the visit, Daddy King grudgingly accepted "that it was real between them, that no amount of discouragement was going to mean anything at all. And so I reluctantly agreed that perhaps they should marry, before anything happened that would force them to rush into a wedding that would bring a lot of embarrassed whispering at the ceremony."

Seven months later, Daddy King conducted the marriage ceremony at the Scott family home. Coretta had become resigned to her decision to give up her career ambitions to become a minister's wife—"Whatever he does, I will be involved in it." But she did decide to wear "a pastel waltz-length gown" rather than a traditional white gown, and she convinced Daddy King to omit "the bride's promise to obey." She saw Daddy King's acquiescence as an indication that "he had learned that, on some issues, the thinking of young people was different from his."

After becoming the wife of the Rev. Martin Luther King Jr., Coretta adjusted to her new role while her husband served as pastor of Dexter Avenue Baptist Church in Montgomery. She played the supportive housewife as her husband's career evolved from being pastor of a small church to becoming the most influential black clergyman of his generation. After Rosa Parks unexpectedly transformed him into a civil rights leader, Coretta quietly supported him. She rejected the entreaties of Daddy King and her own father to leave Montgomery after the 1956 bombing of the parsonage where she was staying with her newborn daughter Yolanda.

During the early 1960s, Coretta was affiliated with Women's Strike for Peace and expressed her opposition to the Vietnam War several years before her husband took a public antiwar stance. Like Martin, she viewed the civil rights struggle in the United States in the broader context of anticolonial movements in Africa and Asia. Both attended the 1957 independence ceremony of Ghana, Africa's first black-ruled nation, and both toured India in 1959 as guests of the Indian government. At the March on Washington, she hoped in vain to be at his side—"I felt that the involvement in the Movement of some of the wives had been so extensive that they should have been granted the privilege of marching with their husbands and of completely sharing this experience together, as they had shared the dangers and the hardships."

After her fourth and youngest child was born in 1963, she gradually expanded her public role. When Martin was jailed in the Selma voting rights protests, she joined the campaign, spoke at a mass meeting, and met with Malcolm X, who was gaining his first experience in the Southern struggle just a few weeks before his death. She joined the climactic march to Montgomery in March 1965. Early the following year, she went to Chicago to join Martin's campaign against Northern de facto segregation, and later in the year their children joined them in the slum apartment Martin had rented. When Martin initially found it difficult to speak publicly against the Vietnam War, he encouraged Coretta to become active in the peace movement, and by 1967 both were involved in the escalating antiwar protests. On March 28, 1968, Coretta participated in an antiwar event in Washington sponsored by the Women's International League for Peace and Freedom. Six days later Martin was assassinated in Memphis, and, four days afterward, Coretta flew to Memphis to take part in a march of striking sanitation workers that Martin had intended to lead. She explained in her memoir: "In the same way that I had given him all the support I could during his lifetime, I was even more determined to do so now that he was no longer with us. Because his task was not finished, I felt that I must rededicate myself to the completion of his work."

On Martin's birthday in 1969, Coretta founded the Martin Luther King Jr. Center in Atlanta to serve as "a living memorial" to Martin, and she moved from the supportive role that she had accepted during Martin's lifetime to a prominent role as chief executive officer of an organization that soon surpassed the declining influence of Martin's Southern Christian Leadership Conference. Although many

Americans saw Coretta as well as her husband in their limited roles as civil rights advocates, I came to see both as visionary leaders. During the 1970s and early 1980s, she played a major role in lobbying Congress to create the National King Holiday. By 1985, when she, as executrix of Martin's estate, asked me to edit and publish his papers, Coretta had indeed proven that she had "something to offer."

Chapter 18

Transitions

*B*y the late 1990s Dexter King had become convinced that James Earl Ray—who had been convicted of assassinating his father—was framed as part of a complex conspiracy that included a Memphis policeman and high government officials. He even visited Ray in jail on March 27, 1997, and stated publicly that he believed Ray was innocent. In November 1999, I went to Memphis to testify at the civil trial of Lloyd Jowers, the restaurant owner Dexter believed conspired to kill his father. The King family had filed a "wrongful death" lawsuit against Jowers asking only for token monetary damages of $100. The family wanted to solicit sworn testimony from dozens of witnesses to refute the official explanation of King's death. William Pepper, who had been James Earl Ray's attorney before Ray's death in prison in 1998, now represented the plaintiff, Coretta Scott King. I had met with Pepper and Dexter the previous June to discuss their claim that Memphis police officer Earl Clark fired the fatal shots as part of a larger conspiracy. I was not convinced but agreed that the official version of the assassination was incomplete. Having already been questioned on the *Charlie Rose Show* and elsewhere about the assassination controversy and knowing how immersed Dexter was in it, I wanted to be better informed on the subject.

I accepted Pepper's invitation to read the materials he was assembling for the trial. When he asked me to enter into evidence the transcript of a *Memphis Commercial Appeal* reporter's interview with a military intelligence officer who witnessed the assassination, I pointed out that I had met neither the reporter nor the officer. He assured me that the judge and the pliant defense attorney were unlikely to object to placing the hearsay evidence into the trial record. I agreed to testify, mostly as an excuse to attend the hearings. I also welcomed the chance to talk with Dexter about the unsettled future of the King Papers Project.

On November 23, the day before I was scheduled to testify, Dexter and I met for lunch at the Peabody Hotel. He seemed exhausted by the first week of the trial. When I asked him how it was going, he expressed disappointment about the lack of press coverage. Some reporters attended Mrs. King's testimony on the opening day, but no major national periodicals had shown interest. As we talked, I could see that the absence of news media reinforced his suspicion about a conspiracy to suppress the truth. He also seemed to accept the possibility that he would not succeed in swaying public opinion regarding the assassination.

"My family has done everything we can to bring out the facts," he explained. He felt hurt by the reports that the family would benefit from the trial, because of their reported financial involvement in a film about the assassination proposed by Oliver Stone. I sympathized with his dismay. He was clearly paying a price for his controversial stand, but I was also troubled that he had moved so quickly from doubts about whether Ray had acted alone to certainty that he was innocent. Embracing the man convicted of killing his father had hardly been an act designed to win public popular support. Even if there had been a conspiracy, I thought it was unlikely that Ray was simply a "patsy" as Dexter believed.

"We've gotten what we wanted," he said with a tone of resignation. "We wanted to have twelve independent jurors hear the information and determine for themselves."

"So you'll accept the outcome?" I asked.

"Whatever decision they come up with after hearing the information, we can live with that. That would help to bring about closure and resolution."

I testified on the afternoon of November 24, 1999. Pepper had already entered into evidence the Memphis reporter's published articles about an army military intelligence group that "shadowed" King's activities in Memphis. The affidavit that Pepper had given me concerned the reporter's interview with two members of a covert Special Forces detachment said to have been connected to this intelligence operation. At the time of King's assassination, according to the affidavit, two Green Berets were stationed at a fire station across from the Lorraine Hotel, the site of King's assassination. Although I had no way of verifying whether the reporter had actually conducted the interviews, some details in the affidavit seemed credible, given the widespread antipathy toward King during his last years. With President Johnson's approval, FBI director J. Edgar Hoover had launched a secret campaign to prevent King and other potential black "messiahs" from uniting to spark a black revolution. According to the affidavit, one of the Green Berets recalled being assigned to Los Angeles in February 1968 when Stokely Carmichael, Maulana Karenga, and other black militant leaders had gathered for a "Free Huey Newton" rally. The FBI's surveillance of me—surely a negligible threat to national security—made it seem likely that military intelligence personnel would be deployed in cities where military force might be used to suppress black rebellions.

The reporter's affidavit did not indicate that the Green Berets participated in King's assassination. Instead, it suggested that they were prepared to kill King and other black leaders "should the situation go in the toilet, and we had a riot on our hands." Under questioning from Pepper, I quoted a key section of the affidavit:

> Doctor King was the leader of a movement to destroy American government and stop the war. We were shown CR, close range photos, of King and Young. Don't know anyone worry about killing those sacks of shit. One buddy on Team 1 remember bragged about him, had him in center mass, this is a sniper term meaning cross hairs and center of chest.

I was not surprised that the mainstream press ignored my testimony. The purported interview stuck in my mind, however. Even if military intelligence personnel were not involved in King's assassination, I found it credible that some were assigned to the nation's volatile urban areas and likely harbored deeply hostile feelings toward him. It reinforced my suspicion that King had come close to the essential truth of his own demise when he commented about President Kennedy's assassination: "While the question 'Who killed President Kennedy?' is important, the question 'What killed him?' is more important. Our late President was assassinated by a morally inclement climate." It is likely that James Earl Ray fired the fatal shot, but everything I knew about the 1960s persuaded me that King had many enemies who were untroubled by his death.

The trial jury took one hour to decide the case in favor of the King family, but the verdict did little to sway public opinion. A *New York Times* account scoffed at "the passivity of the defense, the prevalence of second-hand and third-hand accounts and the propensity of the judge and jurors to apparently nod off during testimony." Dexter and other members of the King family saw the verdict as vindication. "We know what happened," he was quoted as saying. "This is the period at the end of the sentence. So please, after today, we don't want questions like 'Do you believe James Earl Ray killed your father?' I've been hearing that all my life. No, I don't, and this is the end of it."

With the trial over, I hoped that Dexter could focus his attention on the future of the King Papers Project. With the closing of the Emory office and the shift of the project's federal funding from the King Center to Stanford, the project was now a Stanford operation. Its accomplishments had been considerable. Since the publication of the first volume of *The Papers of Martin Luther King, Jr.* in 1992, we had published two additional volumes and completed work on a third. In addition, I had edited, with assistance from some project researchers and former staff members, *The Autobiography of Martin Luther King Jr.*, co-edited *Knock at Midnight*, and nearly completed the manuscript for *A Call to Conscience*. We had also photocopied nearly all of the King Papers at the King Center's archive as well as the documents that had been in Mrs. King's home. We had made hundreds of cassette copies of King's speeches and sermons. The Papers Project had greatly expanded access to King's ideas through its popular website, Liberation Curriculum for schools, King Holiday celebrations, and other public programs, which included dramatic readings based on *Passages of Martin Luther King*. Among those we brought to the Stanford campus during this period were numerous former King colleagues—including Dorothy Cotton, Jesse Jackson, Vincent Harding, C. T. Vivian, and Fred Shuttlesworth—as well as SNCC veterans Bob Moses, James Forman, Connie Curry, Elizabeth Martinez, and Wazir Peacock, who joined with several former members of the SNCC Freedom Singers for a stirring reunion concert. We often invited former SCLC activist Jimmy Collier to our events as well. Another frequent visitor was Herbert Aptheker, the former Communist and pioneering historian who had worked closely with W. E. B. Du Bois while assembling his multivolume *History of the Negro People in the United States*.

Although I was proud that the King Project had done so much despite declining federal funding, I also realized that many of my Stanford co-workers had departed, some of them after rebelling against my tendency to expect too much from them while failing to express sufficient appreciation for their contributions. I knew that the Papers Project could not go on as before. Many staff members were youthful college graduates who had been drawn to the project because of their idealism, a belief that they could contribute to the worthy goal of disseminating King's ideas, but few could sustain their enthusiasm for long. My frequent travels and many commitments—I had by then also contracted to write an African American history textbook—caused me to ignore the fatigue and waning morale of some of those I had recruited, until staff members demanded my attention. After one particularly heated confrontation at a staff retreat, I realized the extent of discontent. I brought in a consultant who recommended a reorganization that created middle levels of responsibility, with appropriate titles and increased pay. I wasn't certain whether the salary increases could be sustained, but the changes were necessary.

Raising the funds needed for the King Papers Project remained a central concern. The foundations and individual donors that had supported us in the past would not commit to funding all fourteen projected volumes of our edition of *The Papers*. Stanford paid for student researchers and some staff, but substantial external support was essential. Since becoming the project's director, I believed that a cooperative effort by the King Center and Stanford would generate ample contributions, but the two institutions had never worked together.

During my Memphis meeting with Dexter, I reiterated my view that the King Center, the King Estate, and the King Papers Project would all benefit from a fundraising campaign that would transform the Papers Project into a permanent, endowed research institute. I told Dexter that Stanford board member and Harvard Law School professor Charles Ogletree supported my idea that the project should seek large endowment contributions from Silicon Valley companies. I explained to him that an institute such as I proposed would have more resources to undertake ambitious public education efforts. Dexter seemed interested in the idea, but I could see that he was distracted, perhaps still thinking about the trial. I promised that I would write to him about my plans after I returned to Stanford.

There were many questions that needed to be resolved. Would the proposed institute be independent of the King Center? Dexter and Phil expected me to collaborate with them on future publishing arrangements, such as the Time Warner deal. How would the project be compensated for the use of its research resources and research staff? If the King Estate made deals to disseminate King's ideas through popular paperback editions and online sales, would the King Papers Project be left with producing only costly hardcover print volumes intended mainly for libraries and scholars? I knew that these questions could not be answered readily. I was approaching sixty and since becoming King's editor, I had published more books of King's writings than King himself had written during his lifetime, but I had only begun to offer my own interpretation of his ideas and had written no books of my own. I wondered whether the position of being King's posthumous editor had devolved from a unique opportunity into a burden. Did I really want to spend the rest of my life producing the remaining volumes of *The Papers*?

In contrast to the nine-month commitment of most faculty members, my decade and a half of work as director of the King Papers Project extended over all twelve months of the year. Indeed, summers were often the most intense period of work, due to the presence of full-time interns and the absence of faculty meetings. I had not had a sabbatical leave since 1979. There were compensations, of course. I was a tenured professor on a beautiful campus and owned a comfortable home in quiet, verdant Palo Alto. After four years of dorm living we moved back to our home in 1995. Our children were now self-supporting adults. Temie married and had two more children—Anthony in 1998 and Helena in 1999—and pursued a graduate degree in social work. Malcolm, a lawyer, married Barbara Ifejika, a former Stanford volleyball star and volunteer researcher at the Papers Project, in 2002. Susan and I could now vacation in interesting places: In 1997 we returned to Paris for the first time since our voluntary exile three decades earlier and indulged ourselves by staying in a comfortable old apartment on Île Saint-Louis. (We discovered that the cheap hotel-brothel where we stayed three decades earlier had been torn down.) The increasing number of speaking invitations I received also allowed me to take breaks from the Papers Project.

When I wrote to Dexter following our lunch meeting in Memphis late in 1999, I urged him to approve the creation of a permanent King research institute at Stanford and proposed launching it with an international conference in 2001 on "Where Does the World Go from Here? An Inquiry Inspired by the Life and Ideas of Martin Luther King Jr." I suggested an ambitious plan to bring together "the world's leading theorists and exponents of King-Gandhian ideals in order to illuminate the continued relevance of King's ideas in the twenty-first century." I suggested naming Nelson Mandela and Mrs. King as honorary co-chairs. I urged Dexter to respond promptly to my proposal in order to take advantage of the "uniquely favorable" economic climate of the late 1990s—"Silicon Valley's economic boom will not last forever," I warned. I never received a formal response to my letter, but Dexter agreed to come to Stanford for an all-day meeting.

By the time we met on May 10, 2000, the "dot com bubble" had burst. Stanford president Gerhard Casper, who had been supportive of the project, had announced that he was resigning, and Provost Condoleezza Rice, who had also been helpful, had departed to join George W. Bush's presidential campaign. It was Dexter's first visit to Stanford. He was accompanied by his new chief aide, Tricia Harris, who was in her twenties. We talked again about possibilities for online distribution of all recorded King speeches and sermons. He expressed some support for the idea of a permanent King research institute at Stanford, but made no commitments. Promising only to stay in close touch, he explained that he needed time to put in place his own plans for the future of the King Center in Atlanta and the King Estate.

Forging a partnership would remain an elusive goal. Dexter and Phil involved me in their discussions with HBO regarding a multipart King series. I wrote a treatment, but HBO never produced the series. I also met with documentary filmmaker Ken Burns, but Dexter and Phil did not reach an agreement with him either. A third opportunity to bring King's life to the screen in a major documentary—this time with Orlando Bagwell, with whom I had worked on *Eyes on the*

Prize—was also met with disappointment. The collaboration with the King Estate fell through, and Bagwell produced the award-winning *Citizen King* without the Estate's approval.

As my meetings with Dexter became less frequent, I also gradually saw less of Coretta King. We would never have much time together again, but I enjoyed meeting with her in February 2000, when she came to the Bay Area for a fundraising dinner for the King Center. When we met in her hotel suite, she seemed favorable to the idea of a King institute. I surmised that she saw this course as the best way to ensure that all the volumes of *The Papers* would be completed. She added, however, that she had given Dexter the responsibility to make such decisions. At the dinner, I was envious of the warm reception that Silicon Valley executives gave her. Although they lived near the King Papers Project, few knew that it existed. In her remarks to the group, I was pleased when she gave the project and its work generous praise. When she announced that the audio edition of *The Autobiography of Martin Luther King Jr.* had just won a Grammy Award for Best Spoken-Word Recording, I basked in the hearty applause, yet I regretted that she was not soliciting funds for both the King Center and the King Papers Project.

Although I saw her briefly when she returned to California to speak in Oakland, it would be two years before I was able to spend time with her again. Susan and I were invited—along with more than two hundred others—to her seventy-fifth birthday celebration, held in April 2002 on the Paddlewheel Riverboat at Stone Mountain Park outside of Atlanta. It was far from an intimate party, but was a joyous event on a wonderful spring day. Before boarding the boat, Susan and I had our photograph taken with the remarkable woman I had finally begun to know as Coretta. I would later treasure the portrait—which she signed "Love + Joy"—because it was the only one to include the three of us. Despite occasional arguments and reconciliations, we had become friends with two decades of memories.

All of the King children were there, although Dexter arrived late from California. He had purchased a stunning hillside home in Malibu overlooking the Pacific Ocean that I visited on one occasion. He and Phil greeted us warmly. It had been eight eventful years since that initial barbed encounter at the Atlanta Hilton. Yolanda rushed over to offer an enthusiastic hug—we had become acquainted during her speaking events in the Bay Area. Martin III, then head of the Southern Christian Leadership Conference, was there with a friendly, attractive young woman named Arndrea Waters. Susan and I later speculated that perhaps he might become the first of the siblings to marry. (He was, in May 2006.) When the birthday cake was served, Yolanda, Martin, Dexter, and Bernice each offered warm, informal toasts to their mother. Despite the large number of guests, she seemed happy and relaxed. Aware of the pressures of her public life, it was a pleasure to see her enjoy the affection of family and friends.

After I returned to California, Susan and I wrote a letter of appreciation that recalled the seventeen years since I accepted her invitation to direct the King Papers Project and especially the five years since we began our work in her basement. We mentioned how much we had appreciated getting to know "the extraordinarily talented and vibrant Coretta Scott—the student activist who campaigned bravely for world peace despite the constraints of the McCarthy era." We applauded her many roles including "the founding president of the Center promoting the ideal of peace with justice, supporting the struggle in South Africa and of course her establishing the King Papers Project." We continued, "Without you, I'm certain, there would be no national holiday honoring Martin." We ended with "Please accept our thanks on behalf of a grateful nation and world."

The last time I remember seeing Mrs. King was at the 2004 King Holiday celebration in Atlanta. On the Saturday evening before the holiday, we spoke briefly during the King Center's annual Salute to Greatness dinner, one of the very few occasions when I wore a tuxedo. I enjoyed the chance to speak with old acquaintances and mingle with celebrities I recognized and the many that I didn't. That year, Bono, leader singer of U2, was one of the honorees. I took a photo of him with baseball legend Hank Aaron and their expressions suggested that neither knew much about the other. Seeing the well-dressed racially diverse attendees reminded me of the changes that had happened since King's death.

The following Sunday morning, I spoke at a televised holiday event at a packed Ebenezer Baptist Church. I followed remarks by Mrs. King, Atlanta mayor Shirley Franklin, and Bernice King, and by the time I rose to speak my goal was simply to hold the audience's attention until Mrs. Farris, Dexter, and Martin got up to bring the event to a close. Although my remarks were by no means memorable, I felt good when the audience applauded after my few minutes in Ebenezer's historic pulpit. At the end of the celebration, I stood next to Mrs. King and Mrs. Farris, and we crossed our arms and joined hands to sing "We Shall Overcome."

After several years of waiting for Dexter's approval of the King Institute proposal, I decided to move ahead with plans to establish the King Institute at Stanford. I had already recognized that my conversations with Dexter were unlikely to bear fruit, and in January 2004, Martin Luther King III, who had been serving as the head of the Southern Christian Leadership Conference, replaced Dexter as the King Center's president. The extent of the gulf between me and the Center was evident in that I learned about the change through newspaper articles.

Soon after Martin's takeover, Harold Boyd, a former Stanford dean and a long-time supporter of the King Papers Project, told me that he had talked with football Hall of Famer Ronnie Lott and discovered the former San Francisco 49ers star's strong interest in Martin Luther King Jr. I met with Ronnie for lunch and learned about his nonprofit educational organization, All Stars Helping Kids. He was particularly interested in the project's efforts to produce educational materials for high school students. After further discussions, Lott agreed in May 2005 to pledge $1 million to create a permanent institute to support the work of the King Papers Project. His pledge led to additional million-dollar pledges from John Mumford's Agape Foundation and former Seagate CEO Steve Luczo. Matched by funds from Stanford's Hewlett endowment for undergraduate education, these pledges resulted in the establishment of the King Research and Education Institute as the King Project's institutional home.

My discussions at Stanford concerning the establishment of the Institute did not involve Martin or Dexter. Although I expected that the new Institute would benefit from a legal agreement with the King Estate, I did not want to wait for one. I decided that without an endowment, the King Papers Project would not have the resources to remain viable, but with adequate financial resources the Estate would view the King Institute as more worthy of collaboration.

I also believed that the King Institute's multifaceted activities were worthy of endowment support. Although producing the remaining volumes of *The Papers* remained the central aspect of the Institute's mission, its public education activities reached students who would probably never read one of the books or ever purchase one of the anthologies. Furthermore, the Liberation Curriculum had always drawn attention not only to King's role but to the vital contributions of SNCC and the grassroots activists in the African American freedom struggle.

The King Institute's public programs continued to expand as we tried new ways of reaching more diverse audiences. Our annual King Holiday celebrations provided opportunities for the staff to take a break from our normal work in order to enhance their understanding and impact of our research. The arrival in 2006 of Clarence Jones as our Scholar in Residence provided a special spark to our celebrations due to his role as one of King's attorneys and occasional speechwriter. In 2007 Tavis Smiley broadcasted his television program from the Institute and featured interviews with Clarence, Dorothy Cotton, and myself. Cornel West also came to this King celebration. The following year, Smiley would feature interviews with Clarence and me in his commemoration of the fortieth anniversary of King's assassination, and several years later he would broadcast his radio program from a summer conference on nonviolence sponsored by the Institute.

We often used our public programs to draw attention to the contributions of lesser known figures in the freedom struggles of the 1950s and 1960s. We began presenting our Call to Conscience award to individuals we thought deserved recognition, including Claudette Colvin, who as a teenager had been arrested for refusing to give up her seat on a Montgomery bus months before Rosa Parks gained lasting fame for a similar protest. We also honored Guy and Candie Carowin, known in Movement circles for popularizing "We Shall Overcome" and the singing and teaching of freedom songs at the Highlander Folk School. We sponsored exhibits of the works of Movement photographers such as Matt Herron and Bob Fitch.

Certainly the most notable of the Institute's visitors was the fourteenth Dalai Lama, who accepted my invitation to stop by our offices after a November 2005 speech at Stanford. Staff members radiated excitement in anticipation of the arrival of this Nobel Laureate at our modest suite of offices. After his motorcade arrived, the Dalai Lama and I sat in chairs in the Institute's reception area enjoying refreshments that my office staff had prepared. During our twenty-minute conversation, with staff members crowding around to listen, I had an emotional response when he spoke of his admiration for King while holding my hand. He mentioned that during a meeting with Mrs. King, she had talked about the "pilgrimage" to India that the Kings had made in 1959 and related that Martin told her afterward about his wish "to dress like Gandhi." The Dalai Lama smiled mischievously as he recalled the conversation, then leaned toward me and confided, "Now, whenever I want to make myself laugh, all I have to do is imagine Martin Luther King Jr. dressed like Gandhi." When it was time to leave, he got into his car, but before the motorcade had traveled far, the cars suddenly stopped, and the Dalai Lama came out and carefully placed a scarf that he had blessed around my neck. It was one of the most moving experiences in my life.

Less than two months after the Dalai Lama's visit, I received the news that Coretta had died at a hospital in Rosarito Beach, Mexico, where she had gone for a controversial form of holistic therapy for advanced ovarian cancer. I didn't learn about her condition until after her death on January 30, 2006. Even so, I was not entirely surprised by the news—she had suffered a stroke and heart attack months before. Her daughter Bernice had been caring for her at the apartment into which she had moved after finally leaving her Sunset Avenue home. Along with Susan and my four longest-serving colleagues at Stanford—editors Tenisha Armstrong and Sue Englander, administrator Jane Abbott, and my assistant, Regina Covington—I immediately made plans to go to Atlanta to commemorate her life.

I was somewhat surprised that the funeral would not take place at Ebenezer Church, where Mrs. King had been a member, but instead at New Birth Missionary Baptist Church, where Bernice King served as an elder. Although New Birth's seating capacity of ten thousand made it a suitable choice for such a major event, I wondered whether Mrs. King would have approved. New Birth's pastor, Bishop Eddie L. Long, was an outspoken opponent of gay marriage, while Coretta had taken firm stands in favor of gay rights. Bishop Long also preached a type of "prosperity gospel" that sharply contrasted with King's social gospel. When the *Atlanta Journal-Constitution* estimated Long's annual income at more than $3 million, he blithely remarked, "Jesus wasn't poor."

After arriving in Atlanta on Sunday, February 5, I learned that President George W. Bush would deliver a eulogy at the funeral service at New Birth on Tuesday, and that former presidents Jimmy Carter, George H. W. Bush, and Bill Clinton would also speak. I knew that security would be tight and checked to confirm that my colleagues and I were indeed on the King Center's list of invitees.

A celebration of Coretta King's life at Ebenezer Church was also held on the evening before the New Birth funeral. When I happened to see the Rev. Cecil Williams, the longtime politically engaged pastor of San Francisco's Glide Memorial Church, he explained that the Ebenezer event provided an opportunity for speakers considered too controversial for the official funeral to call attention to Mrs. King's political activism. I heard rumors that Harry Belafonte, a dedicated supporter of Martin Luther King Jr. during the 1950s and 1960s—and a generous financial supporter of the King family—had not been invited to participate in the official funeral.

Energy and emotion saturated the Ebenezer event as the Morehouse choir warmed up the audience for the invited speakers. I had been asked by Ebenezer pastor Raphael Warnock to speak at the event, but declined. As much as I wanted to express my feelings about the woman I had known for two decades, I could not see myself adding much to a celebration featuring the oratory of Baptist ministers and political leaders who had known her for much longer. Watching Williams, Jesse Jackson, Joseph Lowery, C. T. Vivian, and others, I was thankful to have avoided being sandwiched between these masterful preachers. These people, who called on their years of homiletic experience, were certainly more qualified than I was to express the meanings of Mrs. King's life.

The next day, February 7, 2006, over 14,000 people gathered, including a large congressional delegation, for an eight-hour funeral at the New Birth Missionary Baptist Church in Lithonia, Georgia, where Bernice King was among those to eulogize her mother. The audience warmly applauded President Carter when he mentioned Coretta's lifelong struggle for civil rights and noted that she and her husband had been the target of secret government wiretapping. Reverend Joseph called attention to Mrs. King's vocal opposition to President Bush's Iraq War:

> She deplored the terror inflicted by our smart bombs on missions way afar.... We know now there were no weapons of mass destruction over there. But Coretta knew, and we knew, that there are weapons of misdirection right down here. Millions without health insurance. Poverty abounds. For war, billions more, but no more for the poor.

As I later reflected about the passing of the King Center's founder, I thought of how much had changed in the two decades since I first spoke to Mrs. King on the phone. What would happen now?

The King Institute's future was suddenly thrown into question in June 2006 when the Institute's principal donors became aware of the news that the King documents stored at Sotheby's in New York since the late 1990s had been sold for $32 million. The buyer was a consortium of Atlanta leaders, businesses, and foundations who purchased the papers on behalf of Morehouse College. I learned that Atlanta mayor Shirley Franklin and former mayor Andrew Young had arranged the purchase after discussions with Phil Jones. Franklin had paid $2 million over the appraised value of the collection—"I didn't want to risk losing the papers over a million dollars," she was quoted as saying, "To Atlanta they are priceless."

My initial reaction was surprise that the papers—many of them from Mrs. King's basement—had been sold after being stored at Sotheby's for almost a decade. I knew that several institutions had considered purchasing the collection during that period. The New York Public Library had consulted with me about the collection, and Oprah Winfrey had called me to discuss her interest in buying the papers as well. Some potential buyers were dissuaded by the fact that the King Estate would retain intellectual property rights. Others were concerned that the Sotheby's papers were part of a much larger collection of King's papers still at the King Center. As the years passed, I had become convinced that the collection would not find a buyer willing to pay Sotheby's $30 million asking price. I marveled at the audacity of Dexter and Phil, who had succeeded in their gambit: removing the documents from Atlanta and then selling them back to the city for more than the asking price, while still retaining all rights to determine where the collection could be displayed or used for educational purposes. Although they had sold a few thousand documents that were in the King Center's vault, they still retained the bulk of the original King collection at the Center.

Ronnie Lott and John Mumford, two of the King Institute endowment donors, were disturbed that the King family had sold papers at Sotheby's. They feared that the King Institute would no longer be able to use King's statements in its educational materials. When we met, I assured them that the sale concerned the physical papers rather than the intellectual property, but they remained worried that the King family would ask to be paid for use of King's intellectual property. "I don't want a cent of my money going to that family!" Mumford insisted. I explained that the King Papers Project and the King Institute had been using King-authored documents in its educational materials and its website for over a decade, but my reassurances had little impact. "When the King family sees that the King Institute has an endowment," Mumford asked, "what's to prevent them from asking to be paid for the use of those materials?" I had to admit that I couldn't give him that assurance.

After a meeting with the King Institute's three key donors, we agreed to involve Roger McNamee, a founder of the Silicon Valley venture capital firm Elevation Partners, to assist in seeking an agreement with the King Estate that would clarify the legal relationship between the Estate and the Institute. I thought that Dexter and Phil might be impressed by Bono's close ties with Elevation Partners. In the fall of 2006, I arranged for them to meet with McNamee to work out an agreement, but nothing came of it. Lacking a formal agreement between the King Estate and the King Institute, the three donors suspended their pledges, thereby reducing the Institute's total endowment from the $6 million that had been pledged to less than $2 million.

A year after these discussions with Elevation ended, the King Institute experienced another setback, this one in conjunction with the rest of the world, due to the international financial collapse of 2008. We had expected an annual payout of 5 percent from the endowment, but the sharp decline of stock values precluded payouts for the next few years. Just two years after its founding, the King Institute had lost not only more than two-thirds of its endowment pledges, but also all of its endowment payout.

I had begun the decade with the expectation that the King Papers Project would either forge a permanent agreement with the King Estate or become an autonomous institution. By the end of the decade, I recognized that it would be difficult to achieve either. Although the endowment eventually recovered its initial value, the King Institute would continue to pursue the elusive goal of self-sufficiency. Its future remained inextricably linked to the King Estate, which remained in firm control of the legacy of Martin Luther King Jr. It was no longer always clear who was in control of the King Estate. In July 2008, Bernice and Martin III sued Dexter after alleging that he mismanaged the King Estate and had appropriated estate funds for his own use. Dexter countersued, claiming that Martin had improperly used King Center property for personal use and that Bernice had corrupted their father's legacy by hosting an anti–gay marriage rally at the Center.

Dexter later sued Bernice again, claiming that she was withholding documents needed to complete a biography of Mrs. King—for which the Estate had received an advance of more than $1 million. I surmised that the withheld documents included the love letters Martin had sent to Coretta in 1952 that I had seen while editing *The Autobiography of Martin Luther King Jr.* I sympathized with the comments of the Rev. Barbara Reynolds, who had contracted to write the biography: "There's an African proverb, 'When elephants fight, the grass gets trampled.' These are fights between siblings for control. I'm just a writer caught in the middle."

I recalled their mother's birthday celebration and marveled at the ways the façade of family harmony had been illusory. I wondered why had the legacy left behind by their father stirred rancor rather than a spirit of reconciliation within his own family. Had Mrs. King's lawsuit against Boston University spawned a familial habit of litigation to control their inheritance? I resolved to stay as far away as possible from the internecine warfare.

Part Three

King's Legacy

Chapter 19

Memorial on the Mall

$\mathcal{E}$ven as my contact with the King family and the King Center became more infrequent, I continued to define King's legacy in various ways. The lack of a formal agreement with the King Estate hampered the King Institute's development, but I still found ample opportunities to influence the public's understanding of King. Increasingly, this involved working with other institutions. During the 1990s, I consulted with the designers of the King Visitors Center in Atlanta, and later advised the National Civil Rights Museum in Memphis and also the Center for Civil and Human Rights in Atlanta. When Martin Luther King III established his own organization, Realizing the Dream, I served on its Advisory Board. After the King documents at Sotheby's had been sold and returned to Atlanta, I served on the Morehouse King Collection National Advisory Board and during 2009 as Morehouse's King Distinguished Professor and executive director of the collection. I continued to participate in documentary film projects, such as *Brother Outsider* (2002), about King's movement colleague Bayard Rustin; *Citizen King* (2004); and Tavis Smiley's *MLK: A Call to Conscience* (2008). I co-authored a college-level textbook with Emma J. Lapsansky Werner and my former UCLA professor Gary Nash, *The Struggle for Freedom: A History of African Americans* (2005), which placed King in the broader context of black freedom struggles.

The most important of my efforts to enhance King's legacy started inauspiciously with a phone call early in the spring of 2000. Bonnie Fisher, the Landscape Principal of ROMA Design Group in San Francisco, called me to ask if I would collaborate with her firm to enter the international competition to design the King Memorial on the National Mall in Washington, D.C. The King Memorial Foundation, established by King's Alpha Phi Alpha fraternity to raise the more than $100 million needed to build and maintain the memorial, sponsored the design competition. Bonnie's query was not entirely unexpected given that I had become increasingly well known in the Bay Area due to my role as head of the King Papers Project at Stanford. I was wary of any new distractions from my ongoing effort to publish King's papers—especially since ROMA was only one of many firms that were likely to enter the competition. Nonetheless, I agreed to discuss the proposal over lunch at Palo Alto's MacArthur Park restaurant near the Stanford campus.

When I met with Bonnie and her husband, ROMA's president Boris Dramov, I intended to only offer general advice and wish them well in the competition. However, I was impressed by Bonnie's pert enthusiasm as she described ROMA's "interdisciplinary" approach, bringing together architects, landscape architects, and urban planners to redesign municipal environments. ROMA's previous projects, revitalizing San Francisco's Embarcadero and Santa Monica's Third Street Promenade (a once-declining downtown area near where I had lived during the 1960s), displayed their ability to design spaces that were functional and attractive. Boris, an immigrant born in Bulgaria and raised in Brazil, was somewhat older and, in contrast to Bonnie, more reserved. He had met Bonnie in the early 1980s while both attended Harvard's Graduate School of Design. Each conveyed a thoughtful sense of idealism about their profession and exuded sincere interest in making an enduring contribution to King's legacy. I admired their willingness to commit considerable time and resources to a competition without a large monetary prize that would be judged by a "blind" jury unaware of which team had submitted a particular design.

As our conversation turned to the memorial, I realized how much my views of King had changed since the 1960s, when I championed the grassroots organizing "bottom-up approach" of SNCC. As the director of the King Papers Project I became more appreciative of King's vision. I felt it was important that a King memorial built near the Lincoln Memorial should celebrate the Dream speech and the man who eloquently expressed the larger historical significance of the African American freedom struggle.

Although I had no expertise in landscape design, I recommended that the memorial visualize the vivid metaphorical language of King's 1963 oration. Recalling familiar passages from memory, I suggested some possibilities for visual themes. King's insistence that black Americans would "not be satisfied until justice rolls down like waters and righteousness like a mighty stream," for example, might readily be expressed through fountains and running water. The evocative images— "the table of brotherhood" and "one day every valley shall be exalted"—King used to illustrate his "dream" of a future America offered other visual possibilities. We eventually focused our attention on a less often quoted passage: "With this faith we will be able to hew out of the mountain of despair a stone of hope." This extended metaphor suggested dramatic large-scale elements for a memorial that would celebrate King as an inspirational advocate of racial justice as well as a famous orator. We imagined visitors to the memorial entering through an opening cut through a granite Mountain of Despair. The removed slice—the Stone of Hope—would be thrust forward and turned slightly so that visitors would encounter an inscription of King's words on the slab's smooth surface.

Rather than a familiar passage from the "dream" refrain or from King's dramatic "Thank God Almighty, we are free at last" conclusion, I proposed that we feature a passage near the beginning of his prepared text:

[W]hen the architects of our republic wrote the magnificent words of the constitution and the declaration of independence, they were signing a promissory note to which every American was to fall heir. This note was a promise that all men, yes, black men as well as white men, would be guaranteed the unalienable rights of "Life, Liberty and the pursuit of Happiness."

King's call for the nation to "live out the true meaning of its creed" would, I expected, serve as a continual reminder to Americans that their nation had still not realized some aspects of his dream.

Over a productive lunch, we reached an agreement about key elements of the design. My initial reluctance had given way to an eagerness to work with ROMA's interdisciplinary team. Using diagrams and maps of the National Mall and the Potomac River's Tidal Basin, the ROMA group situated the Mountain of Despair on the four-acre site on the Mall so that it not only served symbolic purposes—it was on the axis from the Lincoln Memorial to the Jefferson Memorial—but also shielded the rest of the memorial from the traffic on Independence Avenue. Placing the Stone of Hope near the edge of the Tidal Basin drew attention to the aquatic background and the Jefferson Memorial across the Basin.

Bonnie and Boris insisted that the memorial not stand apart from its natural bucolic setting, especially the oak, magnolia, and cherry trees that shaded the gentle slope around the Tidal Basin's curved shore. Although constructing the memorial would inevitably alter the site, the large stone structures we envisioned would not overwhelm the existing restful environment. We envisioned the Mountain of Despair covered with landscaping that blended with the setting. A water fountain softened the impact of the long Inscription Wall that extended on each side of the Mountain and served as a tablet for King's notable quotations.

The memorial design offered visitors various vantage points to appreciate this blend of natural and constructed elements. A walkway across the top of the Inscription Wall provided an elevated view of the Stone and the Basin. I indulged my bottom-up perspective of the African American freedom struggle by suggesting that various less-known activists who had devoted their lives to the struggle against the Jim Crow system should be honored by semicircular niches along the walkway. I imagined a public selection process that would increase awareness of figures such as Rosa Parks, Medgar Evers, or the three voting rights workers murdered at the start of the 1964 Mississippi Freedom Summer Project. These two dozen small seating areas would also serve as wells for the water that would flow over the wall.

We disagreed on whether the design would include a statue of King. I resisted the idea of a heroic Great Man representation of someone who often described himself as simply "a symbol of the movement." I was unimpressed with the bust of King I saw unveiled in 1986 at the Capitol Rotunda in Washington but recognized that it was difficult to create a convincing and compelling sculpted image of a man depicted in numerous iconic photographs. For many of his admirers, King's inspiring words made him seem taller and more imposing than his actual stature. Bonnie and Boris persuaded me, however, that many visitors—and perhaps the jurors for the competition—would miss seeing a statue of King. We settled on the idea of sculpting an image of King into the rough edge of the Stone of Hope facing toward the Tidal Basin. Visitors standing at the edge of the Basin would be able to turn back to see King's visage not as a statue but as an integral feature of the Stone. As Boris explained at the time, the image would be "unfinished, allowing people through their own memories to complete the picture."

For a model, I supplied Bob Fitch's portrait of King that was on the cover of my edition of *The Autobiography of Martin Luther King Jr.* This photograph of King standing in front of a desk at the Southern Christian Leadership Conference's Atlanta headquarters depicted him not as a charismatic orator or even as a civil rights protester but as a contemplative intellectual. With his arms crossed and Gandhi's portrait on the wall behind him, King holds a pen in his right hand. ROMA's Stone of Hope drawings based on the photograph depicted King in a pensive pose—we imagined him taking a break from drafting his reference to the "Promissory Note" and looking across time and the Tidal Basin toward Jefferson, one of the nation's founding "architects" and principal author of the Declaration of Independence. The two men would serve as historical frames for a perpetual dialogue about the meaning of American democracy. Upon completion, we were confident that our design exploited the possibilities of the site, gave visual expression to some of King's prophetic insights, and offered inspiration without being overly didactic. Yet, because our basic concept seemed so simple and obvious, I wondered whether other design teams in the competition would also submit proposals that used the rich figurative language of the Dream speech.

The competition attracted almost nine hundred entries from thirty-three countries. Even after I learned that we were among the three finalists invited to attend the September 2000 ceremony in Washington announcing the winner, I still did not want to build up my expectations. When our proposal won the competition, I was excited and relieved. I was also aware that few of those at the ceremony knew my role in the design. As a gaggle of reporters and professional acquaintances gathered around Bonnie and Boris, I refrained from intruding on their moment of triumph. Winning the design competition was a high point of their distinguished careers; for me it prompted a mostly private sense of accomplishment. Yet I could not help feeling a measure of disappointment when Bonnie informed me that only one member of the ROMA team would be able to join Dr. Ed Jackson, the architect who chaired the design jury and headed the King Memorial Project, to appear on the morning news shows.

In the spring of 2001, I traveled to Washington, D.C., with Bonnie and Boris to participate in presentations of ROMA's plan to the U.S. Commission on Fine Arts and the National Capitol Planning Commission. At the Commission hearing, Dr. Jackson firmly asserted himself as chief spokesperson for the memorial design. He asked that the ROMA principals and I limit our remarks to two minutes of personal introductions before he took over the role of explaining the meaning of the memorial and answering questions. We understood the need to convey a consistent message to the planning bodies, but I winced when Jackson's comments about the design or about King seemed ill-informed.

In our discussions at the King Memorial Foundation's headquarters, Jackson made clear that as the memorial's executive architect he had the authority to alter any aspect of our proposal—which now belonged to the Foundation, not to ROMA. I accepted that Jackson expressed the legal reality but worried about how this would affect our vision of the memorial. I recalled Maya Lin's struggle to maintain the integrity of her controversial proposal for the Vietnam Veterans Memorial. I admired her efforts to resist pressures to alter essential elements of her simple, elegant design, even while it was compromised by the addition of superfluous statues near the memorial. Lin gained some leverage from the sympathetic press attention given to her compelling personal story as a Chinese American who had won a design competition while still a Yale undergraduate. ROMA's winning design, in contrast, received little coverage, positive or negative.

Once the planning boards gave it close scrutiny, alterations were inevitable. I was not entirely surprised when Jackson informed us that the walkway and memorial niches I had proposed above the Wall would have to be dropped from the plan because they were costly, possibly unsafe, and difficult to police. He said that such mini-memorials of other civil rights martyrs would also require additional congressional authorization. Our proposal to have water flowing from the niches over the top of the Inscription Wall also faced practical objections, including the high cost of maintenance. Although these changes seemed sensible, they increased my concern about ROMA's limited influence over future decisions regarding the design.

This became even more evident in June 2001, when Bonnie, Boris, and I met with Jackson and other Foundation officials in Washington, D.C. Although some tensions had surfaced in our previous meetings, I expected an amicable discussion about our roles in the memorial project. As Bonnie and Boris resolved design issues with Jackson, I still hoped to play a central role in selecting the quotations that would appear on the memorial. Intending to extend my stay into the following week, I invited Susan and our granddaughter, Dalila, to tour the city while I attended the meetings.

The initial discussion on Friday afternoon did not go well. Bonnie and Boris sought to convince Jackson that the Memorial Foundation would greatly benefit from ROMA's experience with large-scale projects, and I made similar claims regarding the King Papers Project's unique documentary resources while stressing the importance of selecting quotes that were consistent with the memorial's design. For his part, Jackson reiterated that our role would be simply to serve as his advisors. I was disappointed when he announced that he planned to name a committee of historians to suggest appropriate quotations for the memorial.

During a break in the meeting, Jackson pulled me aside. "Are you willing to work independently with the Foundation, even if ROMA was no longer involved?" he asked bluntly. I was caught off guard by the question, wondering whether he intended to eliminate ROMA completely from the process. I could imagine a consulting role apart from Bonnie and Boris with respect to the quotations, but I also felt a sense of loyalty to them. Still confused, I replied, "I prefer to remain part of the ROMA team." When he told me that my participation in the weekend meetings was no longer needed, I realized that I had given the wrong answer. A bit dazed, I called Susan to let her know that I was now available to explore the city with our granddaughter.

When I was finally able to talk to Bonnie and Boris on Sunday, they expressed dismay at my dismissal but remained hopeful that they could remain involved in building the memorial. I sensed that they were used to dealing with people like Jackson who had the drive and political savvy to determine the fate of ROMA's ambitious designs for public places. I realized that I had mishandled my private conversation with Jackson and should have at least discussed possibilities for a separate role as historical advisor. But I felt relieved to be freed from the frustrations I had increasingly felt concerning Jackson and the Foundation.

During the next few years, as the Foundation's fundraising effort proceeded much more slowly than expected, Bonnie and Boris kept me informed about their continuing involvement. With the passage of time, I got over my hurt feelings and came to treasure my memories of the initial collaboration with the ROMA principals and the dinners they hosted at their wonderful home in San Francisco. In November 2005, they invited me and Susan to be their guests at a gala "Dream Dinner" co-hosted by the Foundation and ROMA at San Francisco's Ferry Building. This event raised more than $2 million for the memorial. I felt proud when I saw my name on a large ROMA exhibit of the memorial plan displayed at the dinner.

Soon after the dinner, the Foundation officials contacted me to take part in the Council of Historians, to be headed by Harvard scholar Henry Louis "Skip" Gates Jr. I indicated that I was willing to advise the Council and this led to my appointment in May 2006 as a consultant. Jackson then contacted me to ask that I supply ten quotes that exemplify each of the four themes of justice, democracy, love, and hope. I felt that these thematic requirements were somewhat arbitrary and unduly restrictive, because they excluded other topics important to King, such as peace, nonviolence, poverty, and religion. ROMA's design assumed a chronological rather than thematic arrangement of the quotations. Dr. Jackson also specified that the quotes should be "concise"—consisting of thirty or fewer words—and have "universal and timeless appeal." The word length requirement troubled me because some of King's most significant statements exceeded that length.

When I submitted my recommendations to Jackson, I noted the difficulty of reconciling all of the suggested criteria. I acknowledged that my suggestions included quotes that somewhat exceeded the specified length, explaining, "Some of King's most memorable and profound quotations cannot readily be reduced to less than 31 words." I detailed my concern about the designated themes—"It was also not possible to find equal numbers of highly significant quotations about each of the four designated themes"—and argued for additional themes. I insisted that King's reference at the 1963 March on Washington to the Declaration of Independence as a "Promissory Note" was "central to the meaning of the Stone of Hope." Because King's remarks were addressed to "the architects of our republic," the original design team had intended the Stone of Hope to be oriented so that the sculpted image of King would seem to be looking at the Jefferson Memorial. My list of eleven chronologically arranged quotations traced King's life from the beginning of the Montgomery bus boycott to the eve of his assassination, showing how King's ideas evolved during his public life. I also provided Jackson with the remaining twenty-nine quotations he had requested, and noted that some of these would be appropriate alternatives to the eleven I thought were most suitable.

Although I expected that Jackson or Council members would contact me to discuss my suggestions, I did not hear from them. Then, in February 2007, I read a newspaper story indicating that the Council of Historians had made their selections. When I eagerly searched the Internet to obtain more specific information, I learned that five of my top choices, including a few that exceeded Jackson's word limit, were among the fourteen chosen for the memorial. The other nine were among my alternate selections.

I was pleased that the council chose my recommendation from King's first speech as the leader of the Montgomery Improvement Association, delivered on December 5, 1955, the evening of the first day of the 381-day boycott of Montgomery's buses: "We are determined here in Montgomery to work and fight until justice runs 'down like water, and righteousness like a mighty stream.'" This underappreciated speech was certainly among the most important of King's public life. If it had not been well received, there probably would not be a King memorial today.

The second approved quote, which exceeded the word limit by five words, came from King's speech at the April 18, 1959, Youth March for Integrated Schools: "Make a career of humanity. Commit yourself to the noble struggle for equal rights. You will make a greater person of yourself, a greater nation of your country, and a finer world to live in." The King Papers Project had used this quote, which reflected King's role as an inspirational figure for many young activists, on a T-shirt made for staff members and Stanford student researchers.

An oft-quoted passage from the "Letter from Birmingham Jail" was also included: "Injustice anywhere is a threat to justice everywhere. We are caught in an inescapable network of mutuality, tied in a single garment of destiny. Whatever affects one directly, affects all indirectly."

The fourth quote came from King's Nobel Peace Prize Acceptance Address in Oslo on December 10, 1964: "I have the audacity to believe that peoples everywhere can have three meals a day for their bodies, education and culture for their minds, and dignity, equality, and freedom for their spirits."

Finally, the Council used a forty-six-word passage from King's initial public statement, delivered in Los Angeles, opposing the war in Vietnam. Although not clearly audible in the recording, I later confirmed that King did utter the ambiguous ending. Although King's statement in Los Angeles was not as cogent as his later antiwar speech at New York's Riverside Church on April 4, 1967, the most memorable passages in the latter speech contained even more words than this succinct explanation of his decision to express his antiwar sentiments publicly: "I oppose the war in Vietnam because I love America. I speak out against it not in anger but with anxiety and sorrow in my heart, and above all with a passionate desire to see our beloved country stand as a moral example of the world."

I was not particularly surprised that not all of my top choices had been selected—after all, King said many profound things during his life, and the Council's remaining selections were among the alternatives I had submitted. Nonetheless, I found it odd that I had not been invited to participate in the Council's deliberations and baffled that no one had explained to me the reasons for the final selections. I did not know whether the Council even discussed the Promissory Note passage, which I had deemed essential to the memorial's symbolic meaning. Although valid arguments could be made for the Council's selections, they did not include any passages from several of King's most well-known homilies and orations.

I had suggested this passage from his "I Have a Dream" address at the 1963 March on Washington: "Even though we face the difficulties of today and tomorrow, I still have a dream. It is a dream deeply rooted in the American dream. I have a dream that one day this nation will rise up and live out the true meaning of its creed: 'We hold these truths to be self-evident.'" And the approved quotes did not include the well-known concluding passage from King's final "Mountain Top" oration in Memphis on April 3, 1968: "I just want to do God's will. And He's allowed me to go up to the mountain. And I've looked over and I've seen the promised land. I may not get there with you, but I want you to know tonight, that we, as a people, will get to the promised land."

The replacements for these well-known, emotionally powerful passages seemed weaker in comparison. Rather than selecting quotations that were grounded in the specific context of King's life, many of the approved ones were idealistic abstractions—timeless and universal, to be sure, but lacking the emotional and intellectual weight of King's memorable statements during decisive turning points in his life. For example, two passages attributed to King's "A Christmas Sermon on Peace," delivered at Atlanta's Ebenezer Baptist Church and later broadcast by the Canadian Broadcasting Company, were not nearly as forceful as some of King's other antiwar statements:

> If we are to have peace on earth, our loyalties must become ecumenical rather than sectional. Our loyalties must transcend race, our tribe, our class and our nation; and this means we must develop a world perspective."
> "We must not wage war. It is necessary to love peace and sacrifice for it. We must concentrate not merely on the negative expulsion of war, but on the positive affirmation of peace.

Although both quotes were on my list of alternatives, the latter was not complete and erroneously sourced; it was from King's February 1967 antiwar speech in Los Angeles, where he had added the necessary initial words, "It is not enough to say...."

The approved selections emphasized the theme of love while paying little attention to other elements of King's thought. Three such passages seemed somewhat redundant:

> Darkness cannot drive out darkness, only light can do that. Hate cannot drive out hate, only love can do that.
>
> To return hate for hate does nothing but intensify the existence of evil in the universe. Someone must have sense enough and religion enough to cut off the chain of hate and evil, and this can only be done through love.
>
> Hatred paralyzes life, love releases it. Hatred confuses life, love harmonizes it. Hatred darkens life, love illuminates it.

A fourth quote on the love theme, taken from King's Nobel Acceptance Address, restated a common theme in King's oratory: "I believe that unarmed truth and unconditional love will have the final word in reality. This is why right, temporarily defeated, is stronger than evil triumphant."

I had suggested using a passage from King's rousing speech at the conclusion of the 1965 Selma-to-Montgomery voting rights march, where he conveyed a thought that was similar to the Nobel passage but that more clearly illustrated his distinctive oratorical style (and his tendency to borrow from earlier sources):

How long will justice be crucified, and truth bear it? I come to say to you this afternoon, however difficult the moment, however frustrating the hour, it will not be long, because "truth crushed to earth will rise again." How long? Not long, because "no lie can live forever." How long? Not long, because "you shall reap what you sow."

I felt that the fourteen approved quotations did not adequately represent King during his most challenging moments. Although two quotes from the "Letter from Birmingham Jail" could certainly be justified, it was difficult for me to understand why there were no passages from four of King's most famous and influential orations: his "Dream" speech in Washington, D.C., the voting rights speech, the antiwar address at Riverside Church in New York, and the "Mountaintop" speech in Memphis. Why six references to "love" but not a single passage representing King's final campaign against poverty?

The announcement of the approved quotations for the Inscription Wall attracted little public attention, perhaps because they were made public at the same time as the Memorial Foundation's controversial selection of a Chinese sculptor, Lei Yixin, to carve King's image into the Stone of Hope. Critics of Lei's selection insisted that an African American sculptor should have been chosen for an assignment that required cultural sensitivity in the depiction of the most famous African American leader. A few reporters called me for a reaction to these criticisms, but I was much more concerned about the King quotations than the sculptor's nationality or skin color.

In the fall of 2008, I returned to the memorial site as part of a group of civil rights "Pioneers" for a Foundation-sponsored informational tour. Because ground preparation had not yet begun on the memorial, the visit was largely a symbolic gathering of individuals with special connections to King's legacy. When I saw the large model of the memorial at a luncheon held for the group, my attention was first drawn to Lei's statue of King. Although the original design had focused on King's words rather than his physical presence, the statue was now the memorial's central focus. It was still roughly based on Fitch's photograph, but now King held a scroll in his left hand rather than a pen in his right hand. I was told that Lei sculpted the model for the statue based on a reversed negative of Fitch's image. After becoming aware of that mistake, Lei decided to replace the pen with a scroll as the right-handed King would probably not hold a pen in his left hand. This mirror image meant that King no longer looked toward the Jefferson Memorial, which undermined the notion of King and Jefferson having a conversation.

I was also distressed that Lei had abandoned the concept of King emerging from the Stone in favor of a large-scale heroic representation intended to be the memorial's monumental centerpiece. Rather than a contemplative unimposing relief of King's upper body embedded in the side of the Stone, Lei depicted him as a confrontational, perhaps even an authoritarian figure. His crossed arms suggested rigid stubbornness rather than somber reflection. I accepted that there were many aspects to King's personality that were not reflected in Fitch's photograph, but the statue seemed inconsistent with the Stone of Hope's original symbolic meaning.

I also noticed that the Promissory Note from King's Dream speech was missing from the Stone. Because my interactions with Jackson at the gathering had been amicable, I was as nonchalant as possible when I mentioned the change to him. He explained that the quote was used elsewhere in the memorial but was not used in this prominent location because it was "racially exclusionary"—a reference to King's insistence that the guarantee of equality should apply to "black men as well as white men." I saw this change as a basic misunderstanding of the original design conception of King challenging the racially exclusionary values of "the architects of our republic."

I wrote a letter to Jackson to reiterate my earlier concerns about the other quotations to be inscribed on the memorial. I complained that the decision-making process had resulted in arbitrary thematic requirements and insufficient opportunities for consultations between the Council of Historians and me. I asserted that it was not too late for further research and deliberation before the Council's selections were literally set in stone. More generally, I pleaded for "a more transparent decision-making process that will bring together the creators of the original winning design with those responsible for constructing the memorial. Doing this will result in a memorial worthy of King's intellectual legacy and of the vast financial support that the memorial has received."

Like my previous letter, this one did not receive a response, but in August 2010, Glenn DeMarr of the National Park Service contacted me to confirm the authenticity of the quotations that would soon be engraved on the memorial. When I read his list of questions, I regretted that they had not been raised years earlier. Still, I was impressed by his critical observations, which pointed out a few errors that my colleagues and I had made. For example, the passage from a 1967 speech attacking the Vietnam War, which was among the forty quotations on our list of options, was accurate, but King had earlier used the same words on a far more important occasion—his 1964 Nobel Peace Prize lecture. DeMarr's queries forced me to admit that I should have undertaken further research on the quotations even without consulting with Jackson or the Council. The anger, which I suppressed, at being marginalized in the memorial's completion had made me reluctant to participate at all, even at the risk of allowing an erroneous quote to be inscribed forever. Clearly the research and decision-making process should have been better for a project of such historic importance.

I saw the King National Memorial for the first time on Friday, August 26, 2011. It was two days before its scheduled dedication, and I arrived with Susan and three veteran members of the King Institute staff: associate editor Tenisha Armstrong, administrator Jane Abbott, and director of public programs Regina Covington. Shortly after our arrival, however, we learned that the dedication ceremony and the gala had been cancelled due to the threat that Hurricane Irene might disrupt the event. We were disappointed but resolved to take part in Friday's events before visiting the National Mall. We attended the "Women Who Dare to Dream" luncheon as the entourage of old friend Dorothy Cotton, the effervescent former head of SCLC's Citizenship Education Program. I was surprised when Bernice King happened by with a film crew. She interviewed me, and then I photographed her interviewing Dorothy.

By the time my King Project colleagues, Susan, Dorothy, and I made it to the King Memorial, it was midafternoon. Initially, I was concerned that I would have difficulty judging the completed memorial with an open mind. However, I was impressed by the view that greeted me as I entered through the Mountain of Despair. Visible between the large stone structures was the Stone of Hope with the Tidal Basin and the Jefferson Memorial in the background. I know the entrance will become even more inviting over time as the maturing trees in front soften the stark impact of the large granite elements. Having initially resisted the idea of a statue, I knew it would be difficult for me to make an impartial judgment about Lei's transformation of the Stone of Hope. Lei was certainly more experienced with large memorials and may have been the most talented sculptor available. But why was a memorial for an American icon constructed in China? I wondered what King, who died while supporting a sanitation workers strike, would think of the decision to lower labor costs by outsourcing the construction of his memorial to a nation without independent labor unions.

When we returned to the memorial on Sunday, the mild weather gave little evidence of Hurricane Irene. I had heard earlier in the day that Maya Angelou had criticized the abridgement of the King quotation that was on the side of the Stone of Hope statue. During my previous visit, I hadn't even noticed that the quote—one that I had recommended for the Inscription Wall—had been shortened. It came from King's famous eulogistic "Drum Major" sermon, delivered on February 4, 1968: "Yes, if you want to say that I was a drum major, say that I was a drum major for justice. Say that I was a drum major for peace. I was a drum major for righteousness. And all of the other shallow things will not matter." This had been changed to: "I was a drum major for justice, peace and righteousness."

"The quote makes Dr. Martin Luther King look like an arrogant twit," Maya Angelou remarked. "He was anything but that. He was far too profound a man for that four-letter word to apply." I recalled my dismay about the word limit imposed by Jackson, but this was a far worse decision that I certainly would have disputed, if I had known about it. The *Washington Post* quoted Jackson as saying that the quote was originally planned for the statue's south face—where I had envisioned the Promissory Note passage. He said planners changed their minds and decided to move the "drum major" inscription to the north face. They preferred the statue's other inscription—"Out of the mountain of despair, a stone of hope"—to be seen first, on the south face, because it is the main theme of the memorial's design. When they informed the statue's sculptor, Lei Yixin, he told them that he had already prepared the north face for the short "despair" inscription and the whole "drum major" quote would not fit.

Many questions came to mind as I tried to make sense of Jackson's explanation. Who were the "planners" who "changed their minds" at such a late stage in the construction of the memorial? Why didn't he consult with me or the Council of Historians? (Angelou was a member but admitted that she never attended a meeting.) The fiasco seemed to be another example of the flawed decision-making process that had been evident during the previous decade. "As you move through the process, things happen and you have to make design changes on the spot," Jackson was quoted as saying. Jackson finally admitted that he had made the decision but nonetheless insisted that it was now too late to alter the inscription. After additional complaints and a critical *Washington Post* editorial, Interior Secretary Ken Salazar intervened to order that the mangled quotation be replaced.

Reminiscing over the decade-long effort to build the memorial, I wondered whether my disappointments would matter to the millions of people who visit it. Few will know or care about discarded logistical options any more than visitors to the Vietnam Memorial know or care about its departures from Lin's original vision. Major memorials rarely conform exactly to the original design. Instead, they are usually the products of extensive artistic collaboration and decisions made by people with varied intentions and varied degrees of aesthetic understanding.

Rather than regret the departures from ROMA's original design, I had come to appreciate the King Memorial as the worthy outcome of the collaboration that began more than eleven years ago at a Palo Alto restaurant. I felt privileged to have witnessed the completion of a permanent manifestation of my still evolving understanding of the March on Washington and Martin Luther King Jr. I remain thankful that thousands of people helped to construct the memorial, and millions more contributed to this priceless gift to future generations. Even if imperfectly realized, I saw at least one of my dreams set in stone.

Chapter 20

Bringing King to China

$\mathcal{B}$y the beginning of this century, my unique connection to Martin Luther King Jr. had become a passport to the world. Since then, I have lectured about him in South Africa, Zimbabwe, Tanzania, France, Germany, Belgium, the Netherlands, Israel (including the West Bank), Canada, and Great Britain. In 2008, I traveled to India with a group of Stanford students for a three-week seminar on Gandhi's life and legacy, which helped me understand King's indebtedness to Gandhi's ideas. The following year I returned to India with a congressional delegation that included John Lewis, the former SNCC chair who represented an Atlanta district in the House of Representatives, and Andrew Young, the former King aide, United Nations Representative, and Atlanta mayor who also served on the King Papers Project's National Advisory Board. The trip was organized to commemorate the fiftieth anniversary of King's 1959 pilgrimage to what he called "the land of Gandhi." Martin Luther King III and former Pennsylvania senator Harris Wofford, a longtime acquaintance of mine as well as of Martin Luther King Jr., also joined the delegation.

These travels increased my awareness of King's global significance. I discovered that the King name and the "Dream" refrain were familiar to many people throughout the world, even those who knew little about his background or his role in the Montgomery bus boycott, the Birmingham campaign, or the Selma-to-Montgomery voting rights march. As I have tried to expand awareness of King's ideas in other nations, I've begun to see him less as merely an African American civil rights leader and more as an international symbol of struggles for social justice and human rights.

I gained a special appreciation of the rewards and challenges of translating King's message for a foreign audience when the National Theatre of China in Beijing, the largest and most prestigious drama company in the country, performed my play

Passages of Martin Luther King in 2007. This venture grew out of the determined efforts of Cáitrín McKiernan, a stellar former student of mine at Stanford who worked at the King Papers Project during the summer after her graduation in 2002. A Santa Barbara native, Cáitrín came to Stanford after a childhood that was filled with worldly experiences. Her father, Kevin McKiernan, was a journalist and film-maker best known for his documentary *Good Kurds, Bad Kurds* (2001), made under difficult, often dangerous circumstances, about the Kurdish liberation movement in Iraq and Turkey. Cáitrín had attended an unusual boarding school where students gained a sense of self-reliance living in primitive conditions. At the age of sixteen, she lived for part of a year with a Chinese family and attended Chinese schools despite minimal previous exposure to the language. After graduating from Stanford with a focus on Chinese and African American studies, she became a Fulbright scholar researching the experience of Chinese women during their civil war.

When Susan and I decided to go to China for a three-week visit in 2005, part of the attraction was Cáitrín's offer to meet us in Beijing, arrange an apartment for all of us to share, and then serve as our personal guide. During this visit, we dis-cussed the need to spread awareness of King's ideas in China. Cáitrín recalled how impressed she had been seeing Danny Glover read passages from my play before an appreciative audience at an Oakland church. "Why not perform the play in China?" she asked.

I thought it was an interesting idea but hardly likely to happen. Nonetheless, she seemed determined to explore the possibilities. I imagined that she might convince a small theater group to perform the play in China, but this did not satisfy her. "If we're going to do it, let's do something big!" Although her enthusiasm soon infected me, many questions came to mind: Would the Chinese government allow a play about a human rights advocate and featuring scenes of civil disobedience to be per-formed in China? Could we raise the necessary funding for a production that would involve bringing gospel singers from the United States?

By the time Susan and I finished our visit, Cáitrín had decided to remain in Beijing to work on her ambitious plan. Early the following year, I was surprised to learn that she had contacted the National Theatre and that they had agreed to col-laborate on the project. She had also contacted the American Embassy to secure State Department support for a series of educational programs that would culmi-nate in an eventual full-scale production of the play. I returned to China in March 2006 to deliver lectures in Beijing and Shanghai that Cáitrín and the Embassy had arranged. China's largest web portal, sina.com, conducted an hour-long interview with me. I also had an encouraging meeting with Zhao Youliang, the National Theatre's president. We made plans to stage a dramatic reading of the play using a script that had been translated into Chinese. I agreed to work with Cáitrín to raise about $150,000 needed for travel-related expenses for me and the other American participants, funds to bring key members of the Theatre to the United States for planning discussions, and for the production in China. We also hoped to subsidize the production, so that free tickets would be available for students and their teachers.

The National Theatre performed a dramatic reading in May at Beijing's Oriental Pioneer Theatre before an enthusiastic audience that joined in singing "We Shall Overcome" after the performance. I became more convinced that Cáitrín's ambitious idea might actually come to fruition. It was apparent that Chinese young people—especially those in college—were curious about King. The receptiveness of the government-supported National Theatre encouraged me to believe that Chinese authorities wouldn't object to the production. The fact that Chairman Mao Tse-tung had made positive remarks about King probably influenced some Chinese officials, and I also learned that King's "I Have a Dream" address was widely assigned as required reading in Chinese high schools. Nonetheless, we could not be certain that Chinese authorities would permit the play to be performed until it actually happened.

With the play's international premiere now scheduled for the following spring, Cáitrín and I faced a daunting fundraising challenge. She initially expected that support would come from American multinationals and various Silicon Valley companies, but was disappointed that these companies did not want to risk displeasing the Chinese authorities, even though the National Theatre was taking a considerable risk to support the American initiative. We were more successful in soliciting American foundations, especially George Soros's Open Society Institute, the Rockefeller Brothers Fund, and the Asian Cultural Council. Stanford's president, John Hennessy, also committed funding to the King Institute for the production.

In January 2007 a delegation from the National Theatre arrived at Stanford to begin final preparations for the production in June. In addition to President Zhao, I welcomed Wu Xiao Jiang, the play's director, and Luo Dajun, the script adaptor. We spent several days carefully going over the script to translate its dialogue—infused with religious metaphors—into colloquial Chinese. "What does 'I've been to the Mountaintop' mean?" I recall Luo asking. "Why does King use the phrase 'a drum major for justice'?"

Worried that King's deep immersion in African American culture and religion would make it difficult for the Chinese audiences to understand it, we added a "Narrator" role to provide occasional background information. Some questions stymied us: How would a Chinese audience—and the Chinese censors whose approval was needed—react to a play that took place largely in a black Baptist church? How would they respond to scenes of civil disobedience? Luo also seemed perplexed by my depiction of "Martin" as a leader beset with doubts. "Chinese audiences want leaders to be strong and resolute," he remarked.

Cáitrín used some of our travel funds to take the delegation to Atlanta to attend a Sunday service at Ebenezer Baptist Church to observe the call-and-response interaction between Ebenezer's minister and his congregation. In addition to meeting members of King's family, the delegation also stopped in Memphis for a tour of the National Civil Rights Museum. When the delegation returned to the Bay Area, we took them to a reading of the play in the Rotunda of Oakland's City Hall, where they watched Aldo Billingslea and other African American actors and gospel singers energetically perform the reading in front of a predominantly black audience. They began to imagine how to bring together Chinese actors and African American singers for the first time in China.

Despite these preparations, I was not sure what to expect when I arrived in Beijing in June 2007. Susan decided that returning to Beijing would be too strenuous, given her diabetes, and I soon realized that my schedule was so crowded that I would have had very little time to spend with her. Cáitrín had already experienced difficulties with Luo Dajun over his translated script, which sometimes altered the meanings I had intended. One translated passage that was particularly troubling to us suggested that Martin's father was one of the people who may have contributed to his son's death. I asked for an English translation of the Chinese script but soon realized that Cáitrín would have to speak for me in negotiations over the final text.

When director Wu met with me, he seemed confident that the American singers would work well with his Chinese cast. Cáitrín's bilingual friend Alison Friedman had agreed to become the play's choreographer and served as a bridge in the initial discussion between Wu and the singers. We recruited September Penn, a gospel singer from St. Petersburg, Florida, and a veteran of two previous *Passages* readings, as one of two musical coordinators. I had met her in 2006 when her husband, Ivan, took one of my Stanford classes during his fellowship year in Stanford's John S. Knight Journalism Program. Kenneth Alston, a New York singer Penn recruited, served as the second coordinator. Penn and Alston worked closely with two singers from Stanford: Ré Phillips, a first-year student who was in Stanford's Talisman a cappella ensemble, and Chelsi Butler, co-rector of Stanford's Gospel Choir. Fred Alexander, a former Stanford student, also came to provide keyboard accompaniment.

The two weeks of preparation with the Chinese cast were a grueling endurance test for everyone involved, I was able, however, to leave rehearsals occasionally in order to give lectures to students and faculty members at various Beijing universities. A typical day in the Theatre's insufficiently air-conditioned studio would start in the morning and extend into the evening—longer than would be the case in American productions guided by union rules and far more strenuous than student drama productions. Wu demanded much from his Chinese actors, and their level of dedication was extraordinary.

I was fascinated, watching the actors take on their roles. Cao Li initially had difficulty performing Martin, but I had expected that this role would be especially challenging for someone who was unfamiliar with black ministers and African American oratorical styles. "It's impossible to completely translate Martin Luther King's speaking style into Chinese," Wu admitted. Zhou Ling imbued charm in the role of Coretta, and Du Zhenging deftly conveyed Daddy King's sometimes overweening paternalism. Cui Kai brought Malcolm X to life as Martin's determined antagonist. I had special fun teaching Stokely's Black Power gestures to the youthful Shi Zhan. Despite the rigors of the rehearsals, the Chinese actors were friendly and outgoing, and the choreographed scenes provided opportunities for laughter as the singers showed off dance moves. I was especially impressed that the singers—buoyed by their religious faith—managed to keep pace with their Chinese counterparts. At each day of rehearsals, I watched the bonds become stronger between the singers and the Chinese cast.

By opening night, June 21, 2007, the production had already attracted coverage in the *New York Times, Los Angeles Times, Atlanta Journal-Constitution,* and on National Public Radio. For the most part, the reports marveled at the fact that the play was going to happen in a nation known to suppress protests—indeed, the Oriental Pioneer Theatre was less than two miles from Tiananmen Square, where massive protests had been brutally suppressed by government troops just eighteen years earlier. One article noted that the play would mark the first time that National Theatre actors had ever performed with African Americans. The *Los Angeles Times* reporter mentioned that in previous Chinese plays, black characters had been performed by Chinese actors wearing black makeup—sometimes they would also use "white" makeup to play Europeans or Americans. Zhang Ying, who played King's mother, Alberta Williams King, was quoted as saying that the play gave her "a visceral feel" for how Americans understand the civil rights movement. "Through this process, the historic coming together of Chinese actors and African American singers, we've found a common ground."

Despite such positive feelings, the hours before the first public performance were filled with tension and emotion. Cáitrín was disturbed that the Narrator's implication of Daddy King's complicity in his son's murder had not been excised from the script, despite promises from Wu. I knew that Cáitrín was already upset that Wu and others in the National Theatre had ignored other requests she made. Despite her role as the play's producer, it was apparent that her youth and gender prevented her from gaining the respect that she deserved. When I met privately with Wu to insist that he make the change, I reminded him of the email I had sent several weeks earlier to reiterate my objection. I told him that American Embassy personnel would be at the opening and would find this gratuitous remark offensive. He apologized profusely but claimed that it was too late to alter the script. "The censor has already approved the play, and we can't make changes now," he pleaded.

I couldn't understand why he had not recognized the importance of this issue. There was nothing in my script that had indicated that Daddy King was anything other than a devoted father who was deeply saddened by his son's death. The Narrator character was intended to provide essential and accurate historical information, not to offer wild speculations about an assassination conspiracy. After I reported back to Cáitrín that Wu would not make the changes, I could see that she was even more dismayed than I was. For me, the issue threatened to be an embarrassment, although I could blame the script adaptor; for her, it undermined her sense of what she had accomplished after two years of determined effort.

The premiere and the following four performances were received enthusiastically received. Each night the three hundred seats in the theater were filled, mostly by college-age people. I was extremely proud of Cáitrín when she stood before the audience to introduce the first performance, speaking in both Chinese and English. Her father was there, along with other relatives to record Cáitrín's achievement. The footage shot by Cáitrín's father and Oscar-winning cinematographer Haskel Wexler would later be assembled in the documentary *Bringing King to China* (2011).

I followed the play's dialogue on the caption screen provided for each seat. Hearing the audiences laugh and applaud—thankfully at appropriate moments—allowed me to relax enough to enjoy watching Chinese actors portray the people who had helped shape my life. Despite the language barrier, I felt the force of Martin's sermons and oratory.

I saw that the audiences empathized with Martin and Coretta as they became lovers in Boston during the early 1950s and appreciated Daddy King's domineering affection for his son—and in time, for Coretta. They followed the intense debate between Martin and his ideological opponents, Malcolm and Stokely. I wondered, however, what they thought of Martin's ability to bring his grievances directly to President Kennedy in the White House at a time when Chinese protest leaders were often imprisoned. What did they think of the efforts of FBI director J. Edgar Hoover's use of secret surveillance and illegal tactics to undermine Martin?

I could see the Chinese audience responding emotionally to the play's musical subtext, the sacred songs that became freedom songs that sustained the African American struggle. I felt a special sense of accomplishment when the singers and actors staged the scene based on the 1963 Birmingham protests, carrying "Freedom Now" signs as they confronted Birmingham policemen. When the performances ended with the singing of "We Shall Overcome," I watched as young people stepped forward to talk with the singers, who stayed to teach English-speaking students some of the lyrics or answer questions about Martin and the play's other characters.

During the day before the penultimate performance, the singers and the Chinese cast went on an excursion to the Great Wall of China. I had been there before with Susan, but the unique setting provided the group many opportunities to display their close relationships—and even a few flirtatious ones—that had developed among individuals who had met just a few weeks earlier.

Following the last performance, I was exhausted yet elated that the play had succeeded in conveying King's ideas—and my reflections on the meaning of his life—across cultural boundaries. After a lively cast party—a banquet that went on for hours—I realized that I would probably never see the Chinese cast members again (although I did see Wu and Zhao the following year when they attended the King Institute's celebration of the King Holiday). I regretted that Susan and my King Institute colleagues were not there to witness this historic performance. I knew I could never convey to them the excitement of watching Chinese audiences discover Martin Luther King Jr., his family, and the African American freedom struggle.

Chapter 21

A Palestinian King Drama

I didn't expect that bringing *Passages of Martin Luther King* to the Palestinians in 2011 would resolve their conflict with Israel, but I hoped that audiences consisting of Muslims, Christians, and Jews might enjoy and perhaps find cause for hope in a play about a Christian minister whose ideas transcended sectarian boundaries. *Passages* had not enhanced human rights in China or freed the Tibetans, but I had been encouraged when Beijing audiences gave it an enthusiastic reception. I discovered that King's Dream had distinctive meanings for Chinese audiences and expected that Palestinians, in the midst of their own nonviolent struggle against the Israeli occupation, would also discover their own meanings in King's legacy.

My first visit to the region in December 1991 had been carefully orchestrated by Project Interchange and the American Jewish Committee to familiarize a small delegation of "African American leaders" with Israeli perspectives. I participated because of my long-standing interest in the Israel-Palestinian conflict and its impact on black-Jewish relations. During the 1980s and 1990s I had written several articles on the latter topic, joined a black-Jewish working group organized by Harvard scholar Henry Louis Gates, and appeared in the 1997 documentary *Blacks and Jews*. I came away from the 1991 visit most affected by what I didn't see regarding Palestinian perspectives. We traveled on a bus with curtains drawn, guarded by heavily armed Israeli soldiers, to meet with the Palestinian vice-mayor of Bethlehem during the First Intifada. That grassroots insurgency provided a counterpoint to our discouraging discussion with Likud hardliner Bennie Begin, son of former Israeli prime minister Menachem Begin.

I returned to the region in February 2010 to have substantive discussions with Palestinian proponents of nonviolent resistance. I learned that many of them were influenced by Gandhi and King. Their movement seemed tactically divided along lines that were familiar to me from my 1960s experiences with young activists challenging the more cautious approaches of older leaders. American Consulate officials who arranged my visit dissuaded me, however, from going to any of the protests that were occurring with increasing regularity in East Jerusalem and the West Bank.

During that visit, I proposed that the consulate support a Palestinian production of *Passages*. With financial assistance from the Consulate, the Jerusalem-based National Theatre of Palestine, Al Hakawati, agreed to perform the play. Lacking the time or financial resources that had enabled the key members of the National Theatre of China to work closely with me during the year preceding the Beijing production, I was concerned that my first meeting with the Palestinian director and his company would take place only after my arrival just nine days before the company would perform the first Arabic-language play about King.

Anticipating some difficulty in getting the play's six African American musicians and singers past passport control at the airport, I asked each of them to carry a copy of a letter from the U.S. Consulate requesting that the group receive "every possible courtesy" as participants in "an important U.S. cultural and educational exchange program." After I made it through airport security, however, I learned that Steve Wilson, a member of our group, had been detained. Steve, the musical director of Bethel Community Baptist Church in St. Petersburg, Florida, had never traveled abroad and had just received his passport. When I tried to find him, a security official informed me that the "guy with the Afro" was being questioned in an office near the passport control booths. The official apparently didn't notice Steve's baldness, but I didn't quibble and stood waiting until I was finally allowed to talk briefly with him as he waited for a new interrogator. Steve told me that his beard had prompted repeated questions about whether he was a Muslim. Insisting that he was a Christian, he had responded to additional queries about the purpose of his visit by referring to the Consulate letter. A tall, solidly built, dark-skinned African American, Steve was convinced that racial profiling caused his detention. Aware that Israeli security practice included profiling, I urged him to remain sufficiently calm to convince his interrogators that he really was a Baptist gospel singer rather than a Muslim terrorist. He was grilled for about an hour, and then released and rejoined the group in the airport's "Welcome to Israel" greeting area. The *Passages* contingent had overcome its first obstacle, though I shuddered to think what might have happened if Steve had been a Muslim.

While most of the group checked in at the comfortable Jerusalem Hotel, I moved into the even more comfortable American Colony Hotel (an indulgence I justified with the excuse that Susan would appreciate its history-laden ambience when she arrived later in the week). With the play's opening scheduled for Tuesday, March 22—little more than a week away—I felt relief and confidence that the American performers, in their roles as freedom fighters as well as the chorus of King's Ebenezer Baptist Church, would infuse the play with the same extraordinary energy that freedom songs had injected into the African American freedom struggle.

During our Skype conversations before my arrival, Kamel El-Basha, the Palestinian director, had voiced his concern about how Palestinians would react to the play's Christian context. Similar worries preceded the Beijing production, but the Chinese audiences had not seemed bothered by the play's gospel-inspired singing or its emphasis on King's Christian faith. Kamel advised that Palestinians were especially sensitive about Christian proselytizing, but he accepted that King's story could not be stripped of its Christian elements. I looked forward to seeing how he would integrate the singers' talents with those of his Palestinian actors, who had already been rehearsing for a month.

Three of the African American singers had performed in the Chinese production. September Penn was a featured singer in *Passages* and had played Coretta Scott King in several public readings of the script. Ivan Penn accompanied his wife, as he had on the China trip, intending to write features for his newspaper, the *St. Petersburg Times*. In addition to recruiting Steve Wilson, September had recommended P. Michael Williams, whose personal experience with homelessness added emotional depth to his singing. The play's choir also included Ré Phillips as well as Chelsi Butler, Stanford alums, who also participated in the Chinese production during their undergraduate years. Ré was serving as an American India Foundation Clinton Fellow, helping *dalit* women and children in New Delhi secure sustainable livelihoods through the arts and traditional handicrafts. I invited another singer, Aleta Hayes, a lecturer in Stanford's Drama Department and a noted choreographer, because of her strong voice and singular stage presence.

To document the Palestinian venture, I invited award-winning filmmaker Connie Field, with whom I had collaborated on the Mississippi civil rights documentary, *Freedom on My Mind*, and the recent multipart series on the anti-apartheid movement, *Have You Heard from Johannesburg?* Although Connie and the singers had agreed to participate in return for modest compensation to cover their expenses, their levels of engagement with Palestinian issues varied. Several of the singers were evangelical Christians who knew little about Palestinian concerns but welcomed the opportunity to visit the Holy Land and tour the Christian historical sites in Jerusalem's Old City. Connie, a Jewish leftist, looked forward to investigative forays into the West Bank with a Palestinian film crew. Her documentary film would later be released as *Alhelm: Martin Luther King in Palestine* (2012).

As we recovered from jet lag on our first full day in Jerusalem, our high expectations confronted the reality that we knew little about what was going to happen. An
orientation meeting arranged by the Consulate provided assurances that Jerusalem
was, for the most part, safe for tourists, but a security official also warned of the
dangers facing Americans venturing into the West Bank. I sensed that some of the
cast members were understandably concerned that the play would be performed
not only in Jerusalem but also in the West Bank towns of Jenin, Nablus, Bethlehem,
Hebron, Tulkarem, and Ramallah.

For myself, I hoped that this visit would offer opportunities to deepen my understanding of the Palestinian nonviolent movement, not only through the scheduled
events but also through unsupervised travel. I expected to learn more about the ways
in which King's Christian beliefs would affect how Palestinian Muslims received his
ideas. I knew from King's account of his 1959 visit to the Holy Land that he sympathized with the plight of the Palestinians, yet also saw Jerusalem through the
prism of his religious beliefs. In a sermon he delivered after returning, he recalled
the "captivating quality" he found there: "[T]here was something that overwhelmed
me, and before I knew it I was on my knees praying.... Before I knew it I was weep-
ing. And this was a great world shaking, transfiguring experience."

After the orientation, Kamel greeted me warmly. Articulate in English, the fifty-
year-old director made clear his great admiration for King "as a ray of light to all
believers in peaceful resistance around the world." He outlined his vision of the
play. He had already told me that he planned to adapt the script to make it more
accessible for Palestinian audiences, but I was wary about unexpected changes. The
dispute over the Chinese script implicating Daddy King in his son's assassination
still bothered me. Something always gets lost in translation, but it is also troubling
when something unexpected is added. Although Kamel assured me that 80 percent
of the text was still mine, I was eager to review the remaining 20 percent.

I later skimmed through my copy of the English version of the Arabic script, and
found that Kamel had created his own play as a frame for *Passages*. Using impro-
vised dialogue drawn from discussions with the Palestinian actors, he had written a
farce about disgruntled cast members rehearsing to perform a King play supported
by an American cultural exchange program and directed by a blind American who
could speak to the actors only through her Palestinian assistant. His concept enabled
the Palestinian actors to inject their own sentiments about their characters in my
play and, more generally, about, in Kamel's words, "the reality of the Palestinian
actors and their relationship with the American director." My play had become a
play within a Palestinian play. The play-within-the-play idea was hardly innovative,

but it was stunningly risky, given the challenge of blending a contemporary farce with the King story, using Palestinian and American performers, with only one week for rehearsals.

That afternoon, as I considered the implications of Kamel's ambitious vision, Jamal Ghosheh, the theater's general manager, drove me to Ramallah to withdraw money from the grant funds that the Consulate had supplied to cover the expenses of the American participants. He used the opportunity to express some of the frustrations that I had come to expect when a Palestinian confides in a foreigner assumed to be sympathetic. He pointed to the Jewish settlements crowning the surrounding hills, making certain that I could distinguish between established Palestinian towns and the large housing complexes constructed during the past few decades as part of Israel's effort to establish permanent Jewish-only Jerusalem suburbs. Jamal remarked that the Israeli government had constructed security fences and walls on confiscated Palestinian land that was typically far from the residences they were intended to protect. As we drove past the Qalandia checkpoint, Jamal stopped in front of the nearby refugee camp so that I could photograph the graffiti on the wall—fading expressions of Palestinian resentment amid the vast expanse of gray concrete.

After we withdrew the funds from a bank housed in one of Ramallah's ubiquitous modern towers with their stone façades, Jamal invited me to join him for tea. He explained the difficulty Al Hakawati faced as it tried to create a distinctively Palestinian theater. "There isn't much of a tradition of theater here," he noted, mentioning the difficulty of raising funds from Palestinian sources. Instead the theater relied on foreign institutions that were more interested in cultural exchanges rather than in nurturing Palestinian artists. Although he didn't mention my play, his comments reinforced the tone of Kamel's remarks earlier in the day. I knew that the pioneers of African American theater had faced similar difficulties when support was more likely to come from well-meaning white leftists than from the small number of affluent blacks. I asked Jamal whether Ramallah's rapid economic growth would eventually enable Al Hakawati to gain support from affluent Palestinians. He stated that Ramallah's Western financial backers wanted to tie the Palestinians to the world economy, rather than reinforce a culture of resistance to Israeli occupation.

As we returned to Jerusalem, Jamal explained that his permit to reside in the city meant that he didn't have to leave his car to walk through the Qalandia checkpoint. He said that this privilege hardly compensated for the fact that he was a stateless person, neither a Palestinian citizen nor an Israeli. His identity permit could be taken away for a variety of reasons, including political crimes or extended stays away from Jerusalem. Israeli West Bank policies encouraged Jews to commute from the West Bank to Jerusalem, while strongly discouraging this for Palestinians. "If they make it difficult enough for us, the Israelis believe that all Palestinians in Jerusalem will decide to leave," Jamal lamented. I had seen the checkpoints and the security fences on my previous year's visit, and I could not imagine becoming habituated to them. The walls provided safe, exclusive corridors for speedy travel by Israelis between the West Bank and Jerusalem, while simultaneously separating Palestinians from other Palestinians and breaking up neighborhoods.

The next morning I returned to Ramallah, this time with Connie, to attend a demonstration scheduled for that day in central Manara Square. I looked forward to witnessing a significant event in the Palestinian resistance movement and reuniting with my former Stanford student, Fadi Quran, one of the initiators of the demonstration. Fadi had participated in my 2008 overseas seminar in India while an undergraduate student. Even then, he had told me of his desire to apply the ideas of Gandhi and King to the Palestinian situation. When Fadi became ill in India, we developed a special bond while flying from Delhi to Ahmedabad to wait for the rest of the group to arrive by train. He told me about his experiences living in the West Bank and about his encounters with Israeli soldiers when traveling to and from the United States. His willingness to forgive the indignities sometimes inflicted on him by Israeli soldiers amazed me. He informed me by email that he had organized a group of young people for a hunger strike that would culminate in a major demonstration on March 15, and I knew I had to be there.

Connie and I arrived at the square by 10:00 A.M. Despite several days without food, Fadi looked remarkably energetic as he conferred with his associates. He had just finished his undergraduate work at Stanford the previous June, but he seemed more mature than his colleagues, many of whom looked to him for guidance. After he hugged me warmly, he expressed concerns that the demonstration, which had been initiated by young people infused with the principles of nonviolence, would be hijacked by Fatah and other groups.

Palestinian police tried to keep the streets open to traffic, but they eventually gave up as hundreds more protesters arrived. Fadi mentioned that his group had been harassed by the Palestinian Authority police, who refused to allow them to set up tents or even bring mattresses. He said the protest was not only against the Israeli occupation but also against Palestinian leaders who wanted the demonstration to show unity between Fatah and Hamas, the factions that had fought a bloody internecine war after Hamas prevailed in the 2006 Palestinian legislative council elections.

Fadi's fears were realized when a sound truck arrived blasting music. Soon afterward, large organized groups of protesters wearing black and white head scarves signifying Fatah affiliation flooded into the square. By early afternoon, the hunger-strikers were struggling to avoid being trampled by the ever-expanding crowd—which included government employees who were given time off to participate. Fatah leaders used loudspeakers to lead chants that were picked up by their followers, many of them waving the red, white, black, and green Palestinian flags. News reports paid little attention to the young hunger-strikers, although *Time* magazine later featured Fadi as "the face of the new Middle East"—surely a heavy burden of expectation to be placed on a twenty-three-year-old. While Fadi looked on in dismay, Mahmoud al-Aloul, a senior Fatah official, addressed the crowd and then embraced Hamas leader Abu Kweik. Instead of a mobilization of bottom-up people power, the demonstration became a show of top-down unity.

I made it back to Jerusalem in time to read through the script before the first rehearsal of the full cast. I was startled by Kamel's decision to cut the character of Martin's mother, Alberta Williams King. He later explained that no middle-aged female Palestinian actors could be found to play the role. The script also indicated that the Palestinian actors—or perhaps Kamel—had very little understanding of the characters in my play or the racial oppression King fought against. In Kamel's script, when the American director asks Ramzi Maqdisi, who plays Martin, to describe his character, he responds that Martin had been "fucked in the ass" by the FBI, a comment that might have been metaphorically appropriate but one I could not imagine being spoken on a Palestinian stage. Kamel's script also suggested that Martin was trapped into marrying Coretta, although I could not think of anything in my script that would justify such a harsh judgment about the woman Martin had ardently courted. At various points in the script, actors suddenly shifted out of their roles in my play: a Birmingham policeman arresting King begins speaking Hebrew rather than Arabic; the actor performing Malcolm models his gestures on those of Muammar Gaddafi; Coretta becomes Violet, a Palestinian radical strenuously objecting to the American flag draped on President Kennedy's casket, which was not mentioned in my script.

When Coretta/Violet loudly insists that the flag represents the American image—"it's ugly"—the American director, Leticia, responds by escalating the verbal confrontation:

LETICIA: What about your image? Terrorists!
VIOLET: If we are terrorists what are you doing here?
LETICIA: I don't believe you are terrorists. You're resisters.

VIOLET: Yeah, right.

LETICIA: I'm here as an artist, doing a cultural exchange…

VIOLET: We have a lot of those.

LETICIA: ….If we were doing a play about a Palestinian in America, wouldn't there be a Palestinian flag?

VIOLET: But you killed Martin Luther King and Kennedy. You Americans kill each other, every day.

LETICIA: You Palestinians kill each other, every day. This is only one face of America. There are many faces. We have 300 million people, fifty states.

VIOLET: ….The only face that we see is the veto face.

I expected that such dialogue might elicit emotional responses from Palestinian audiences, but I worried that this would overwhelm King's story. Were Kamel and his actors thumbing their noses at the American government that was helping to sponsor the play? When I voiced my concern that Kamel's script seemed to work at cross purposes from my own, he insisted that his adaptation would "serve the drama" of my play. "I know my audience," was his consistent theme. When I commiserated over drinks at the American Colony Cellar Bar with Mik Kuhman—the blind Leticia in Kamel's script—she expressed confidence in Kamel's talent as a director. "He trusts his actors, and they trust him," she explained, "even when he doesn't always make clear how it's all going to come together." Mik, who called herself a "movement and conceptual artist," had worked with Kamel on a previous play. She reassured me that Kamel could "get miracles out of people," even if the process was going to be difficult. She understood why I resisted major changes in my script but advised me that Palestinians had little regard for intellectual property considerations when adapting Western works for their own purposes. "It doesn't matter what play a Palestinian theater does," she explained, "it is always seen in reference to the situation here."

Uncertain whether a miracle would emerge from the rehearsals, the American cast members and I had several opportunities to learn more about the Palestinian situation. A visit to Bethlehem included a stop at the Church of the Nativity, an emotional experience for many of the singers. Then we took a guided tour of the Bethlehem area arranged by Sami Awad, the thirty-nine-year-old American-born son of Palestinian refugees, who was executive director of the Holy Land Trust. The nephew of Mubarak Awad, a pioneering figure in the Palestinian nonviolent movement and a dedicated proponent of the ideas of Gandhi, King, and Mandela, Sami Awad talked about his group's numerous but mostly unsuccessful protests to stop Israeli confiscation of Palestinian land. We visited a Palestinian sheep farm nestled in a valley that had been divided by a security fence installed to protect an elevated road to a settlement. In order to leave or return to their home, the family that owned the land had to ask Israeli soldiers for a key to a door in the fence. Despite protests and court rulings on behalf of the family, their prospects for remaining on the land looked dim. We also spent time with another Palestinian, whose home had been separated from the land he owned by the concrete walls that towered over a nearby settler road. His dire plight brought tears to the eyes of more than one of the singers.

We also visited the oddly named Abu Jihad Museum for Prisoners Movement Affairs on the campus of Al-Quds University in Abu Dis adjacent to Jerusalem. After I spoke to an animated audience of Al-Quds students and faculty members, our group was treated to an outdoor lunch that allowed me to exchange ideas with a variety of intellectual figures in the Palestinian resistance movement. The most prominent of these were the university's president, Sari Nusseibeh, a member of one of Jerusalem's most prominent Palestinian families, and his British-born wife Lucy Nusseibeh, the founding director of the influential organization, Middle East Nonviolence and Democracy (MEND). As I talked with Sari and Lucy, I became aware of the gulf between the guarded optimism of the Nusseibehs, Sami Awad, and the generation of activists convinced of the efficacy of nonviolent resistance and the disillusionment felt by many younger people who deprecated prospects for Palestinian liberation, through either violent or nonviolent means. Fadi and his comrades in Ramallah represented only a small minority of a Palestinian generation that, mostly, seems resigned to seeking basic human rights and career advancement rather than Palestinian nationhood.

Back in Jerusalem, the rehearsals moved ahead slowly during the weekend before the Tuesday opening. The difficulty of bringing the Americans and the Palestinians together when neither group spoke the other's language, as well as Kamel's script additions, caused my ninety-minute, one-act play to run at least two hours. The final dress rehearsal dragged noticeably, despite Kamel's decision to call a halt before the cast reached the concluding scene. "The rehearsal was terrible," Kamel admitted, "but sometimes a bad final rehearsal leads to a great opening night."

I had heard this before, but I was nonetheless dismayed that the final rehearsal did not include the conclusion I had written. My play ended with a powerful King sermon climaxed by a fantasy scene in which two of his strong antagonists, Malcolm and Stokely, join King as he proclaims, "If you have not found something worth dying for then you aren't fit to live." But in the new script, this passage came after most of the cast members had walked off the stage in protest over their failure to be paid (the Palestinian actors, ironically, were actually engaged in a wage dispute). The two characters who remain onstage then engage in a brief dialogue about whether they have a dream. When one of them says that his dream would be to perform a play about King without engaging in petty disputes, his fantasy is realized when the other actors return to finish the King play. Both plays, mine and Kamel's, had concluded with a fantasy—one to balance tragedy with hope, the other to balance farce with commitment.

Opening night went better than I could have expected. The mostly enthusiastic audience included many who were personally invited—including Al Hakawati board members and supporters, Consulate personnel, journalists, intellectuals, artists, and political activists. The broad humor of Kamel's script went over well, as did the spirited singing of the choir, which drew strong applause. As had been the case in China, African American music did not seem to require translation in order to have an emotional impact. The Christian religious context of the play also did not seem to be a problem, perhaps because the audience undoubtedly included a larger proportion of Christians and secularists than would be in attendance at subsequent performances.

Ramzi Maqdisi was also effective as Martin, exhibiting the necessary emotion and conviction in his declamations yet also exposing Martin's inner doubts. He later told me that his devoutly Islamic parents attended the play and recognized the common elements that linked King's faith to their own. Cynthia Harvey, the cultural affairs officer at the Consulate and the person most responsible for securing the funding, did not seem bothered by the outburst over the American flag. Amid the overall enthusiasm, my wife and I were among the few members of the audience who were aware that the fantasy ending of my play had been cut, but I still felt a sense of relief as I walked back to the American Colony Hotel.

I spent most of the following day in Bethlehem, where I spoke to a class on "Democracy and Human Rights" at Bethlehem University, but soon after returning to Jerusalem, I learned of an explosion in a central bus station where Susan and her longtime friend, Joni Reid, had caught a tour bus a few days earlier. The bomb took the life of a British Bible student living in Jerusalem and wounded more than thirty others. Although no organization took responsibility for the bombing, television reports soon linked the act to the escalating violence in Gaza, where Israel had launched air attacks against Hamas to retaliate for rockets fired into Israel. For the American singers, the bombing may have confirmed their submerged fears about coming to the region, but no one spoke openly about their concerns. Many Palestinians responded to the bombing by avoiding checkpoints that were set up afterward, and this reduced the size of the audience that came to the performance that night.

The evening performance left me completely deflated; Kamel had changed the play once again, moving Martin's concluding sermon to the play's beginning. I watched in shock as Ramzi, playing his Palestinian alter ego, Subhi, came onstage alone to "rehearse" his monologue. Caught off guard, I wondered how the play would end, only to discover that there was no conclusion—at least to my play.

After the performance, Kamel noticed me sitting glumly in my seat. He explained that he decided to shorten the play after seeing about fifty people leave during the final thirty minutes on opening night. "There's only two doors to the theater, Kamel," I responded angrily. "Don't you think I would have noticed fifty people leaving?" I reminded him that my original play was shorter and suggested that I would have preferred some cuts in his script. "Why do you think that moving the conclusion to the beginning solves the problem?"

Kamel responded that Palestinians could not absorb so much information at the end. "They need to get it when their minds are fresh," he explained. "They can put it in context later." I pleaded against the notion that a concluding monologue could be convincingly delivered by a character supposedly practicing a part. Kamel was just as insistent that he was making my play more accessible, but he finally conceded, "It's your play. If you want the ending changed back, we'll do it." We agreed that we would meet again the next day at 4:00 P.M., just three hours before the final evening performance in Jerusalem.

I did not sleep well and rose early the next morning to write an email to Kamel proposing that my original ending be restored but also suggesting that Daddy King's introduction of his son's final sermon be cut along with a few passages in the sermon itself. I also suggested cutting some of Kamel's additions, including the playing of a segment of Spike Lee's *Malcolm X* film showing the assassination.

I later learned that Kamel did not read my email before our meeting. While returning that afternoon from media interviews and meetings with youth groups in Ramallah, I heard that the matinee performance, before an audience mostly comprised of students, went well. I wondered whether this would strengthen Kamel's belief that he understood his audience, but I nonetheless looked forward to discussing it with him. After Kamel said everyone was welcome, including all the cast members who wanted to come, about twenty people crowded into the office.

Kamel explained his revisions, and I reiterated the concerns I had already expressed to him and then asked whether any of the cast members wanted to speak. Gina Asfour (Violet/Coretta) spoke up first, firmly supporting Kamel's view that the revised beginning would be more successful in reaching Palestinians. She repeated what I had heard from Kamel: "The Palestinians do not have a long history of theater, it is only thirty years old or so, and it's too much information to digest." Firas

Frah (Malcolm X) supported the revised opening by mentioning the way parables are presented in the Qur'an and cited the positive response of the afternoon's youthful audience.

Just as it seemed as though the entire cast would support the director, one of the American singers spoke up and suggested another option. I was stunned that P. Michael, one of the youngest of the cast members, would join the emotionally charged discussion. "Why don't we stay with the actor rehearsing Martin's speech in the beginning, but, at the end of the play, have him repeat the final lines, with Malcolm and Stokely joining him," he proposed. "This would satisfy both perspectives and tie it all together."

There was a moment of silence in the room before I interjected, "That sounds like a workable compromise—that is, if the new ending can be worked out during the next two hours." I suspected that Kamel and most of the cast members were pleased mainly by the prospect of finalizing the script after the multiple changes that had occurred during the last rehearsals and the first two days of public performances. When I returned that evening, the theater lobby was crowded, as it had been opening night. Security precautions associated with the bombing had apparently abated. After the performance, cast members agreed that it was the best night yet. "The show felt like an opening; it became our show, all of ours," Mik enthused. She attributed the increased energy of the cast to "having an open meeting, from being in on the discussion and being in on the solution." In contrast to the performers, I felt numb and exhausted after the long day.

The next morning I met with Ramzi. We had talked about King several times during the week, and I was pleased to learn that he had consulted Internet materials, including videos of King's speeches. He was the only one of the cast members who sought my views as a King scholar. Ramzi had also told me about his activist background as a Hamas sympathizer, his time in an Israeli jail, and the death of a younger brother, but he indicated that he wanted to move ahead in new directions. He mentioned his initial enthusiasm for President Obama: "I thought he was a savior, like Jesus, that he would understand our situation and help us." Like many Palestinians, he was devastated by the American veto of the United Nations resolution denouncing Israeli settlements as illegal. (I refrained from mentioning that the vote was cast by Susan Rice, one of my former students.) I asked him what he would tell Obama, if he were at the table with us. "I would not sit at a table with him," he replied quietly. "We would have nothing to say." Yet he also did not have a high opinion of the Palestinian Authority. "I would prefer to have the Israelis directly in charge," he remarked. "At least then we would know who our enemies are."

After Ramzi left, Cynthia Harvey, her associate Suzan Nammari, and Frank Finver, the Counselor for Press and Cultural Affairs, came by to take me and the other Americans for a relaxing outing at the Dead Sea. We needed a break, and the Palestinians perhaps needed a break from us. It was our first full day since our arrival that did not involve meetings related to the play. Along the way, P. Michael was able to fulfill his childhood dream of riding a camel. Mik and the singers covered themselves with Dead Sea mud and floated in the salt-saturated water. No one talked about the script. I enjoyed photographing their fun, even though I did not join in.

The next day I tried to gather my thoughts for a presentation at the MEND conference in Ramallah organized by Lucy and her colleague Walid Salem. After the unexpected issues relating to the play, I wondered whether I could contribute anything useful to the Palestinian resistance movement. If I had learned anything during the previous week, it was that many Palestinians saw the world rather exclusively in the context of their own oppression. I had arrived with a sense that they could learn important lessons from the African American freedom struggle, but I had begun to conclude that each sustained freedom movement tended to view itself as unique and understandable truly only from the inside. Yet I persisted in believing that my own activism and my career studying liberation movements had produced at least a few insights of universal significance.

My presentation at the conference was cautious and restrained, but it contained what I considered were the play's lessons for the Palestinians: that King was, like other great movement leaders, a flawed, vulnerable human being caught up in a mass movement whose greatness derived from his ability to argue persuasively for his principles. I talked about my early involvement with King's youthful critics and my generalized suspicion of charismatic leaders, even visionaries such as King. I thought of Fadi when I urged Palestinians to build a liberation movement that did not replicate existing "pyramids of power" under new leaders. The successful twentieth-century movements that had succeeded in turning peasants (and the children and grandchildren of peasants) into citizens had produced visionaries such as Gandhi, King, and Mandela, but it had also produced liberators who became tyrants using force to stay in control of "people's" democracies.

I saw little likelihood that the few hundred proponents of nonviolence who gathered at the Ramallah conference posed any immediate threat to the power of Fatah or Hamas or, even less, Israel. For proponents of bottom-up movements, evidence of success typically comes in small increments. I could only hope that Palestinians could accept useful lessons from the past and pass on the enduring lessons of their struggle.

Although the cast had another week of performances in the West Bank ahead of them, my involvement with the play ended on Sunday night, March 26, at the Freedom Theatre inside the Jenin refugee camp. The bus ride from Jerusalem took us through the beautiful hills of the northern West Bank. The cast was more relaxed and amiable than ever, with Americans and Palestinians interacting as friends rather than the strangers they had been less than two weeks earlier. (The cast in China connected similarly during their day together at the Great Wall.) We stopped at a small art fair at one of the attractive Palestinian towns, a location that would be a magnet for tourists if it were located anywhere else in the world. When we arrived at the Freedom Theatre, we were greeted by a colorful poster for a previous production of *Alice in Wonderland*, and then, warmly, by the small staff.

Juliano Mer-Khamis had established the Freedom Theatre in 2006, working with Zakariya Zubeidi, the former local military leader of the Al-Aqsa Martyr Brigades. Juliano's father, Saliba Khamis, was a Christian Palestinian, while his mother, Arna Mer, was a Zionist Communist who became an activist for Palestinian rights and worked with her son to raise funds for the building. Juliano's 2003 documentary, *Arna's Children*, had dramatized his mother's efforts to bring theater to refugee children, many of whom were victims of the bitter fighting that had taken place at the camp during the Second Intifada.

Seeing the youngsters playing near the theater building as we familiarized ourselves with the new venue, it was possible for us, at least for a moment, to ignore that tragic history. I handed out King Institute buttons to the kids, and soon they came back gesturing for more—pointing to their friends and siblings. Inside the theater there was bench seating for perhaps 150 people, with the small stage located close to the first row. With only two hours to prepare, cast members explored the set that had been moved from Jerusalem. The singers joked with each other, loudly belting lyrics from popular songs as the children outside listened with curiosity.

I'll never forget the Jenin performance. Drawn together by the intimate setting, the mostly youthful audience intently watched the actors and singers perform the play with a confidence they had not previously shown. The earlier disputes over the script were supplanted by the joy of bringing the play to an audience that appreciated a brief diversion from Palestinian reality and perhaps felt the force of King's enduring message.

The next day, after a farewell luncheon with the cast members, Susan and I flew back to California. Although I regretted having to miss the final performances, I was relieved that the experiment in cross-cultural collaboration had gone well, despite unexpected difficulties.

A week later, as I was about to deliver a speech at Virginia Tech marking the four-year anniversary of the massacre on that campus, I heard that Juliano Mer-Khamis had been shot and killed near Jenin, reportedly by Islamic militants. Palestinian friends suggested that the killing may have been a fundamentalist response to the Freedom Theatre's encouragement of women and girls to watch and participate in theatrical performances.

I learned that cast members were understandably stunned by the killing, and some of the American singers questioned whether they would go ahead with the final performance in Ramallah. I felt guilty that I had departed before the play had finished its run. Nonetheless, I was pleased and proud that the cast members decided to perform the show. Several singers told me that the final performance went very well, all things considered. I found myself wondering what would have happened if we had been aware of the imminent possibility of deadly violence before the Freedom Theatre performance. Would I have wanted the play to go on? What if the Freedom Theatre's decision to welcome an American-sponsored play about a Christian advocate of nonviolence had been the final provocation for Juliano's killers? Upon reflection and after thinking about all that had happened since I had arrived, I decided that I would never know whether the killing had anything to do with us or the play. Perhaps it was something only Palestinians could truly understand.

Chapter 22

Obama's Conscience

*E*arly in the morning of October 16, 2011, after a red-eye flight from San Francisco, I arrived in Washington, D.C., to participate in the dedication of the Martin Luther King Jr. National Memorial. Hurricane Irene had briefly threatened the nation's capital in August, causing the cancellation of the original dedication ceremony that would have coincided with the forty-eighth anniversary of the March on Washington. The excitement I initially felt when Susan and my King Institute colleagues accompanied me that weekend was now replaced with an eagerness to finish what had been postponed. I had already experienced the thrill of seeing the King Memorial for the first time and had come to terms with the fact that while it was not quite what I had imagined it was nonetheless an impressive new addition to the National Mall. On this occasion, my expectations were modest: attend the dedication ceremony, exchange greetings with acquaintances, listen carefully to what President Barack Obama has to say, and then catch a late-afternoon flight back to California.

I realized of course that attending the dedication was not something I should take for granted. So much had changed since that day in 1963 when I participated in the March on Washington, but I was still in many respects the wide-eyed observer I had been as a teenager. I felt fortunate that I could afford to fly rather than hitch rides across the country and that I had a special invitation to the event. After being briefly deflated when I was told that my name was not on the VIP list, I was relieved that Harry Johnson, head of the King Memorial Project Foundation, intervened to get me through the security checkpoints into the small cordoned-off area in front of the memorial where Obama would give his speech.

At the 1963 march, I had been alone amid a mass of strangers, but now I recognized many acquaintances among the several hundred people who sat in assigned seats or mingled in the area. The familiar faces reminded me of various stages of my improbable journey from novice activist to editor of King's papers to participant in the design of the King Memorial. I spoke briefly with several SNCC veterans, including Bob Zellner, the group's first white staff member, and Julian Bond, the group's former communications director who had since become the NAACP's board chair. I waved to SNCC's former chair John Lewis, who was one of the many members of the Congressional Black Caucus in attendance. I had become better acquainted with him during our 2009 visit to India to commemorate King's trip fifty years earlier. Representatives Shirley Jackson Lee and Al Green, who had also participated in the commemoration, waved in recognition.

I was especially pleased that Bonnie Fisher and Boris Dramov of ROMA Design Group were there, because they were most responsible for what, I thought, was best in the memorial. They seemed pleased and gave no hint of disappointment that some of their ideas had not been implemented in the final design. Later in the day, I would meet Lei Yixin, the sculptor of the Stone of Hope. Although I remained disappointed that his stern-looking statue of King failed to capture the essence of the Bob Fitch photo I had recommended, I found Lei friendly and engaging when we talked briefly. (By a happy coincidence, Cáitrín McKiernan, who had brought *Passages of Martin Luther King* to Beijing, was there to translate.)

When I saw Dorothy Cotton, she excitedly told me that she had been invited to go to the White House after the ceremony. During the previous two decades, Dorothy had often visited Stanford, and sometimes stayed with Susan and me. I was pleased that she was finally finishing the memoir that we had helped edit. I expected that her account of the achievements of SCLC's Citizenship Education Program would bring her the attention she deserved.

I made a special effort to exchange greetings with members of the King family seated in the front row. King's sister, Christine King Farris, who was the King Center's treasurer when I first started there, caught my attention with her stylish dark-blue suit and eye-catching hat. After the event we had a chance to chat when I introduced her to Bonnie and Boris while standing next to the Stone of Hope. Mrs. Farris's gregarious son, Isaac Jr., who had served as the King Center's president a few years earlier, greeted me with a warm hug.

It was good to see Martin Luther King III, his wife Arndrea, and their daughter Yolanda again. Susan and I had spent a wonderful afternoon at their home while I was a visiting professor at Morehouse in 2009. I met with Martin again in June 2011 when we discussed an ambitious new effort, funded by J. P. Morgan, to digitize all of the historical materials at the King Center. The King Papers Project had, with far fewer resources, made progress toward this goal during the 1990s, and I tried unsuccessfully to convince Martin to make the new venture a collaboration with the King Institute. (Soon after the 2012 King Holiday, Martin would fall victim to continued internecine familial conflicts and resign as the King Center's president after Dexter and other members of the Center's board stripped him of much of his authority and named his sister Bernice King as the Center's CEO.)

In the minutes before Obama's arrival, I noticed Jesse Jackson sitting near me with a somewhat glum expression on his face. I remembered how vibrant he had been while campaigning to be president and when we spent time together in Dakar, Senegal, during the 1994 African and African American Summit. He had visited the King Papers Project's office at Stanford on several occasions, but I had seen little of him since 2006, when our paths crossed at the commemoration of the 1966 Chicago Campaign. I wondered what Jesse thought as he sat there largely ignored, pushed from the limelight by the younger speakers at the dedication. He must have realized that Obama's presidency would not have been possible without his own presidential campaigns of the 1980s. I attended the 1984 Democratic National Convention when Jackson delivered his stunning evocation of the American "rainbow": "Our flag is red, white and blue, but our nation is a rainbow—red, yellow, brown, black and white—and we're all precious in God's sight." Two decades later Obama issued a similar call at the 2004 Democratic National Convention: "There's not a black America and white America and Latino America and Asian America; there's the United States of America." Jesse had shown how black voters and other racial minorities could be mobilized to participate in the political process while still attracting a significant number of white voters. Jesse's historical significance would never equal that of King or Obama, but he was certainly the most important link between the two.

Jesse's downcast demeanor contrasted with the ebullience of Al Sharpton when he entered the seating area after speaking to the large crowd gathered in an open area near the memorial. I had once seen him as Jesse's protégé during the time when we were all together in Dakar, but he had quickly risen in stature and influence while Jesse faded from national prominence. Like Jesse, he had always been friendly toward me and had recently spent a day at the Stanford office interviewing me for a television program he was producing.

By the time Obama made his entrance, I was tired from walking around but still wanted to stand close to the front of the podium to take photographs of the dedication speech. I was eager to hear what the president would say about the memorial and King's legacy. I had been impressed by Obama's ability to speak knowledgeably about King and the Movement in some of his addresses. Many politicians I heard at King Holiday events used King quotes—often from the "I Have a Dream" oration—to embellish otherwise dull speeches or to support positions that King would have found vapid or even objectionable. I was disturbed, for example, when opponents of affirmative action policies cited King's vision of a future when his children would be judged "by the content of their character, rather than the color of their skin." I often lamented that King's "Dream" had become a reassuring affirmation of racial progress rather than a disquieting reminder of unrealized ideals.

During Obama's extraordinary presidential campaign, I became convinced that his success as a candidate was in some way related to his understanding of King's oratory and of King's role in the modern African American freedom struggle. I knew, of course, that there were many differences between King, the son, grandson, and great-grandson of Baptist preachers, and Obama, who grew up with little knowledge of his father and paternal roots. King was born into a close-knit, extended family in a Southern black urban community during the culminating decades of the long struggle to overcome the Jim Crow system. Obama, in contrast, was raised by his white mother and white grandparents, mostly in the multicultural milieu of Hawaii, and came of age more than a decade after the passage of major civil rights reforms.

As was true for many African Americans of Obama's generation, King's legacy became a central element of his identity as a black man and as an American. In his memoir, *Dreams of My Father*, he had written movingly about finding his life's purpose as a young man by thinking of "romantic images" of the Southern freedom struggle, and of college students

> placing their orders at a lunch counter teetering on the edge of riot. SNCC workers standing on a porch in some Mississippi backwater trying to convince a family of sharecroppers to register to vote. A country jail bursting with children, their hands clasped together, singing freedom songs. Such images became a form of prayer for me, bolstering my spirits, channeling my emotions in a way that words never could.

As they did for me in my youth, these images convinced Obama that he wasn't alone in his struggles. We both came to realize that black communities could be "more than just the place where you'd been born or the house where you'd been raised. Through organizing, through shared sacrifice, membership had been earned."

I had put off the notion of becoming a SNCC worker to finish my college education, but Obama had persisted in his dream of contributing in some way to the remnants of the Movement that still remained in the 1980s. He eventually saw that the Movement of his dreams "had died years ago, shattered into a thousand fragments." When he attended a lecture by Kwame Toure, formerly Stokely Carmichael, he was put off by the dogmatism he heard. "It was like a bad dream." Nonetheless, his desire to become a community organizer eventually landed him a job organizing black residents in Chicago.

Obama's life story seemed to bring together the two large themes of my own life: the bottom-up perspective of SNCC combined with the visionary ideals of Martin Luther King Jr. As in my case, Obama came to admire King after first being influenced by Malcolm X and black activists who challenged King's ideals of nonviolence and interracialism. He would come to see that King was the most profound spokesperson to emerge from a historic freedom struggle that was beyond the control of a single charismatic leader. Obama learned, as I belatedly realized, that King's central role had been to link the aspirations of black Americans to the nation's traditional egalitarian and democratic values.

In *The Audacity of Hope*, Obama recalled that during visits to the Lincoln Memorial he would "look out over the Reflecting Pool, imagining the crowd stilled by Dr. King's mighty cadence." Such occasions strengthened Obama's sense of connection to "those like Lincoln and King, who ultimately laid down their lives in the service of perfecting an imperfect union." Obama's mother, his biracial identity, and the creation of the King Holiday all contributed to his awareness of King's importance as a symbol of the nation's effort to overcome racial oppression and realize its egalitarian ideals.

As a presidential candidate, Obama had continued King's dialogue with "the architects of our republic" about the meaning of the American Dream. He drew inspiration from an American tradition of democratic thought that extended back through King to Lincoln, whose great speech at Gettysburg provided a template for King's prepared remarks at the March on Washington, and then to Jefferson. Both King and Lincoln had recognized that the nation's destructive racial divisions could be bridged only if Americans resolved to "make real" the promise of universal human rights that justified their nation's Declaration of Independence. The source of King's greatness as an orator and of Obama's as a politician was their ability to transcend contemporary issues and access the timeless shared ideals of Americans of all races.

I had watched live on television as Barack Obama gave his acceptance address at the Democratic National Convention in Denver on August 28, 2008—exactly forty-five years after I saw King deliver his "I Have a Dream" oration. There were more than 80,000 supporters packed into the stadium. It was already the following morning in New Delhi, India, where I was staying at the Gandhi Darshan guesthouse with a group of Stanford students enrolled in my Overseas Seminar on Gandhi's contemporary relevance. My travels and talks in India made me aware of the enormous interest there was in Obama, who had quickly become the most widely admired African American leader since King.

Given his evident admiration for King, Obama was aware of the coincidence that the Denver speech, the most widely watched speech of his political career, occurred on the same August date as King's most famous oration. The main portion of his speech was characteristically lucid and certainly uplifting. I found, however, that it lacked the metaphorical richness and intellectual depth that I associated with King's speeches or even Obama's best speeches. He reiterated his basic campaign theme: "Change happens because the American people demand it, because they rise up and insist on new ideas and new leadership, a new politics for a new time." Although his forceful criticisms of Republican candidate John McCain as well as of "the broken politics in Washington and the failed policies of George W. Bush" elicited sustained cheers and applause, there was, I thought, little in the speech that was likely to be long remembered.

Obama waited until his conclusion before referring to the anniversary of King's speech. As he turned from partisan politics to his overriding theme of overcoming the nation's divisions, he transcended the transitory partisan concerns of the moment and offered a brief reference to King's 1963 speech. Adapting King's Dream for his own purposes, he spoke for a generation that understood King not as the controversial dissenter I had seen in the flesh but as the revered national icon he would become after his assassination. Obama spoke with confidence that Americans of all races would accept his linkage of King with "that American spirit, that American promise that pushes us forward even when the path is uncertain; that binds us together in spite of our differences." His speech reflected the transformation of the nation's racial attitudes since King's death. He mentioned those of us who had gathered at the Lincoln Memorial to "hear a young preacher from Georgia speak of his dream," and observed that we "could've heard words of anger and discord" or "been told to succumb to the fear and frustration of so many dreams deferred." Instead, he asserted "people of every creed and color, from every walk of life" heard "that in America, our destiny is inextricably linked. That together, our dreams can be one."

I wondered at the time whether Obama was consciously diminishing the centrality of King in his political consciousness as he came nearer to the presidency.

Would he have the confidence to become a boldly transformative president who could fuse SNCC's bottom-up organizing ethos with King's visionary message? Would fear of scaring off white voters with talk of grassroots mobilization and egalitarian ideas prevent him from adopting Jesse Jackson's strategy of building a new electoral majority by vigorously encouraging the political participation of those who rarely or had never voted?

These questions were still on my mind when Susan and I traveled to Washington for Obama's inauguration in January 2009. In the weeks before that historic day, I pondered the significance of his election. It was not just that he was the first president with known African ancestry; he was also the first president with a non-European father and the first son of an immigrant to the United States. More important to me, he was the first president who had come of age after years of freedom struggles in the United States and elsewhere in the world that had transformed colonial subjects and victims of racial discrimination into citizens with the right to shape the destinies of their nations.

Standing in the cold that day, I thought back to the march in 1963 when I had been at the other end of the Mall in front of the Lincoln Memorial. Then we had been seeking to grab the attention of those elsewhere around the National Mall— President Kennedy, who had no black members of his cabinet, and a Congress with only five black members. Many of the demonstrators who had been at the Lincoln Memorial in 1963 were now seated in places of honor behind the platform where Obama would take his oath of office.

I was pleased just to have a ticket to one of the areas in front of the Capitol, although the ticket turned out to be of little use in the chaotic bustle of more than a million people also trying to be witnesses to history. Susan fell and hurt her arm as we scurried to reach one of the checkpoints with a color that matched the color on our ticket. We finally found a place where we could at least see the Capitol steps, though not the speaker's podium. Unlike in 1963, I couldn't just squeeze my way past the crowd to get a better view, but I had once again become distracted by the time the main speech on the program began. Rather than thinking of how to find my bus to take me back to Indianapolis, I was worried about how Susan would get medical attention for her aching arm, which we later learned was broken.

Obama's inauguration speech was somewhat of a letdown. It was as if his success in winning the nomination and then the presidency had moved him away from the attributes I thought he shared with King and the Movement. It wasn't a bad speech—he seemed incapable of delivering one on an important occasion. He said many of the things that needed to be said by an able and earnest president facing daunting challenges. The best passage came early in the speech when he said,

> On this day, we gather because we have chosen hope over fear, unity of pur-
> pose over conflict and discord. On this day, we come to proclaim an end to
> the petty grievances and false promises, the recriminations and worn-out
> dogmas that for far too long have strangled our politics. We remain a young
> nation. But in the words of Scripture, the time has come to set aside child-
> ish things. The time has come to reaffirm our enduring spirit; to choose our
> better history; to carry forward that precious gift, that noble idea passed on
> from generation to generation: the God-given promise that all are equal, all
> are free, and all deserve a chance to pursue their full measure of happiness.

It was the closest he would come to the themes that were central to SNCC's organizing and King's oratory and to the historical dialogue about the evolving meaning of the Declaration of Independence. But the passage was submerged in a speech that seemed rooted in an older vision of America that predated King. Except for a few contemporary references—mostly about foreign policy concerns—the rest of the address might have been delivered by any Democratic president going back to Franklin D. Roosevelt.

Perhaps it was inevitable that Obama's presidency could not live up to the idealis-tic hopes of his campaign. Promising to transcend destructive partisanship was easier than finding effective ways to accomplish this goal. Once he became president, he would make fewer references to King's Dream as he confronted the partisan conflicts that prevent serious efforts to deal with the nation's problems. Only when the occa-sion required did he have much to say about the ideals that had shaped his identity as a young man. He seemed unwilling to apply King's principles to the political realities he encountered. When he accepted the Nobel Peace Prize in 2008, he mentioned King while at the same time insisting that he could not be guided by King's principles.

> As someone who stands here as a direct consequence of Dr. King's life's
> work, I am living testimony to the moral force of non-violence. I know
> there is nothing weak—nothing passive—nothing naïve—in the creed and
> lives of Gandhi and King. But as a head of state sworn to protect and defend
> my nation, I cannot be guided by their examples alone. I face the world as
> it is, and cannot stand idle in the face of threats to the American people.
> For make no mistake: evil does exist in the world. A non-violent movement

could not have halted Hitler's armies. Negotiations cannot convince al Qaeda's leaders to lay down their arms. To say that force is sometimes necessary is not a call to cynicism—it is a recognition of history; the imperfections of man and the limits of reason.

I found it difficult to accept Obama's argument that King's ideas were good enough to win the presidency yet not suitable as guides for his presidency. King, like Gandhi, knew about social evil and terrorism through personal experience. King's notion of nonviolence was not a capitulation to evil. He based his strategy of nonviolent resistance to evil on political as well as moral insights. His critique of American foreign policy called not for unilateral disarmament but for "a radical revolution of values" that would transform the nation "from a thing-oriented society to a person-oriented society." If he had lived to see Obama's election, he might have reminded the president that such a revolution of values would lead American leaders to "look uneasily on the glaring contrast of poverty and wealth," to question the "Western arrogance of feeling that it has everything to teach others and nothing to learn from them," and to "lay hands on the world order and say of war: 'This way of settling differences is not just.'"

By the time Obama spoke at the King Memorial dedication his failure to bridge the ideological divide in American electoral politics had defined his presidency. But he reminded me that morning of what had attracted me to his candidacy four years earlier. Perhaps realizing that his speech at the memorial would probably receive little press attention or affect the overall narrative of his presidency, he allowed himself to be more reflective than oratorical. Since the audience in front of him consisted of a few hundred invited guests rather than the thousands watching on television screens a short distance away, he displayed little of his characteristic energy. He acknowledged that King's contributions as a leader came in the context of a mass and sustained social movement:

> Dr. King would be the first to remind us that this memorial is not for him alone. The movement of which he was a part depended on an entire generation of leaders. Many are here today, and for their service and their sacrifice, we owe them our everlasting gratitude. This is a monument to your collective achievement.

I was pleased when Obama praised King's speech at the march on Washington, stating that: "because of Dr. King's moral imagination, barricades began to fall and bigotry began to fade"—while also insisting that progress did not come from words alone: "Progress was purchased through enduring the smack of billy clubs and the blast of fire hoses. It was bought with days in jail cells and nights of bomb threats." Obama's words paralleled my own feelings, as expressed in *Passages* and in many speeches, about the importance of King's final years:

> We forget now, but during his life, Dr. King wasn't always considered a unifying figure. Even after rising to prominence, even after winning the Nobel Peace Prize, Dr. King was vilified by many, denounced as a rabble rouser and an agitator, a communist and a radical. He was even attacked by his own people, by those who felt he was going too fast or those who felt he was going too slow.

I could see that Obama appreciated the complexities of King's historical role. He understood that King's Dream encompassed not simply civil rights reform but a basic reordering of American values and a restructuring of American society. "I raise all this because nearly 50 years after the March on Washington, our work, Dr. King's work, is not yet complete," he remarked:

> In too many troubled neighborhoods across the country, the conditions of our poorest citizens appear little changed from what existed 50 years ago— neighborhoods with underfunded schools and broken-down slums, inadequate health care, constant violence, neighborhoods in which too many young people grow up with little hope and few prospects for the future.

The speech he delivered at the dedication conveyed goals that had been the central themes of his domestic agenda: "fixing our schools so that every child—not just some, but every child—gets a world-class education, and making sure that our health care system is affordable and accessible to all, and that our economic system is one in which everybody gets a fair shake and everybody does their fair share." Obama, I was sure, wanted Americans to see that King saw "his charge not only as freeing black America from the shackles of discrimination, but also freeing many Americans from their own prejudices, and freeing Americans of every color from the depredations of poverty." He acknowledged the tension between his own optimistic calls for the end of partisan divisions and his realization that his goal should not be "false unity that papers over our differences and ratifies an unjust status quo."

Dr. King understood that peace without justice was no peace at all; that aligning our reality with our ideals often requires the speaking of uncomfortable truths and the creative tension of nonviolent protest. But he also understood that to bring about true and lasting change, there must be the possibility of reconciliation; that any social movement has to channel this tension through the spirit of love and mutuality. If he were alive today, I believe he would remind us that the unemployed worker can rightly challenge the excesses of Wall Street without demonizing all who work there; that the businessman can enter tough negotiations with his company's union without vilifying the right to collectively bargain.

Obama's speech reminded me of King's cautionary remark at the March on Washington about "drinking from the cup of bitterness and hatred." In 1963 King had reason to fear a turn toward destructive black militancy, but he was more willing than Obama to welcome "whirlwinds of revolt" that would "shake the foundations of our nation until the bright day of justice emerges." I realized that Obama won the presidential election despite his background as a community organizer rather than because of it. He admired King's nonviolent idealism, but as president he did not want to risk encouraging a nonviolent protest movement in support of global peace and social justice. Ironically, the right-wing Tea Party rather than the Occupy campaign became the most politically effective mass movement of Obama's presidency.

I was not surprised that Obama did not use King as a model for his presidency, but I was disappointed that his unique virtues as a candidate lamenting partisan divisions had proven so ineffective in bridging them once he became president. Although his Republican opponents painted him as a radical, he sought to govern as a conciliator but lacked the political skill to reduce partisan conflict—an achievement that would have guaranteed his second term. As a candidate, he insisted that the nation's long-term problems required bipartisan solutions, but as president he distanced himself from the findings of his own bipartisan budget commission. Instead of boldly announcing that he would sign major pieces of legislation only after proposals put forward by a majority of congressional Republicans had been incorporated, he expended his political capital to gain passage of moderate legislation without any Republican support. Obama's greatest achievement during his first term was to enact a health-care law modeled on Mitt Romney's Massachusetts plan, but the mandate to purchase private insurance disappointed many of his strongest supporters, greatly strengthened his most implacable opponents, and revealed his inability to translate campaign rhetoric into an effective political strategy to guide his presidency.

Obama's thoughtul speech in front of the memorial recieved polite but unenthusiastic applauase. Disappointed by Obama's passionless delievery, the Movement veterans in the audience, I am certain, were thankful that the commemoration speech was delievered by a president who appreciated King's visionary ideals. Obama had not yet become the transformational leader many of us expected or hoped for, nevertheless, I remembered a time when I was disappointed that King did not display SNCC's brash boldness. However, I judged him more favorably dueing his final years, when he willingly sacrificed his popularity on behalf of his ideals. As Ella Baker once warned, leaders sometimes have feet of clay, but I have long believed that the great movements to achieve a more just world should rely on bottom-up activism rather than top-down leadership.

Chapter 23

An Enduring Dream

*I*expect to return to the National Mall on August 28, 2013, the fiftieth anniversary of the March on Washington. I will be sixty-nine years old and a much different person than the nineteen-year-old student who found a way to get to the march without a clear sense of how to get home. Since then, faded memories have been sharpened by a better understanding of what I saw and what I wished I had seen. It is difficult for me to imagine what I would have done with my life if I had not attended; yet it was largely serendipity that brought me to the march and often serendipity that got me to this point in my life. Biographers and historians often point to contingencies as well as intentions in order to explain what happened in the past. Certainly my adulthood is evidence that poor planning, good timing, and lots of luck—or, as some would say, grace—can produce a rewarding life. I could not have expected that my formative experiences growing up in a town with only a handful of black residents would prepare me to participate—even as a foot soldier—in the African American freedom struggle. Or that my somewhat haphazard education would prepare me to write about African American history, to edit the papers of a leader who was deeply rooted in that history, and to convey that leader's visionary ideas to the world. Only in retrospect can I see that the incorrigible youthful curiosity of my childhood led me to a historic freedom struggle that gave me as well as countless other people a compelling sense of purpose and mission.

Perhaps I would have become involved in the struggle even if I had not met Stokely Carmichael on the eve of the march. I was fortunate that my first impression of a SNCC worker was so indelible and that my first demonstration was, as Martin put it in his speech, "the greatest demonstration for freedom in the history of our nation." It was also fortunate that I had my first encounter with Bob Moses, an exemplar of SNCC's bottom-up organizing ethos, soon after the march. At first, I viewed the Movement from SNCC's perspective as the "great revolution" that John Lewis mentioned in his speech at the march and as the culmination of years of Southern grassroots organizing and activism. SNCC's influence attracted me to Ella Baker's idea of "group-centered" leadership rather than "leader-centered" groups. I learned through studying SNCC's history that resistance to subordination and to oppressive conditions is ubiquitous and universal, even though sometimes isolated, ineffective, and hardly noticed. SNCC's best organizers recognized the potential power of such resistance and encouraged the grassroots leaders who mobilized the mass movements of the 1960s. SNCC's influence not only guided my historical research but also affected my teaching as I tried to nurture the skills of my students, to encourage them to question authority (especially that of their teachers), and to free their minds from outmoded ways of thinking. *In Struggle: SNCC and the Black Awakening of the 1960s* and my other scholarly writings have focused on the ways in which seemingly ordinary people in the South were encouraged to unleash their latent abilities and thereby make extraordinary contributions to the African American freedom struggle of the 1950s and 1960s.

I realize now that because of SNCC's profound influence on my worldview, I initially gave insufficient attention to Martin Luther King Jr. Even after accepting Coretta Scott King's 1985 invitation to become editor of Martin's papers, my rejection of "Great Man" notions of historical change made it difficult for me to recognize that Martin's role in the struggle was indeed extraordinary. After pointing out in my writings that he did not initiate the Montgomery bus boycott, the sit-ins, the freedom rides, or the black voting rights movement in the South, I struggled to specify exactly what accounted for his rapid rise to national and international prominence.

Yet, as I became more and more immersed in King's papers, the nature of his contribution became clear. While the freedom struggle provided opportunities for ordinary people to accomplish extraordinary things, Martin's roots in African American religious traditions—as the son, grandson, and great-grandson of Baptist preachers and as the intellectual descendant of Benjamin Mays, George Kelsey, and Howard Thurman—prepared him to answer the unexpected call to become the principal spokesperson for a mass protest movement that he did not initiate. He inspired black residents of Montgomery to believe that their protests had a moral and spiritual significance and that they were part of a global struggle to resist subordination and injustice. He transformed prosaic, transitory expressions of discontent into inspiring oratory that has endured.

Perhaps because Martin's deep family roots in the African American past contrasted so sharply with my own sense of being cut off from racial and religious roots, it took a while for me to respond to the power of his biblical imagery and language. I gained an extraordinary familiarity with Martin's voice and diction while editing *The Papers of Martin Luther King, Jr.*, writing *Passages*, and assembling *The Autobiography of Martin Luther King Jr.* Reading Martin's published and unpublished writings, listening countless times to his speeches, and talking extensively with those who knew him best has given me access to at least some of those places he once called "the quiet recesses of my heart."

Martin's first speech as a leader of the Montgomery boycott, delivered on December 5, 1955, at the initial mass meeting of the Montgomery Improvement Association (MIA), displayed this singular ability to link the modest initial goals of the boycott with transcendent principles and major historical trends. At a time when some bus boycott leaders were still unsure about whether to directly challenge segregation, Martin provocatively identified the boycott with the nation's democratic and egalitarian ideals. "If we are wrong, the Supreme Court of this nation is wrong," he insisted. "If we are wrong, the Constitution of the United States is wrong. If we are wrong, God Almighty is wrong." Martin also imbued the boycott with religious significance: "If we are wrong, Jesus of Nazareth was merely a utopian dreamer that never came down to earth." Using a phrase similar to the one he would make famous at the 1963 March on Washington, he urged his listeners "to work and fight until justice runs down like water and righteousness like a mighty stream."

While other black Montgomery leaders limited themselves to clarifying the MIA's immediate goals and plans, Martin galvanized black Montgomery residents by encouraging them to believe that they were part of a struggle with global importance. At the conclusion of his speech, he made an audacious prediction about the historical importance of the bus boycott: "Right here in Montgomery, when the history books are written in the future, somebody will have to say, 'There lived a race of people, a black people...who had the moral courage to stand up for their rights. And thereby they injected a new meaning into the veins of history and of civilization.'" Martin's sense of history was astounding, given that it was the first day of a boycott that faced concerted opposition from white segregationists and that had not yet directly challenged segregation laws. His stirring oratory helped ensure that the Montgomery movement would indeed become worthy of mention in history books.

Following the successful conclusion of the 381-day boycott, Martin made even more audacious claims regarding its significance. When the MIA hosted a gathering of Southern activists in December 1956, he announced proudly, "Little did we know that we were starting a movement that would rise to international proportions." The Montgomery movement, he proclaimed, "would ring in the ears of people of every nation...would stagger and astound the imagination of the oppressor, while leaving a glittering star of hope etched in the midnight skies of the oppressed." Although some national black leaders resisted acknowledging the growing stature of a pastor from a small church in a medium-sized Southern city, King's prophetic speeches enabled him to move beyond his role as a local protest leader.

A few months later, when King traveled to London on his way to attend the independence ceremony of the West African nation of Ghana, he met with C. L. R. James, the idiosyncratic West Indian socialist and Pan-Africanist who had spent most of his adult life promoting radical causes and interacting with revolutionaries throughout the world. James came away from that meeting highly impressed with the unity displayed in Montgomery. "It was one of the most astonishing events of endurance by a whole population that I have ever heard of," he gushed in a letter to his associates. James went on to compare the Montgomery bus boycott to the independence struggle in Ghana led by Kwame Nkrumah. Both movements, he said, demonstrated the "unsuspected power of the mass movement," a power that radical political leaders often failed to recognize. He rejected the notion of many Marxists that workers needed ideologically sophisticated leadership and argued instead that the mass movements in Ghana and Montgomery served as "a warning to all revolutionaries not to underestimate the readiness of modern people everywhere to overthrow the old regime."

Martin's ever-deepening understanding of Christian and Gandhian principles gave him the intellectual tools to expand his vision beyond the African American struggle. Due to the documentation of the King Papers Project, I have learned to appreciate the importance of Martin's family roots in the African American Baptist church, his academic experiences, and his ever-expanding network of Christian and Gandhian acquaintances. He was always ready to adapt his ideas to the changing needs of a mass struggle he could influence but not control.

Of course, I could not see all this when Martin spoke at the 1963 march. I know now that he was speaking less to me and the thousands who heard him that day than to "the architects" of the American republic and all democratic republics. I and many others were unwittingly listening to a perpetual dialogue about the role of government in extending and protecting "the unalienable rights of 'Life, Liberty and the pursuit of Happiness.'" Martin did not expect his listeners to see themselves as a passive audience for his dialogue. He was a model for citizens willing to boldly speak truth to those in power. "The whirlwinds of revolt will continue to shake the foundations of our nation until the bright day of justice emerges," he warned, even

while advising against allowing "creative protest to degenerate into physical violence" rather than "meeting physical force with soul force."

While the initial passages of Martin's speech addressed the Founding Fathers
and the middle passages spoke to the participants in the African American struggle, the extemporaneous conclusion of his speech painted a vivid portrait of a future
America that he believed would someday come into existence. Martin's Dream
extended far beyond President John F. Kennedy's pending civil rights bill that would
become the Civil Rights Act of 1964. Instead he offered an inspiring glimpse of a
transformed America, at a day when the nation would "rise up and live out the true
meaning of its creed—we hold these truths to be self-evident that all men are created equal," when even Mississippi would become "an oasis of freedom and justice,"
when his children and children everywhere would "not be judged by the color of
their skin but by the content of their character."

Even if I had been able to comprehend Martin's Dream when I first heard him at
the March on Washington, I would have found it difficult to keep pace with its continued evolution after 1963. When he received the Nobel Peace Prize at the end of
1964, he broke free of some of the constraints that his role as an African American
civil rights leader had placed upon him. Many of those who admired him did not
recognize that he, like Mohandas K. Gandhi, had transcended the movement and
the nation that spawned him. Martin now clearly expressed his "abiding faith in
America" as well as his "audacious faith in the future of mankind." He had "the
audacity to believe that people everywhere can have three meals a day for their
bodies, education and culture for their minds, and dignity, equality, and freedom
for their spirits." He saw that the African American struggle for civil rights was "a
relatively small part of a world development."

> The deep rumbling of discontent that we hear today is the thunder of dis-
> inherited masses, rising from dungeons of oppression to the bright hills
> of freedom, in one majestic chorus the rising masses singing, in the words
> of our freedom song, "Ain't gonna let nobody turn us around." All over
> the world, like a fever, the freedom movement is spreading in the widest
> liberation in history. The great masses of people are determined to end the
> exploitation of their races and land. They are awake and moving toward
> their goal like a tidal wave.

Speaking only months after the passage of the 1964 Civil Rights Act, he used
biblical language to warn that African Americans may "have left the dusty soils
of Egypt," but, before reaching the Promised Land, they faced "a frustrating and

bewildering wilderness ahead." He warned that violence was "both impractical and immoral" as a way of achieving racial justice. Though nations have achieved independence through it, he asserted that "violence never brings permanent peace" because "it is a descending spiral ending in destruction for all." He cited the example of Gandhi, who used nonviolence "to challenge the might of the British Empire and free his people from the political domination and economic exploitation inflicted upon them for centuries."

In addition to calling for a global struggle against racial oppression, Martin also announced that "the time has come for an all-out world war against poverty": "The rich nations must use their vast resources of wealth to develop the underdeveloped, school the unschooled, and feed the unfed." He identified war as "the third great evil" and expressed alarm "that nations are not reducing but rather increasing their arsenals of weapons of mass destruction." He advised "that the philosophy and strategy of nonviolence become immediately a subject for study and for serious experimentation in every field of human conflict, by no means excluding the relations between nations. It is, after all, nation-states which make war, which have produced the weapons which threaten the survival of mankind, and which are both genocidal and suicidal in character."

Martin closed his Nobel lecture by referring to the idea of a "world house"—an idea that has become even more relevant in our era of globalization and Internet communication. The "world house," he explained, was

> the great new problem of mankind. We have inherited a big house, a great "world house" in which we have to live together—black and white, Easterners and Westerners, Gentiles and Jews, Catholics and Protestants, Muslim and Hindu, a family unduly separated in ideas, culture, and interests who, because we can never again live without each other, must learn, somehow, in this one big world, to live with each other.

Martin urged that our loyalties "become ecumenical rather than sectional" and proclaimed that "worldwide fellowship that lifts neighborly concern beyond one's tribe, race, class, and nation is in reality a call for an all-embracing and unconditional love for all men."

Although many SNCC workers also broadened their perspectives as they exchanged ideas with their activist counterparts elsewhere in the world, some others retreated into a narrow vision of liberation that focused on the particular oppression of black Americans or perhaps black people throughout the world. This was perhaps inevitable, since participants in all mass movements tend to see their circumstances as unique and to see a deep and unbridgeable gulf between themselves and those who have not experienced their oppression. During the 1960s, I saw that SNCC's early Gandhian idealism gave way to the racial separatism and black-versus-black internecine conflicts of the Black Power era.

Even as he faced increasing criticism from Stokely Carmichael and other Black Power proponents, Martin refused to abandon his conviction that black Americans were part of a global ongoing freedom struggle. He identified himself not only with poor black people, but with poor people of all races and with the world's peasants—"the shirtless and barefoot people," he called them in his Nobel lecture—who were engaged in a long struggle to become citizens rather than subjects, "developing a new sense of 'some-bodiness' and carving a tunnel of hope through the dark mountain of despair."

This was the global vision that Martin took to Memphis in 1968, when he joined forces with that city's striking sanitation workers, many of them less than one generation removed from peasantry. As he spoke to them on April 3, 1968, the last evening of his life, he once again performed the role he had performed in Montgomery more than a dozen years earlier. He inspired the strikers by convincing them that their labor struggle was connected to historic liberation struggles throughout the world. Despite seeing the world as "all messed up," he drew attention to positive aspects of what was happening in the world, finding solace in his "panoramic view of the whole of human history up to now."

If God gave him the choice, he announced, he would not prefer to live in any previous era—not the biblical Exodus from Egypt, the age of classical Greek philosophy, the "great heyday" of the Roman Empire, the Renaissance and Reformation, the Civil War, or the Great Depression. "Strangely enough, I would turn to the Almighty and say, 'If you allow me to live just a few years in the second half of the twentieth century, I will be happy.'" Although he acknowledged that he lived in difficult times—"The nation is sick, trouble is in the land, confusion all around"—he still saw reasons for hope:

> But I know, somehow, that only when it is dark enough can you see the stars. And I see God working in this period of the twentieth century in a way that men in some strange way are responding. Something is happening in our world. The masses of people are rising up. And wherever they are assembled today, whether they are in Johannesburg, South Africa; Nairobi, Kenya; Accra, Ghana; New York City; Atlanta, Georgia; Jackson, Mississippi; or Memphis, Tennessee, the cry is always the same: "We want to be free."

Martin's global historical vision led me to see that the African American freedom struggle was only one aspect of what I have come to see as history's greatest
freedom struggle. During the past two and a half centuries, a majority of humanity overcame major systems of oppression—notably inherited forms of status based
on class, race, and gender. The transformation of the world's peasants and their
descendants into citizens has been the most important achievement of the modern
age. I have learned to appreciate that this transformation was accomplished not only
through freedom struggles but also through the mass migration that brought my
parents out of the South to greater opportunities elsewhere. This great transformation still continues.

Martin chose to end his two greatest orations with extemporaneous visions
of a Dream that he would never see fulfilled and of a Promised Land he would
never reach. His Dream and his vision of a Promised Land were rooted in the "self-
evident" "truths" that had justified the American Declaration of Independence and
in the faith-based truths of religious scripture. His final speech in Memphis was
meant for all human beings seeking to break free of the oppressive forces that constrain their lives, their freedom, and their pursuit of happiness.

Understanding the extent to which Martin's vision had expanded by the end of
his life, I could see that his Dream still endures in the freedom struggles of our time
and in all future freedom struggles. We can imagine him speaking of the day when
freedom will ring in "every village and every hamlet" throughout the world and
thereby "speed up that day when all of God's children" of all races "will be able to
join hands and sing in the words of the old Negro spiritual, 'Free at last, free at last.
Thank God Almighty, we are free at last.'"

Acknowledgments

*A*lthough *Martin's Dream* is a personal story, writing the book was a collective venture that brought me closer to some of the people who were part of my life. I appreciated the opportunity to learn more about them, and I hope they have gained a new understanding of me.

For most of the past three decades, my dedicated colleagues at the Martin Luther King Jr. Papers Project and its current institutional home, the King Research and Education Institute, have in various ways made it possible for me to devote my professional life to studying King's life, ideas, and legacy. This memoir is based largely on the extensive research effort associated with the King Project's definitive multivolume edition of *The Papers of Martin Luther King, Jr.* The hundreds of individuals who contributed to *The Papers* are acknowledged in the published volumes, but I wish to offer special thanks to three current King Institute staff members who have worked closely with me for more than a decade. I was able to take the time needed to complete this book only because I could leave the day-to-day management of the King Institute in the capable hands of Associate Director Tenisha Armstrong, Administrator Jane Abbott, and Public Programs Director Regina Covington. As I traced the history of the King Papers Project, I relied heavily on my research assistant, Sarah Overton, and received occasional help from Assistant Editor Stacey Zwald Costello. During the final stages of copyediting this memoir, two newly hired research assistants, Catherine Petru and Dr. Michael Eze, provided greatly appreciated help.

When my initial enthusiasm for the book concept gave way to weariness, family members and friends volunteered the assistance I desperately needed in guiding the book through the publication process, and I am extremely grateful. My wife, Susan, who is the love of my life, was there at the conception of this book project and remained until the end. She has always been my best and most reliable collaborator on my major writing projects, starting with my doctoral dissertation.

She has the organizational abilities I lack, and her editing skills have often saved me from embarrassing errors. On this particular project, her contributions were manifold. She encouraged me to undertake this blend of autobiography and history when a conventional historical narrative would have been easier to accomplish, and her generous advice has served as a necessary corrective to my fading memory and stubborn biases. Most importantly, she always remained confident, in the face of contrary evidence, that the book would be finished in time for the fiftieth anniversary of the March on Washington.

During the spring, summer, and fall of 2012, my sister, Gail Wentler, and my daughter, Temera Carson, volunteered for the grueling process of checking for errors and responding to copyediting queries—a task Gail also performed when I published my first book three decades ago. My love and appreciation for them deepened as I witnessed their determination to devote long days and nights to reading and checking the manuscript as deadlines approached. On many occasions, my brother-in-law, Bruce Wentler, joined the editorial brigade. During one weekend, my son, David Malcolm Carson, came to visit with his six-month-old son, Isaac, and pitched in to read portions of the text. All of them tolerated my propensity to rewrite even as they sought to finalize the manuscript. At the end of the summer, Rosalind Wolf, a friend from the sixties, offered helpful editorial assistance while Susan and I were guests in her home in Pacific Palisades. As those closest to me discovered previously unknown aspects of my life, I also learned much about them and came to appreciate their love and friendship even more than before.

This book would not have been possible without the support of my agent, Sandra Dijkstra, editor, Luba Ostashevsky, and the other members of the Palgrave Macmillan editorial staff.

Finally, I am thankful for the insights that many veterans of SNCC and associates of Martin Luther King Jr. have shared with me. I have made clear my indebtedness to many of them in this book, but I will always especially treasure that my life crossed paths with Stokely Carmichael, Bob Moses, Vincent Harding, Dorothy Cotton, Connie Curry, C. T. Vivian, Andrew Young, and my longtime King Institute colleague Clarence Jones. As my role in disseminating King's legacy has expanded, I have also continued to appreciate the opportunity I have had to know and collaborate with Coretta Scott King, Dexter Scott King, Martin Luther King III, Bernice Albertine King, and the late Yolanda Denise King.

Index